BEHOLD THE CHRIST

Seeing Jesus Clearly in the Gospel of Mark

Jonathan Sole

Pleasing God Press

BEHOLD THE CHRIST

Copyright © 2025 Jonathan Sole

Printed in the United States of America

ISBN: 979-8-9941959-0-1

Publisher: Pleasing God Press

North Kingstown, Rhode Island

Cover design: Katelyn Sole

Interior design: Jonathan Sole

Contents

FOREWORD

Introduction

Chapter 1..1

   Presenting Jesus the Christ 1

   Divine Authority Displayed 5

   Divine Care Displayed 9

Chapter 2.. 14

   Questioning Jesus: Who Does He Think He Is?........14

   Questioning Jesus: Why Do You Eat?....................18

   Questioning Jesus: Fasting and the Sabbath 23

Chapter 3..28

   The Great Conspiracy 28

   Falling Before Him..33

   Jesus' Calling: Purpose of His Call – Part 1 37

   Jesus' Calling: Purpose of His Call – Part 2 42

   The Folly of the Scribes and the Unforgivable Sin 47

   True Family..52

Chapter 4..58

   The Word at Work: Kingdom Building 58

   This Big Light of Mine..63

   An Unshakable Kingdom 68

   All Creation Submits 74

Chapter 5..79

   An Unlikely Convert..79

When Faith and Fear Collide 84

Chapter 6 90

The Reality of Ministry: Facing and Embracing
   Rejection 90

The Reality of Ministry: It Will Cost You Everything
  95

The Reality of Ministry: Caring for Others 100

The Reality of Ministry: Being Patient With People
  105

The Reality of Ministry: Bringing People to Jesus 110

Chapter 7 116

The Demise of True Religion, Part 1 – Legalism... 116

The Demise of True Religion, Part 2 –
   Traditionalism 121

You Aren't What You Eat 126

Grace Beyond Borders 131

Marvel Beyond Measure 136

Chapter 8 141

Jesus Is Enough 141

Why Do You Doubt? 146

From Confusion to Clarity: Progressing in the
   Christian Life 151

Who Do You Say That He Is? 155

It Will Cost You Everything 161

Chapter 9 167

Jesus Christ, The Son of God 167

Help My Unbelief 172

Living in the Kingdom of Christ.................................177

Salty, But Not Sinful 182

Chapter 10...**187**

The Truth About Divorce, Marriage, and
    Remarriage 187

Jesus Loves the Little Children...............................192

The Great Exchange 197

The Prophets' Prediction: The gospel According to
    Jesus 202

Greatness in Service, Not Status 206

The Making of a Disciple of Jesus Christ.................211

Chapter 11...**216**

The Messiah's Royal Procession 216

A Phony or a Follower?.....................................220

Faith Seeking Understanding 225

Chapter 12 ....**232**

Love's Final Call..232

Dual Citizenship: When Kingdoms Collide............238

Relationships and Resurrection in the Life to Come
   244

Above All, Love 250

Beware of Pastors and Preachers...........................256

Giving to the Glory of God................................263

Chapter 13 ....**271**

It Is Not the End of the World as We Know It 271

It Is Not the End of the World as We Know It – Part 2...276

It's the End of the World as We Know It – Part 1..281

It's the End of the World as We Know It – Part 2 .287

Chapter 14 ....**292**

Three Hearts Toward Jesus 292

Conspiracy and Communion: Lessons from the Last Supper...297

The Fall and Rise of Peter and the Disciples..........302

The Agony in Gethsemane.......................................306

The Kiss of Betrayal 311

Guilty as Charged: Truth on Trial...........................316

Chapter 15 ....**322**

Justice Denied: A Scandalous Gospel 322

You Shall Bruise His Heel, Part 1 327

You Shall Bruise His Heel – Part 2...........................332

You Shall Bruise His Heel – Part 3...........................336

Chapter 16 ....**341**

He Shall Bruise Your Head 341

Conclusion..**346**

For Katelyn

my biggest supporter, whose encouragement sustained me as I preached through the Gospel of Mark.

FOREWORD

Why another commentary on the Gospel of Mark? Isn't there already enough books in print for the pastors, teachers, and laypeople called to equip God's people in His church? One may answer "yes," but that is short-sighted, as God continues to raise His gifted people for His church through the printed page. This excellent commentary is one of those equipping tools. Written with biblical precision and devotional warmth, Pastor Jonathan's commentary on Mark's gospel, titled *Behold The Christ: Seeing Jesus Clearly in the Gospel of Mark*, will do just that for the thoughtful and prayerful reader.

I highly recommend this book for two reasons. First, my relationship with its author. I am his father, yet more than that, a colleague in pastoral ministry, having been privileged to sit under the sermons on Mark from which this commentary is birthed. I have also observed the maturing of Pastor Jonathan, not only as a preacher but in pastoral ministry. He has developed a pastoral heart for God's people through a deepening passion to rightly handle the Word of God to feed and equip the saints. This commentary is the fruit of his laborious study, along with the practical application in his own life, an essential element in effective pulpit and pastoral ministry.

As one dives into this commentary, a statement that Pastor Jonathan makes in his introduction sets the course for beholding the Christ in Mark and its implications for daily Christian living. He writes, "*The gospel of Mark calls us to lift our eyes from the temporary to the eternal, to behold the glory of the unseen Savior revealed in flesh. It confronts us with the reality that discipleship is costly, but worth it. It challenges our assumptions about greatness and shows that true greatness is found in humble service. And it comforts us with the reminder that Jesus is still near, still ruling, still redeeming broken lives by His grace."*

Another feature in this commentary is the short, direct, and clear explanation and application of the text. A person is not bogged down or confused. Wonderful headings introduce the exposition, which serves as a compass unfolding the text. With precision and skill, Pastor Jonathan brings us face to face with Jesus in a lovingly confrontational, challenging, and stirs the heart to want to see more and more of Jesus in this shortest of the synoptic gospels.

Yes, this is another commentary on Mark, but one that should find its way into the preaching and teaching libraries and ministries of those called by God to shepherd and instruct His people. I highly recommend it —not as an endorsement of a father for a son, but as a fellow pastor always looking for excellent tools for the equipper of God's people to equip God's people. This is one of them!

In the affection of Christ Jesus,

Pastor Jim Sole

Quidnessett Baptist Church

North Kingstown, RI

Behold The Christ: Seeing Jesus Clearly in the Gospel of Mark

Introduction

There is no greater pursuit in life than to know Jesus Christ. From the first page of Scripture to the last, the central figure of God's redeeming plan is His Son, our Savior, our King, our Lord. Yet, in a world filled with competing voices and endless distractions, it is easy to lose sight of who He truly is. The gospel of Mark calls us back to behold Him afresh.

Mark writes with urgency and simplicity. His favorite word is *immediately*, and his storytelling is vivid and fast-paced. He doesn't begin with a genealogy or long introduction; instead, he opens with a bold declaration: *"The beginning of the gospel of Jesus Christ, the Son of God"* (Mark 1:1). Every word that follows invites us to see Jesus clearly, to understand not only what He did, but who He is and why He came.

Mark's gospel is not merely a historical record of miracles and teachings. It is a theological portrait of the Christ who came not to be served but to serve, and to give His life as a ransom for many (Mark 10:45). It is the story of the Son of God who took on human flesh, walked among sinners, demonstrated divine authority, and willingly suffered the cross for our salvation. Through Mark, the Holy Spirit paints a portrait of Jesus that demands a response of faith, repentance, and wholehearted devotion.

Many readers have called Mark's gospel the "action gospel" because of its brisk movement from one scene to the next. But beneath that pace lies profound purpose. Mark shows us Jesus' power over disease, demons, nature, and death, all to reveal His authority as the Son of God. Yet just when we might expect triumph, Mark slows down. Nearly half the book is devoted to the final week of Jesus' life, reminding us that His greatest act of power came through His willing submission and sacrificial death. The path to glory ran through the cross.

To study Mark is to follow Jesus on the road to Calvary and beyond. It is to watch Him heal the broken, confront hypocrisy, restore sinners, and redefine what true discipleship means. Along the way, we are forced to ask ourselves the same question Jesus asked His disciples: *"Who do you say that I am?"* (Mark 8:29). Everything depends on how we answer.

This book, *Behold the Christ*, is written to help you see Jesus more clearly, to slow down long enough to reflect on who He is and what He has done. Each chapter walks through a section of Mark's gospel, drawing from the text to show how every story, every miracle, every conversation leads us to the cross and the empty tomb. My prayer is that, as you read, you will not only gain understanding but also experience transformation, and that your heart will be stirred to love Christ more deeply and follow Him more faithfully.

BEHOLD THE CHRIST

"For the things that are seen are transient, but the things that are unseen are eternal."

—2 Corinthians 4:18

The gospel of Mark calls us to lift our eyes from the temporary to the eternal, to behold the glory of the unseen Savior revealed in flesh. It confronts us with the reality that discipleship is costly, but worth it. It challenges our assumptions about greatness and shows that true greatness is found in humble service. And it comforts us with the reminder that Jesus is still near, still ruling, still redeeming broken lives by His grace.

This book is a product of preaching verse by verse through the entire gospel of Mark in my church. I was constantly brought face-to-face with Jesus, which deepened my love for him, Scripture, and his church. The church was also incredibly blessed by encountering Jesus afresh each week as we unpacked Mark's masterpiece.

I hope that this journey through Mark's gospel will renew your awe of Jesus Christ. May you come to see Him as the suffering Servant, the sovereign Lord, and the risen Son of God. May the Spirit open your eyes to behold His beauty, your heart to embrace His truth, and your life to reflect His glory.

Come, then. Open your Bible to the gospel of Mark. Let us walk the dusty roads of Galilee, sit at the feet of the Master, and stand at the foot of the cross. Let us behold the Christ, and in beholding Him, be changed.

Chapter 1

Presenting Jesus the Christ

Mark 1:1–13

The Gospel's Opening Announcement (Mark 1:1–3)

Mark begins his gospel like a runner bursting out of the blocks: "The beginning of the gospel of Jesus Christ, the Son of God." He doesn't start with a genealogy like Matthew or a birth narrative like Luke. He doesn't begin in eternity as John does. He announces, "This is the start of the good news." And that good news centers on a Person: Jesus, the Messiah, the Son of God.

That title "Son of God" is not incidental. It's central. It tells us from the outset that Jesus is not just a moral teacher or miracle worker. He is divine. Mark doesn't build up to that conclusion. He starts there and says, "Now watch what Jesus does."

Then Mark anchors this good news in the promises of the Old Testament. He quotes Isaiah and Malachi to demonstrate that Jesus' arrival is not random—it is the fulfillment. God had promised to send a forerunner, a voice in the wilderness, who would prepare the way. That voice belongs to John the Baptist. The gospel doesn't begin in a vacuum; it starts as the climax of centuries of waiting.

1

John the Baptist's Ministry (Mark 1:4–8)

John appears just as the prophets said he would: in the wilderness, calling people to repentance. He wears camel's hair and a leather belt. He eats locusts and wild honey. He's not refined, but he is righteous. His very appearance is a sermon; it's not style, attire, or a fancy building that draws a crowd, but conviction and truth.

People flock to him, not for entertainment, but for awakening. They come confessing their sins and are baptized by him in the Jordan River. But John is clear: he's not the point. He's not the Savior. He says, "After me comes one who is mightier than I." In fact, John says he's not even worthy to untie His sandals, a task reserved for the lowest of servants.

John baptizes with water, a symbol of cleansing. But he speaks of One who will baptize with the Holy Spirit, a baptism of new birth. John's message was confrontational. He preached repentance. But it was also preparational. He was clearing the way for the King.

What's striking is that John doesn't try to hold the spotlight. He knows his place. He must decrease so Christ can increase. That kind of humility is rare. It's tempting in ministry to want recognition. But John teaches us that greatness in God's kingdom means being content to shine the spotlight on someone else, especially Jesus.

The Baptism of Jesus (Mark 1:9-11)

Then, Jesus shows up. Quietly. Humbly. He comes from Nazareth of Galilee, a town so obscure that a disciple later asked, "Can anything good come out of Nazareth?" And yet, this is where the Messiah comes from.

He presents Himself to John for baptism. That should give us pause. Jesus had no sin to confess. He didn't need cleansing. So why does He get baptized?

Because He came to stand in the place of sinners, from the very beginning of His ministry, Jesus identifies with those He came to save. He doesn't wait for the cross to take our place. He begins that work the moment He steps into the water.

Jesus didn't need to receive baptism because He was sinless. But he got in the water anyway. He stood where sinners stood. That's what He came to do. He came to identify with us, to step into our mess, to take our place.

As Jesus comes up out of the water, something astonishing happens. The heavens are torn open. The Spirit descends like a dove. And a voice from heaven declares, "You are my beloved Son; with you I am well pleased."

This is one of the most beautiful Trinitarian moments in the New Testament. Father, Son, and Spirit are all present. All united. All affirm that the mission is underway.

It's also deeply personal. Before Jesus does a single miracle, preaches a single sermon, or calls a single disciple, the Father says, "I am pleased with You." That's grace. And it's a reminder that God's approval is not based on performance, but on position. If you are in Christ, the Father says the same over you: You are My beloved child.

The Temptation in the Wilderness (Mark 1:12–13)

Immediately after His baptism, the Spirit drives Jesus into the wilderness. That word "driven" is strong. It wasn't optional. This was a divine appointment. The wilderness was part of God's plan.

For forty days, Satan tempts Jesus. He is surrounded by wild animals and ministered to by angels. Mark doesn't give us the details like Matthew and Luke do. He doesn't record the three temptations. Instead, he gives us the atmosphere—the weight of it.

But the message is clear: Jesus goes where humanity has failed. Israel was tested in the wilderness for forty years and failed. Adam was tested in the garden and failed. But Jesus, the true and better Adam, the faithful Israel, succeeds. He resists the devil. He remains obedient. He proves Himself to be the worthy Son.

This wilderness scene reminds us that following Jesus involves struggle. Baptism may be followed by battle. Affirmation may be followed by testing. But Jesus goes before us. He is not only our Savior, but He is our example and strength when the wilderness comes.

Reflection & Response

Why do you think Mark begins his gospel with such urgency and brevity?

What does Jesus' baptism reveal about His mission and our identity in Him?

How does John the Baptist's humility challenge your view of ministry or leadership?

In what ways do you see Jesus identifying with humanity in this passage?

How does Jesus' victory in the wilderness give you confidence in your own spiritual battles?

Divine Authority Displayed

Mark 1:14–34

The Time Is Fulfilled (Mark 1:14–15)

After the arrest of John the Baptist, Jesus begins His public ministry. Mark doesn't delay; he records Jesus stepping into the scene with clarity and conviction. "The time is fulfilled, and the kingdom of God is at hand; repent and believe in the gospel." These are the first words of Jesus in this gospel, and they're packed with urgency and significance.

The "time" is not just chronological, it's theological. God's redemptive plan has reached its next chapter. The waiting is over. The kingdom of God has arrived not in its fullness, but in its presence. The King is here, and His reign has broken into the world. But this kingdom doesn't come by sword or politics. It comes by repentance and faith.

Jesus' message is clear: turn and trust. Turn from sin. Trust the good news. This is the same call that goes out today. The gospel is not simply a historical announcement; it is a personal invitation. We are called to repent and believe in the gospel of Jesus Christ.

The Calling of Disciples (Mark 1:16–20)

Jesus walks along the Sea of Galilee and sees Simon and Andrew casting a net into the sea. Then James and John, mending their nets with their Father Zebedee. These are fishermen, ordinary men. Not religious scholars. Not political elites. Just everyday laborers.

Jesus says to them, "Follow me, and I will make you become fishers of men." That phrase is radical. In those days, disciples chose rabbis. But here, the Rabbi chooses the disciples. Jesus calls them not just to believe, but to *follow*, to leave behind their old life and step into a new mission. Jesus didn't offer a five-year plan. He didn't negotiate their schedules. He called them, and they dropped their nets. That's what His authority demands immediate obedience.

And notice the transformation. Jesus doesn't just call them to a task; He calls them to Himself. "Follow *me*," He says. The relationship comes first. But He also gives them a new identity: "fishers of men." He will make them into something they are not yet. That's the pattern of discipleship Jesus calls us to follow, and He forms us in it.

Teaching with Authority (Mark 1:21–22)

They enter Capernaum, and on the Sabbath, Jesus goes into the synagogue and begins to teach. The people are astonished not because He was louder or more energetic than the scribes, but because He spoke with authority. He didn't quote other rabbis. He didn't hedge or speculate. He declared the truth.

This was different. The scribes were professional teachers. They knew the Scriptures, but their teaching often felt secondhand, safe, recycled, deferential. But Jesus spoke like someone who wrote the word. Because he did, his authority wasn't borrowed; it resided within him.

We still need that kind of teaching today, the truth that comes with conviction, clarity, and divine weight. Not because the preacher is impressive, but because the Word of Christ is being proclaimed with the authority it already possesses.

Authority over Darkness (Mark 1:23–28)

As Jesus is teaching, a man with an unclean spirit interrupts the service. The demon cries out, "What have you to do with us, Jesus of Nazareth? Have you come to destroy us? I know who you are, the Holy One of God."

Isn't it striking? The people are still wondering who Jesus is, but the demons already know. Jesus doesn't engage in debate. He says, "Be silent, and come out of him." And with a convulsion and a cry, the demon obeys. The people are amazed. They've never seen anything like this. Teaching with authority is one thing, but commanding unclean spirits? That's a whole different category. Jesus isn't just a teacher. He's a conqueror. His authority isn't just over minds, it's over the spiritual realm.

The synagogue was a place of worship, and yet that's where the demon was hiding. That tells us something: we can't assume that religious spaces are automatically spiritually safe. But where Jesus is present, the darkness is exposed and expelled.

Healing with Compassion (Mark 1:29–34)

After the synagogue, Jesus enters the house of Simon and Andrew. Simon's mother-in-law has a fever. Jesus takes her by the hand, lifts her, and the fever leaves her. Immediately, she begins to serve.

There's something beautiful in that response. She isn't healed just for comfort—she's healed for purpose. And Jesus didn't just speak the word. He touched her hand. His authority is not distant. It's personal and compassionate.

That evening, the whole city gathered at the door. Word has spread. People bring their sick and demon-possessed, and Jesus heals many. He casts out demons, but He doesn't let them speak, because they know who He is.

Jesus is in complete control. He's not overwhelmed by the crowd. He's not rattled by the demonic. He is deliberate, compassionate, and sovereign. And yet, even in this burst of ministry success, Jesus is not chasing popularity. His mission is deeper than miracles. He came to preach. He came to redeem.

Reflection & Response

What stands out to you about the way Jesus called His first disciples?

How does Jesus' authority in teaching and casting out demons strengthen your confidence in Him?

In what ways do you need to "drop your nets" in response to His call?

How does Jesus' compassion in healing shape the way you think about His heart for the broken?

What do you learn from the contrast between the religious crowd and the spiritually afflicted man in the synagogue?

Divine Care Displayed

Mark 1:35–45

I. Jesus Prioritized Prayer (v. 35)

Mark tells us that "rising very early in the morning, while it was still dark," Jesus went out to a desolate place, and there He prayed. After a long evening of ministry healing the sick, casting out demons, and teaching crowds, Jesus doesn't sleep in. He seeks solitude with the Father.

This is the first recorded moment of Jesus' prayer life in Mark's gospel, and it's striking. The Son of God, filled with power and compassion, still prioritized private prayer. If anyone could've coasted on His divine authority, it was Jesus. But he withdrew to pray. Prayer wasn't just something Jesus did to check off a spiritual box; it was His lifeline. He rose early, in the dark, not because it was convenient, but because it was necessary.

This shows us that intimacy with the Father was more important to Jesus than the applause of the crowd. Ministry success didn't substitute for spiritual depth. Even amid constant demands, Jesus made time to be alone with God.

It challenges us. When we're tired, when our schedule is full, do we pull away to pray or press ahead in our own strength? If Jesus needed communion with the Father, how much more do we?

II. Jesus Resisted the Urgency of the Crowd (vv. 36–39)

While Jesus is praying, Simon and those with him pursue Him. "Everyone is looking for you," they say. The implication? *You're in high demand. Let's go back and keep the momentum going.* The crowds had tasted healing and power, and they wanted more.

But Jesus doesn't return to Capernaum. Instead, He says, "Let us go on to the next towns, that I may preach there also, for that is why I came out." This response might seem surprising. Wouldn't more miracles bring more belief? But Jesus isn't driven by popularity. He's committed to His mission. Jesus was never in a rush to please the crowd. He wasn't motivated by their expectations. He was anchored in the Father's will, not pulled by public pressure.

This moment teaches us something profound about spiritual priorities. Jesus had compassion on the crowds, but He didn't confuse popularity with purpose. He came to preach the kingdom, calling people to repentance and faith, not just to heal bodies. Healing was a sign of the kingdom, but preaching was the heart of the mission.

It's easy to be swayed by the loudest voices or the biggest opportunities. But Jesus reminds us that faithfulness often means saying no to good things to say yes to the best things. His authority was rooted in clarity of calling, not the approval of others.

III. Jesus Displayed Compassion to the Outcast (vv. 40–42)

A leper comes to Jesus, begging Him and kneeling before Him: "If you will, you can make me clean." This man doesn't question Jesus' power; he questions His willingness. He's desperate, but unsure if someone like Jesus would care for someone like him.

Leprosy was more than a physical disease; it was a social and spiritual sentence. Lepers were isolated, cut off from the temple and the community. They were untouchables. People avoided, feared, and forgot them. Yet this man approaches Jesus, kneeling in faith and desperation.

And Jesus responds most stunningly. "Moved with pity, he stretched out his hand and touched him." Before He says a word, Jesus does the unthinkable. He touches the leper. That touch was everything. It was healing, yes, but more than that, it was dignity. Compassion. Love. Jesus could've healed him with a word, but He chose to reach out His hand.

"I will," Jesus says. "Be clean." And immediately the leprosy left him, and he was made clean. This moment shows us the heart of our Savior. Jesus is not just willing to heal. He's willing to touch the untouchable. He's not just powerful, He's compassionate. He moves toward the broken, not away. He restores the outcast with both word and touch.

We live in a world filled with modern-day lepers that society ignores, isolates, or casts aside. And the church must learn from the Lord. We are called to extend grace and dignity to the forgotten, not just in theory, but in action. The touch of Jesus is still extended through His people.

IV. Jesus Obeyed the Father's Timing (vv. 43–45)

After healing the man, Jesus gives him a strong warning: "See that you say nothing to anyone, but go, show yourself to the priest and offer for your cleansing what Moses commanded, for a proof to them." This may seem puzzling. Why the secrecy?

It wasn't time yet. Jesus wasn't interested in stirring up premature fame. He wanted the man to obey the law and follow the steps outlined in Leviticus 14 to be formally restored to the community. Jesus was not abolishing the law. He was fulfilling it.

But the man disobeys. He goes out and begins to talk freely, spreading the news. And what happens? "Jesus could no longer openly enter a town, but was out in desolate places, and people were coming to Him from every quarter."

The result of disobedience was a shift in Jesus' ability to minister freely. And yet even when He was pushed to the margins, people still sought Him out. His fame grew, but so did the pressure.

This section teaches us something important about the tension between faith and obedience. The healed man was understandably excited, but he was also instructed. Gratitude should never override obedience. And for us, there's a lesson: even after Jesus transforms your life, His voice still guides it.

Reflection & Response

How does Jesus' early morning prayer life challenge your priorities?

What are some ways you're tempted to follow the crowd's urgency instead of God's calling?

Who are the "untouchables" in your life—people you've avoided but Jesus would move toward?

What does Jesus' healing of the leper teach you about His heart toward the outcast?

Why do you think obedience to Jesus' instructions matters, even after He's shown you mercy?

Chapter 2

Questioning Jesus: Who Does He Think He Is?

Mark 2:1–12

I. Faith That Finds a Way (vv. 1–4)

Jesus returns to Capernaum, and word spreads quickly that He is at home. Soon, the house is overflowing with people, so packed that even the door is blocked. Then four men arrive, carrying a paralyzed friend on a stretcher. They're too late to get in through the door. But they don't give up. They climb to the roof, dig through it, and lower their friend down right in front of Jesus.

This moment is more than impressive creativity. It's a picture of faith that refuses to be deterred. These men didn't just believe Jesus could heal; they acted on that belief. They saw the obstacles and overcame them because they believed the reward was worth it.

Their faith wasn't passive. It was persistent. It tore through barriers. Literally, they weren't going to let crowds or ceilings stop them from getting their friend to Jesus.

We learn something here about genuine, active faith. It doesn't wait for ideal conditions. It moves. It takes risks. It finds a way. And notice Jesus saw *their* faith, not just the paralytic's. There's something powerful about friends' faith in behalf of someone who can't walk to Jesus on their own.

II. Forgiveness Before Healing (v. 5)

When the paralytic is lowered before Him, Jesus doesn't start with what everyone expected. He doesn't say, "Get up and walk." Instead, He says, "Son, your sins are forgiven."

This is shocking. Not just because the man's obvious need was physical, but because Jesus is doing something no one else had the authority to do. Only God can forgive sins. Yet Jesus pronounces forgiveness right there on the spot. Jesus looks past the surface and goes straight to the soul. Everyone else saw a paralyzed man. Jesus saw a man spiritually dead in sin.

This is a profound moment. The man came for healing, but he got something greater. He got forgiveness. Jesus is showing us that the greatest need any person has is not physical healing, but reconciliation with God.

Many today want Jesus to fix their circumstances, but they overlook their own sin. They want relief more than redemption. But Jesus came not just to improve your life, but to give you new life. That begins with forgiveness.

III. The Thoughts of the Scribes (vv. 6–7)

As soon as Jesus pronounces forgiveness, the scribes silently fume. They don't say anything aloud, but in their hearts, they accuse Him of blasphemy. *"Who can forgive sins but God alone?"* And in a sense, they're right.

Only God can forgive sins. So they inwardly ask Who does He think He is?

But what they failed to see was that God was standing right in front of them.

This is one of the first conflicts between Jesus and the religious leaders in Mark's gospel. It won't be the last. But it's telling how it starts —not over something He *does*, but over something He *claims*. Jesus isn't just a healer or teacher. He's claiming divine authority. The scribes had great theology, but they couldn't connect the dots. They knew only God could forgive sin, but they didn't believe Jesus *was* God.

Sometimes we can be guilty of the same thing. We know the correct answers. We know the verses. But when Jesus challenges our categories or our comfort, we stiffen. Like the scribes, we stay on the edges, evaluating, instead of falling at His feet.

IV. Proof of Power (vv. 8–12)

Jesus, knowing their thoughts, calls them out. "Why do you question these things in your hearts?" And then He asks a powerful question: *"Which is easier, to say to the paralytic, 'Your sins are forgiven,' or to say, 'Rise, take up your bed and walk'?"*

It's a rhetorical trap. Saying "your sins are forgiven" is invisible; there's no way to prove it on the spot. But telling a paralyzed man to get up and walk? That's testable. That's visible. So Jesus chooses the harder one to prove the unseen. Jesus doesn't just talk. He shows. He gives visible evidence of invisible authority. He doesn't back down. He doubles down.

16

Then He says, "But that you may know that the Son of Man has authority on earth to forgive sins. "He turns to the paralytic, "I say to you, rise, pick up your bed, and go home." And the man does exactly that. The crowd is amazed. They glorify God, saying, "We never saw anything like this!" And truly, they hadn't. This wasn't just another healing. This was a revelation. Jesus has the authority to forgive sin. And He proves it by reversing the curse of sin, brokenness, disease, and paralysis with a single word.

V. Who Is This Man?

This entire episode forces the question: Who does Jesus think He is?

He forgives sins, something only God can do. He reads hearts, something only God knows. He heals with power, something only God commands. And He accepts worship, something only God deserves.

Mark wants us to wrestle with that question because the answer will shape everything else. Jesus is not a life coach. He's not a moral example. He's not a genie for your comfort. He is God in the flesh. And He came to forgive sinners and restore the broken. The crowd saw a miracle. The scribes saw a threat. The friends saw hope. And the man on the mat? He saw grace. His body was healed, but his soul was saved.

Reflection & Response

What obstacles might be keeping you—or someone you love—from coming to Jesus?

How does Jesus' priority of forgiveness over healing challenge your view of your own needs?

Why do you think the scribes missed the truth about Jesus, even though they knew Scripture?

What visible fruit in your life reflects the invisible work of forgiveness Jesus has done?

How would you answer the question: Who does Jesus think He is?

Questioning Jesus: Why Do You Eat?

Mark 2:13–17

I. Jesus Goes to the Margins (v. 13)

Mark tells us that Jesus went out again beside the sea, and the crowd came to Him, and He taught them. At first glance, this sounds familiar: another seaside moment with Jesus and the crowds. But pay attention to the location and movement: Jesus leaves the town center and moves toward the edge of town. Toward the margins.

There by the water sits Levi, also known as Matthew, a tax collector. And Jesus doesn't just notice him, He calls him. "Follow Me," He says. And Levi rose and followed Him. We don't know whether Levi had heard Jesus before or what internal struggle he was experiencing. But the call of Jesus breaks through all of that. And Levi walks away from his booth, his wealth, and his old life to follow the Son of God.

This was no small decision. Tax collectors were among the most despised people in Jewish society. Many saw them as traitorous Jews who worked for the Roman oppressors and often extorted money from their own people. They were religiously unclean, socially shunned, and morally suspect. And yet Jesus calls Levi.

It's a pattern we see throughout Jesus' ministry. He doesn't start with the religious elite or the morally polished. He begins with the outsiders. The misfits. The forgotten. The ones the world has written off. Jesus doesn't avoid the mess. He walks straight into it.

II. Jesus Dines with Sinners (v. 15)

Soon after, Jesus is reclining at the table in Levi's house, along with many tax collectors and sinners. And they weren't just occasional guests, Mark says, *many* of them were following Him.

This is stunning. Jesus doesn't just tolerate sinners; He *eats with them*. He enters their homes, reclines at their tables, shares their bread. In ancient cultures, eating with someone was to identify with them. It was an act of relational acceptance. Jesus didn't become a sinner by eating with sinners. He didn't compromise His holiness. But he showed that he isn't afraid of proximity. He engages. He reaches out because He came to seek and to save the lost.

And it wasn't just Levi. His whole crew shows up. The other tax collectors. The outcasts. The sinners. The broken people of society. And Jesus isn't uncomfortable. He doesn't keep His distance. He's right there with them, not to affirm them, but to transform them. This is what the kingdom of God looks like. It moves outward. It tears down the barriers between the clean and the unclean, the insider and the outsider. It invites people into fellowship not because they've earned it, but because grace has come to their table.

III. The Question of the Righteous (v. 16)

But not everyone is happy. The scribes of the Pharisees, those meticulous keepers of religious law, see what's happening, and they're offended. "Why does He eat with tax collectors and sinners?" They can't fathom a holy man associating with the unholy. For them, righteousness was about separation. Avoiding contamination and keeping your distance from anything or anyone that might tarnish your purity. Jesus' behavior confuses and angers them.

They weren't asking for information. They were accusing. This wasn't curiosity; it was condemnation. In their minds, Jesus had compromised Himself by even sitting at that table. This is one of the earliest clashes between Jesus and the religious establishment, and it sets the tone for the rest of the gospel. They want control. They want categories. Jesus disrupts all of that. He reaches across the lines they've drawn and invites people they've excluded.

Their question is rooted in pride. They think they're above those at the table. They assume their righteousness is intact. But they don't see that their hearts are just as sinful, only more disguised.

IV. The Mission of the Great Physician (v. 17)

When Jesus hears the question, He responds with one of the most important statements in all of Mark's gospel: *"Those who are well have no need of a physician, but those who are sick. I came not to call the righteous, but sinners."*

This is not just a defense, it's a declaration. Jesus is saying, *This is precisely why I came.* Like a doctor who goes to the sick, Jesus goes to the sinner. Not to affirm them, but to heal them. Not to participate in their sinfulness, but to restore them to wholeness. He's not saying the Pharisees are truly healthy. He's saying they think they are. They don't see what they need. The tax collectors and sinners know they're broken. They know they're unworthy. And that humility is the doorway to grace.

Jesus didn't come to congratulate the morally successful. He came to save the spiritually desperate. This is the heart of the gospel. The grace of Jesus is not for those who have it together. It's for those who know they don't. It's for people like Levi, who walked away from comfort and corruption to follow Christ. And it's for people like us, who know our own sin and come to the table hungry for mercy.

V. So Why Does He Eat with Sinners?

The answer to that question is clear now because that's who He came for. Because the table is where grace meets guilt. Because sinners aren't saved from a distance. They're saved by a Savior who draws near. Jesus eats with sinners not to endorse sin but to extend

21

salvation. He's not afraid of the mess because He's the one who can clean it. He's not worried about their guilt; he will bear it. He's the Lamb of God who takes away the sin of the world.

This changes how we think about the church, about outreach, about discipleship. We're not called to create sanitized religious bubbles; we're called to follow Jesus into the margins. To invite the outcast. To offer grace at the table. If Jesus has forgiven you, you're not just a guest at the table, you're a host. You carry His welcome. You extend His invitation. You live as proof that mercy sits with sinners. Who sits at your table?

Reflection & Response

What does Jesus' call to Levi teach you about who is welcome in His kingdom?

How does Jesus' presence at Levi's table challenge the way you view evangelism and hospitality?

In what ways might you be tempted to act like the Pharisees, judging who's "worthy" of God's grace?

Who in your life might be a modern-day "Levi" waiting for someone to invite them to follow Jesus?

How does Jesus' identity as the Great Physician shape your view of your own need for grace?

Questioning Jesus: Fasting and the Sabbath
Mark 2:18–28

I. An Unruly Discipline (vv. 18–22)

Mark sets the scene with another question, this time from the disciples of John and the Pharisees. They ask Jesus, "Why do John's disciples and the disciples of the Pharisees fast, but your disciples do not fast?" At first glance, it is a straightforward religious question. But beneath it lies a growing unease. Jesus doesn't seem to play by the expected rules. The Pharisees fasted twice a week. John's disciples, serious about repentance, also fasted. Fasting was seen as a mark of devotion. So why did Jesus and His followers seem so relaxed?

They were asking, "If you're really from God, why aren't you more religious?" Their assumption was: *Godly people fast, mourn, and live disciplined lives. Jesus isn't doing that.* Jesus responds with a powerful metaphor: "Can the wedding guests fast while the bridegroom is with them?" In other words, now is not the time for fasting, because now is a time of joy. The bridegroom has come. The long-awaited Messiah is here. You don't fast at a wedding feast.

Jesus isn't rejecting fasting entirely. He's redefining its timing and purpose. He acknowledges, "The days will come when the bridegroom is taken away... and then they will fast." There will be a time for mourning, but this isn't it. Jesus is saying, "You're missing what's right in front of you. God has come near. This is not the moment to focus on your religious effort. This is the moment to rejoice in divine presence."

Then Jesus gives two illustrations to drive the point home: the patch on the old garment and the new wine in old wineskins. They reinforce His central point: the kingdom of God isn't an add-on to the old religious system. It's something entirely new. If you try to fit Jesus into the old categories, He'll tear them apart. If you pour the new wine of the gospel into the brittle wineskins of legalism, everything bursts. Jesus didn't come to patch up old religion. He came to fulfill and surpass it.

This is what made His ministry so "unruly" to the religious establishment. It didn't meet expectations. It broke categories. It replaced ritual with relationship. The formality of fasting gave way to the intimacy of feasting with the bridegroom. And yet, this wasn't lawlessness; it was the fulfillment of God's promises. Jesus brought joy, not because He ignored sin, but because He would deal with it entirely. The cross was coming. The bridegroom would be taken away. But in this moment, it was time to celebrate.

II. An Unruly Observance (vv. 23–28)

Mark then moves to another confrontation about the Sabbath. As Jesus and His disciples walk through grainfields on the Sabbath, His disciples begin plucking heads of grain. The Pharisees quickly accuse them: "Look, why are they doing what is not lawful on the Sabbath?"

They weren't stealing. The law allowed travelers to pick grain by hand (Deut. 23:25). The issue was that it was the Sabbath, and in the Pharisees' eyes, this counted as work. Their interpretation of Sabbath law had become rigid, extending far beyond the original command. The Pharisees had built fences around God's law. Their traditions were meant to protect obedience, but eventually the fences became the law themselves.

Jesus answers their accusation not with argument, but with Scripture. He recalls the story of David in 1 Samuel 21, when David and his men ate the bread of the presence, which was supposed to be eaten only by priests. Jesus points out that David broke the ceremonial law in a moment of need, and yet he wasn't condemned.

Why bring up David? Because David was the Lord's rightful king, and his actions, though technically unlawful, were upheld because of who he was and the circumstances he was in. Jesus is identifying with David here. He's saying, "I am the true king. I'm greater than David. And what's happening now is even more significant."

Then Jesus delivers a massive theological correction: *"The Sabbath was made for man, not man for the Sabbath."* In other words, the Sabbath was a gift, not a burden. It was meant to restore people, not oppress them. The Pharisees had reversed it. They made the Sabbath about rules, not rest. About restrictions, not refreshment. But Jesus brings the Sabbath back to its purpose: to serve humanity, not enslave it.

And then comes the climax: *"So the Son of Man is lord even of the Sabbath."* This is staggering. Jesus claims authority over one of Judaism's most sacred institutions. The Sabbath was rooted in creation (Gen. 2:2–3) and codified in the Ten Commandments. And

Jesus says, "I'm Lord over that. "This isn't just unruly, it's divine. Jesus is claiming that He stands above the Sabbath, not beneath it. He's not breaking the law. He's fulfilling it and revealing its true purpose.

The Sabbath pointed forward to the rest we would find in Christ. Jesus doesn't abolish Sabbath rest; He becomes it. He invites the weary to come to Him and find true soul rest. So when the Pharisees questioned His disciples, they revealed their blindness. They were so committed to religious form that they missed the Lord of the Sabbath standing right before them. They clung to the shadow and ignored the substance.

The Larger Conflict

These two moments about fasting and the Sabbath are not isolated. They reveal a growing tension between Jesus and the religious leaders. At every turn, Jesus seems to be upending their system. He redefines righteousness, worship, and devotion. And they can't handle it. What they saw as disorder, Jesus knew was restoration. What they called unruly, Jesus called redemptive. He was doing something new, something beautiful, and the old wineskins, too bound, could not contain it.

We can fall into the same trap. We can confuse tradition with truth. We can cling to our forms and miss the transforming presence of Jesus in the process. Jesus doesn't discard spiritual disciplines. But he infuses them with life. Fasting becomes about longing for His return. The Sabbath becomes a window into His rest. The kingdom of God isn't about religion; it's about a relationship with the king.

Reflection & Response

What does Jesus' response to fasting reveal about His priorities in worship?

How might we try to fit Jesus into old "wineskins" in our own lives or churches?

In what ways have we turned God's gifts—like rest or discipline—into burdens rather than blessings?

What does it mean that Jesus is "Lord of the Sabbath," and how does that shape how we view rest and worship?

Are there any areas where you're resisting the newness Jesus brings because it challenges your expectations?

Chapter 3

The Great Conspiracy

Mark 3:1–6

I. A Setup in the Synagogue (vv. 1–2)

Jesus enters the synagogue, and immediately Mark notes that a man there has a withered hand. The tone of the passage is This isn't just another healing opportunity. This is a setup. The Pharisees are watching Him closely. Not to learn or worship, but to catch Him.

Mark tells us plainly: *"They watched Jesus, to see whether he would heal him on the Sabbath, so that they might accuse him."* The man's disability becomes a pawn in their trap. That's how hardened their hearts were; they were willing to exploit a suffering man to try to undermine Jesus.

This isn't curiosity. It's a conspiracy. They didn't doubt that Jesus could heal; they expected it. But instead of celebrating that, they used it against him. To them, healing on the Sabbath wasn't mercy; it was a violation. They had elevated their traditions above compassion, above people, above God Himself.

II. A Call to Stand (v. 3)

Jesus, knowing their hearts and intentions, doesn't retreat. He doesn't whisper or wait. Instead, He calls the man with the withered hand to *"come here."* Literally, "rise and come forward." He brings the man to the center of the room. He could have waited until after sundown. He could have healed quietly later. But Jesus chooses this moment to confront their hypocrisy. This isn't just about physical restoration; it's about moral and spiritual clarity. Jesus doesn't avoid conflict when bad players are present. He doesn't dodge hard questions. He steps into them, truthfully and courageously.

The man rises and stands. He doesn't argue. He doesn't ask questions. He trusts Jesus enough to respond. Imagine standing in front of your entire religious community, with a visible deformity, in the middle of a theological standoff. But he obeys. Jesus brings him to the center because He's about to reveal what's really at stake, not just the healing of a hand, but the hardness of hearts.

III. A Question of Law and Mercy (v. 4)

Jesus turns to the religious leaders and asks a pointed question:

"Is it lawful on the Sabbath to do good or to do harm, to save life or to kill?"

It's a masterful question. He frames it not as "Is healing allowed?" but "What is the Sabbath for?" Is it a day for goodness, or for rigid observance? For mercy or for legalism? And how do they respond? *"But they were silent."*

They have no answer. Because if they say, "It's lawful to do good," they justify Jesus. If they say, "It's unlawful," they reveal their callousness. So they say nothing. Their silence speaks volumes. They weren't interested in truth—they were guarding their control. They would rather cling to their system than submit to the Savior.

And isn't that the danger of all religion without relationship? It turns sacred things into systems. It hides behind rules instead of reaching out in love. It silences the voice of God to preserve man-made observances.

IV. A Grieved Savior and a Restored Hand (v. 5)

Then we read one of the most emotional verses in the Gospels:

"And he looked around at them with anger, grieved at their hardness of heart."

Jesus is not indifferent here. He is righteously angry. But he's also deeply grieved. The word Mark uses speaks of sorrow that cuts deep. This is not the anger of an offended man—it's the sorrow of a holy Savior who longs for His people to see. Jesus was angry not because they disagreed, but because they were blind. They loved their rules more than their neighbor.

Then he says to the man, *"Stretch out your hand."* And as he does, the hand is restored, completely whole. Jesus never touched him. He spoke. That's how powerful His word is. The man who stood in shame is

30

now standing in healing. The center of the trap has become the stage for God's grace. And all of this happened on the Sabbath. The day of rest. The day of renewal. The very day these leaders thought Jesus was violating, He was fulfilling.

V. The Conspiracy Begins (v. 6)

And how do the Pharisees respond? *"The Pharisees went out and immediately held counsel with the Herodians against him, how to destroy him."*

This is chilling. The Herodians were not religious people. They were political allies of Herod, aligned with Roman power and often despised by the Pharisees. But here, religion and politics unite in their hatred of Jesus. The enemy of my enemy is my friend. That was their logic. Jesus was a threat to both camps, so they joined forces to eliminate Him. Notice the irony. Jesus asked if it was lawful to *save life or kill* on the Sabbath. They refused to answer. But now, they begin plotting murder on the Sabbath.

Their hearts are so hard that they don't see the contradiction. The Sabbath is broken, not by healing a man, but by conspiring to kill the Son of God. This is the beginning of a growing opposition that will lead to the cross. The tension that started with questions is turning into action. The conflict is no longer just theological; it's life-or-death.

The Bigger Picture

This brief scene carries significant theological weight. It reveals the core of the gospel. Jesus came not just to heal bodies, but to expose hearts. Not just to confront sin, but to call sinners to Himself. Not just to challenge the system, but to fulfill the law with truth and grace. And it asks every reader the same question: Will you stand with Jesus in the center, or will you stay silent in the shadows?

There's no neutrality with Jesus. The man with the withered hand had to stand up. The Pharisees had to make a choice. And so do we. Will we cling to our control or surrender to Christ? The great conspiracy was not just political; it was spiritual. The powers of darkness saw the Light of the World, and they hated it. But what they didn't know was that their conspiracy would become the very path of redemption. The cross wasn't the end of Jesus; it was His victory.

Reflection & Response

What do the Pharisees' motives in this story reveal about the dangers of hardened hearts?

How does Jesus' emotional response—anger and grief—shape your understanding of His character?

In what ways do we sometimes use religion to avoid real mercy and love?

What does it mean for you to "stand up" and obey Jesus in front of others, even when it's uncomfortable?

How does this scene point forward to the ultimate conspiracy at the cross—and why is that good news?

Falling Before Him

Mark 3:7–12

I. A Shift from the Synagogue to the Shore (v. 7)

Following the explosive confrontation in the synagogue where Jesus healed the man with the withered hand and exposed the Pharisees' hardness of heart, Mark tells us that Jesus withdrew to the sea. This wasn't a retreat out of fear. It was a strategic redirection. Jesus isn't abandoning ministry; He's broadening it. The synagogue, once the center of religious life, had become a place of opposition. But at the shore, Jesus draws people from every corner of Israel and even beyond.

Jesus doesn't stop ministering because of opposition. He shifts the venue. When the religious walls close in, He opens the doors wide to the world. This movement to the sea symbolizes something significant: the kingdom of God is not confined to religious institutions. It reaches far and wide across the lands.

The crowds follow from Galilee, Judea, Jerusalem, Idumea (to the south), the region beyond the Jordan (to the east), and even Tyre and Sidon (Gentile territories to the north). People come from everywhere. The word is spreading fast. Jesus' reputation is expanding quickly. The sheer magnetism of Jesus—his authority, his compassion, his power—is drawing people from all directions. And they're not coming to be entertained. They come in desperation and expectation.

II. Crushed by the Crowd, Driven by Need (vv. 8–9)

Mark gives us a vivid picture of the chaos. The crowd was so large and intense that Jesus told His disciples to prepare a boat as a getaway vessel in case things got out of control. That's how overwhelming the need was. The people were pressing in, not because they were curious, but because they were convinced. They needed Jesus to touch them. To heal them. To help them. And they were willing to crowd Him to get it.

This wasn't a calm religious assembly. It was a throng of hurting humanity reaching for hope. Some came with twisted limbs. Others with tormented minds. Some have lifelong illnesses. Perhaps others are carrying loved ones on stretchers. And all of them are moving toward one man. Jesus doesn't recoil. He doesn't rebuke the crowd. He prepares for it. He continues to minister, heal, and teach. But the pressure is intense. The desperation is real.

This is the weight of ministry. Jesus doesn't stay in pristine spaces. He enters the real need. He allows himself to be surrounded, pulled on, and crowded by the pain of the people. And yet, even here, He's not overwhelmed. His compassion keeps flowing. His power never runs dry.

III. Falling Before Him (v. 11)

Then Mark adds a surprising detail. *"Whenever the unclean spirits saw him, they fell before him and cried out, 'You are the Son of God.'"*

This is the second time in Mark's gospel that demons declare who Jesus is (see Mark 1:24). But this time, the image is even more striking; they fall before Him. Even in rebellion, they must bow. The demons' physical reaction is a theological truth: Jesus is Lord, even over the powers of darkness. They can't stand in His presence. They collapse under His authority.

The Greek word used here for "fall down" (πίπτω, *pipto*) is the same word used elsewhere in Scripture for worship or total submission. And though their allegiance is not genuine, their posture is revealing. The demonic realm recognizes something that the religious leaders refuse to see. Jesus is not just a healer. He's not just a teacher. He is the Holy One of God—the divine Son with sovereign authority.

They name Him correctly, *"You are the Son of God."* But Jesus silences them. Not because the statement is false, but because the timing is wrong. The crowd's understanding of "Son of God" is incomplete, and Jesus will reveal His identity on His own terms, ultimately through the cross. There is a sobering lesson here: It's possible to hold correct theology and still be opposed to Jesus. The demons had a better Christology than the Pharisees, but they lacked faith. They did not bow in surrender, only in fear.

Don't settle for being impressed by Jesus. Fall before Him in faith. Surrender. Worship. Obey.

IV. Power that Draws and Divides

This short section captures the growing tension in Jesus' ministry. On one hand, His power is drawing people like never before. On the other hand, it is exposing the true nature of hearts. The crowd is massive, but not all are there for the right reasons. Some want healing. Some want hope. Others want spectacle. The demons fall before Him, but not in repentance. The religious leaders remain on the sidelines, plotting destruction.

Jesus stands in the middle of all of it, composed, Compassionate, and Commanding. He is calling people not just to admire Him, but to follow Him. Mark's gospel often paints the contrast: between belief and unbelief, between curiosity and commitment, between confession and conspiracy. And here, that tension continues to rise.

V. Who Do You Say That He Is?

The crowds came because they had heard of what Jesus could do. The demons fell because they recognized Jesus. The question for us is: What will we do in response?

Falling before Jesus is more than a physical posture. It's a heart posture. It means acknowledging His authority and submitting our lives to Him. The crowds were amazed. The demons were terrified. But the true disciple falls before Him in worship, recognizing that this Jesus is not only powerful but worthy.

If even the demons fall before Him, how much more should we? Not in fear, but in faith. Not because we must, but because we get to. Jesus is not content to be a spectacle. He is Savior and King. And He calls us to more than admiration, he calls us to allegiance.

Reflection & Response

What does the growing size and desperation of the crowd tell you about the human condition and about Jesus' compassion?

Why do you think the demons consistently recognize Jesus' identity before others do?

How does Jesus' response to being overwhelmed (v. 9) model faithful ministry under pressure?

In what ways are we tempted to admire Jesus without falling before Him in surrender?

Jesus' Calling: Purpose of His Call – Part 1

Mark 3:13–19

I. The Mountain of Calling (v. 13)

Mark tells us that Jesus "went up on the mountain and called to him those whom he desired, and they came to him." Mountains in Scripture are significant. They're often places of revelation, where God meets with His people. Think of Sinai with Moses, or the Mount of Transfiguration. Here, Jesus chooses a mountain for the moment. He's not escaping the crowds; He's preparing leaders. In the Gospels, Jesus never gathers a crowd. He calls disciples. He's not looking for spectators. He's raising servants.

The phrase "He called to him those whom he desired" conveys an intimacy and sovereignty. This wasn't a mass invitation. It was an intentional selection.

Jesus chose them, not based on their qualifications, education, or charisma, but because He desired them.

That truth brings both humility and assurance. Our calling begins not with our merit, but with His mercy. Discipleship is about responding to the One who calls. If you belong to Jesus, it's because He called you. He desired you. He drew you to Himself. "And they came to him." Simple. Powerful. They responded. Jesus' call demands a response. The disciples didn't just hear the call; they left what they were doing and came.

II. The Purpose of Discipleship (v. 14)

Verse 14 is one of the most explicit expressions of Jesus' strategy for discipleship: *"And he appointed twelve (whom he also named apostles) so that they might be with him and he might send them out..."*

Don't miss the order:

To be with Him

To be sent out

Before Jesus sends them to preach or cast out demons, He calls them to Himself. Discipleship starts with closeness to Jesus. The primary purpose of following Jesus is to be with Jesus. Ministry without intimacy is empty. Before Jesus wants your service, He wants your heart. Your nearness. Your attention.

This flies in the face of our productivity-driven culture. We equate effectiveness with activity. But Jesus knows that power flows from proximity. The twelve will one day stand before rulers, perform miracles, and suffer for the kingdom. But first, they must learn to sit with Him. This "being with" is about formation. Their character will be shaped not just by what Jesus teaches, but by how He lives. They'll see His prayer life. His compassion. His endurance. His grief. His joy. And all of that will mold them. The call to discipleship is a call to closeness. You cannot be transformed by someone you keep at a distance.

III. The Commission to Proclaim and Push Back Darkness (v. 15)

Next, Jesus gives them purpose beyond presence: *"and he might send them out to preach and have authority to cast out demons."*

These two tasks —preaching and spiritual warfare — sum up the mission. They're not just followers. They're ambassadors. And their message is more than information; it's confrontation. To preach is to declare the good news of the kingdom. It's not just teaching moral principles. It's proclaiming that the reign of God has come in Jesus Christ. That sin can be forgiven, and life can be transformed.

To cast out demons is to push back the kingdom of darkness. The disciples are given real spiritual authority because of who sent them. The same power that was on display in Jesus' ministry is now extended through them. Discipleship is not a spectator sport. Jesus calls you to Himself, but then He sends you out with a message that saves and has the power to set free. This is a reminder that Christian discipleship is both relational and intentional. You are close to Jesus so that you can share Him with others. You sit at His feet, and then you stand in His name.

IV. The Twelve He Appointed (vv. 16–19)

Mark then lists the twelve by name. Each name carries history, personality, and a future story of both failure and faithfulness.

Simon (Peter) – Impulsive, bold, and deeply human. The rock that would deny, weep, and eventually lead.

James and John – Sons of Thunder. Zealous. Protective. Sometimes short-tempered. But Jesus would shape their passion into courage.

Andrew, Philip, Bartholomew, Matthew, Thomas, James (Son of Alphaeus), Thaddaeus, Simon the Zealot, and Judas Iscariot – A mix of fishermen, tax collectors, skeptics, political extremists, and unknowns.

This is not a dream team. It's a mess of ordinary men with rough edges and complicated pasts. And yet they were the ones Jesus chose. He appointed them. He called them by name. Jesus doesn't build His kingdom with the impressive. He builds it with the willing, available, and surrendered.

Each of these men would carry the gospel across the known world. All but one would die for it. Their stories remind us that calling doesn't require perfection. It requires obedience. And at the end of the list, Judas Iscariot, "who betrayed him."

Even here, we see the shadow of the cross. Jesus called Judas, knowing full well what he would do. This reminds us that God's purposes are never thwarted by betrayal. Even the greatest act of treachery would be woven into the tapestry of redemption. Jesus didn't make a mistake with Judas. He made a plan. The cross wasn't a backup; it was the mission.

V. What It Means for Us

This passage is more than a historical account. It's a window into how Jesus still works. He still calls. Still forms. Still sends. And the pattern remains:

He calls whom He desires

He invites us to be with Him

He equips us to go out for Him

He uses the weak, the flawed, the overlooked

He builds His kingdom with faithfulness

If you belong to Jesus, your calling starts with the same invitation: *Be with Me.* Everything else, ministry, mission, purpose, flows from that. Don't rush past the call to be with Him. Before you try to do big things for God, spend time with God. That's where the power is. That's where the change begins.

Reflection & Response

How does Jesus' invitation to "be with Him" challenge your view of discipleship?

In what ways have you been tempted to value doing for Jesus more than being with Jesus?

Why is it significant that Jesus chose ordinary, flawed people to carry out His mission?

How does it encourage you to know that Judas' betrayal didn't derail God's plan?

Jesus' Calling: Purpose of His Call – Part 2
Mark 3:13–19

In Part 1, we saw that Jesus called the Twelve not first to preach or act, but *to be with Him*. From this nearness flows their ministry. In Part 2, we step deeper into the implications of that calling. Who were these men? What does their story tell us about the kind of people Jesus chooses and what He expects?

Mark lists the Twelve not as background characters, but as a foundational moment in redemptive history. These are the ones Jesus appointed. Not because they were extraordinary, but because He is.

I. Jesus Appointed Twelve (v. 14)

The Greek word translated "appointed" means "making" or "creating." Jesus isn't just gathering a group; He is forming something new. These twelve are more than assistants; they represent the restored people of God. Just as there were twelve tribes in Israel, so too are there twelve apostles who will serve as foundational witnesses in the new covenant community. Jesus is doing more than selecting servants. He's signaling something: God is remaking

His people, and He's starting with a dozen ordinary men.

Their appointment is both symbolic and strategic. Jesus will pour into these Twelve more deeply than anyone else. They will carry His message, represent His kingdom, and apart from Judas suffer for His name. The disciples aren't just called *to* something. They are called *for* something. And that distinction matters.

II. From Unremarkable to Essential

When you look at this list of names, there's not much that would stand out in the ancient world:

Peter, known for being impulsive and deeply flawed

James and John, hot-tempered "sons of thunder"

Andrew, quieter and often in the background

Philip and Bartholomew are barely mentioned beyond the lists

Matthew, a former tax collector

Thomas, mainly remembered for doubting

James (Son of Alphaeus), **Thaddaeus**, and **Simon the Zealot**—largely unknown

Judas Iscariot, the betrayer

There's no prestige in this lineup; No theologians or trained scribes: just fishermen, tradesmen, and a tax man. Jesus didn't call the impressive, he called the available. He didn't need degrees; He needed disciples. This is how Jesus builds His kingdom: through surrender and willing hearts. And here's the miracle: These men, flawed, fearful, and forgettable, would become the foundation of the church. Their words would spread across empires. Their faithfulness would change the course of human history. Their obedience would cost them everything.

III. Judas Iscariot: Chosen and Yet Lost

Mark ends the list with a sobering line: *"and Judas Iscariot, who betrayed him."*

Jesus knew from the beginning. And yet He called him. For three years, Judas followed, listened, and watched. He held the money bag. The group trusted him. But his heart was never truly with Jesus. You can be near Jesus in proximity and still far from Him in your heart. Judas is proof that religious activity is no substitute for genuine faith.

This raises a theological mystery: Why would Jesus call someone who would betray Him?

The answer is twofold:

To fulfill Scripture and divine purpose, Judas' betrayal would set in motion the cross. God's sovereignty was never in danger.

To remind us of the danger of external discipleship—Proximity to ministry does not equal saving faith.

Judas's inclusion is a warning. But it also highlights the unmatched grace of Jesus. He washed Judas' feet. Broke bread with him. Loved him. And still, Judas walked away. Judas' story should humble us. It should make us examine our own hearts. Am I following Jesus or just around others who do?

IV. The Pattern of Discipleship

In these verses, we see the recurring shape of discipleship in the gospel of Mark:

Called by Jesus – "He called to Him those He desired."

With Jesus – "That they might be with Him."

Sent by Jesus – "To preach and have authority."

This same pattern holds for us today.

Calling is personal and gracious. We are saved not because of what we offer, but because of what He gives.

Being with Jesus is the foundation. We cannot give what we don't have.

Being sent is the overflow. Every disciple is sent. Not all are preachers, but all are proclaimers.

If you're a follower of Jesus, you are called to more than belief. You're called to be with Him and to go for Him. You are both loved and launched.

This pattern guards us against two common errors:

Activism without intimacy – doing for Jesus without being with Jesus

Comfort without calling – sitting with Jesus but never going for Him

Healthy discipleship holds both together. Time with Jesus fuels the mission for Jesus.

V. Application for Today

This passage is a mirror. It asks us to see ourselves in these Twelve.

Are you...

Willing like Peter, even if flawed?

Zealous like James and John, needing refinement?

Hidden like Thaddaeus, but available?

Struggling like Thomas, but still showing up?

Close to Jesus in proximity, like Judas—but far in heart?

Jesus still calls disciples today. He still appoints and sends. And he's not looking for spiritual all-stars. He's looking for people who will trust Him, follow Him, and be transformed by being with Him. Don't believe the lie that God can't use you. If he used this group, He can use you. What matters is not your background, but your obedience.

Mark's list ends quietly, but these men's lives exploded into action in the book of Acts. And that's the call for us too: ordinary people with an extraordinary Savior, carrying His message into a dark world.

Reflection & Response

Which of the Twelve do you relate to most right now, and why?

Why is it significant that Jesus chose such ordinary people to launch His kingdom mission?

How does the pattern of discipleship (called → with Him → sent out) shape your understanding of what it means to follow Jesus?

What's one way you've been tempted to follow Jesus outwardly but not inwardly?

What will it look like for you to be with Jesus and be sent by Him this week?

The Folly of the Scribes and the Unforgivable Sin

Mark 3:20–30

I. Misunderstood by His Own (vv. 20–21)

Mark tells us that Jesus entered a house and the crowd gathered again, "so that they could not even eat." The pressure of public ministry is relentless. The crowds are so overwhelming that Jesus can't take a break for basic needs. But the most surprising detail is what happens next: *"When his family heard it, they went out to seize him, for they were saying, 'He is out of his mind.'"*

His own family thought He had lost it. Not his enemies. Not the Pharisees. His family. It's a sobering reminder: even those closest to Jesus misunderstood Him. Mary and his brothers were concerned, maybe embarrassed. The intensity of His ministry, His controversial claims, and His high level of productivity all seemed irrational.

And in a culture built on honor, this behavior would reflect on the whole household. The family goes to take charge of Jesus. The word *"seize"* is strong; it implies force and intervention, almost as if restraining someone for their own safety. The crowds do not just misunderstand Jesus. He's misjudged by those who share His blood. The ultimate issue is unbelief. Faith in Jesus doesn't come through biology. It comes through belief. Proximity to Christ doesn't guarantee clarity about Him.

II. Accused by the Scribes (vv. 22–27)

As if being misunderstood by His family weren't enough, the religious elite now slanders Jesus. The scribes from Jerusalem —the theological watchdogs — don't deny His power. That's what makes this passage so chilling. They see the miracles. They hear the teaching. And they don't call Him a fraud; they call Him demonic.

"Beelzebul possesses him," they say, *"and by the prince of demons he casts out demons."*

They attribute the work of the Holy Spirit to Satan himself. It's one thing to doubt Jesus. It's another thing to watch Him cast out demons and say, "That's the devil's power." This is deliberate blindness; a heart hardened by pride.

Jesus answers them with a parable. He exposes the logical absurdity of their accusation:

"How can Satan cast out Satan?"

"If a kingdom is divided against itself, that kingdom cannot stand."

"If Satan has risen against himself and is divided, he cannot stand, but is coming to an end."

In other words, Jesus says, "Why would Satan work against his own agenda? Why would he cast out his own forces?" This is more than a defense; it's an exposure. The scribes aren't thinking clearly. They're not trying to be accurate. They're trying to discredit Jesus, even if it means embracing contradiction.

Then Jesus gives them the correct interpretation: *"No one can enter a strong man's house and plunder his goods, unless he first binds the strong man. Then indeed he may plunder his house."*

Jesus is saying: "You're seeing exorcisms not because I'm demonic, but because I've invaded Satan's territory and bound him." The casting out of demons is proof that Jesus has authority over darkness. The kingdom of God has come, and it's not negotiating with evil—it's conquering it.

III. Warning About the Unforgivable Sin (vv. 28–30)

Then Jesus makes one of the most sobering statements in all of Scripture:

"Truly, I say to you, all sins will be forgiven the children of man, and whatever blasphemies they utter..."

"...but whoever blasphemes against the Holy Spirit never has forgiveness, but is guilty of an eternal sin."

This is an extreme warning; It's a red alert.

Jesus is warning the scribes, his family, and all of us that there is a line. A line where the heart becomes so hard, so self-assured, so resistant to truth, that it calls light darkness and darkness light. Let's be clear: Jesus begins with grace. *"All sins will be forgiven..."* That's good news. Jesus forgives liars, adulterers, murderers, deniers, and doubters. There is no sin too deep for His mercy. But then comes the warning: *"...whoever blasphemes against the Holy Spirit never has forgiveness."*

What is this "blasphemy against the Holy Spirit"? It is the willful, settled rejection of the Spirit's testimony about Jesus. In this case, the scribes saw Jesus' miracles, which the Spirit empowered, and instead of believing, they attributed them to Satan.

It is not just unbelief, it is active resistance. It's calling the Spirit's work evil. It's rejecting the only path to forgiveness and, in doing so, making forgiveness impossible. The unforgivable sin is not a moment of doubt or a season of rebellion. It's the hardened, willful rejection of the Spirit's witness to Jesus. It is a settled unbelief. Jesus gives this warning: "because they were saying, 'He has an unclean spirit.'" The warning isn't theoretical. It's direct. The scribes are walking dangerously close to that line.

IV. A Word of Pastoral Clarity

Many believers have read this passage and panicked:

"Have I committed the unforgivable sin?"

"Did I say something wrong about the Holy Spirit?"

"Is there no way back?"

Let me give you a clear pastoral word:

If you're worried you've committed this sin, that's a strong sign you haven't.

Why?

Because the unforgivable sin requires a heart so hardened that it no longer cares. It no longer listens. It's not concerned about repentance or forgiveness. It is settled in its rejection of Jesus and His Spirit. The person who fears they've sinned is often the very person who's sensitive to the Spirit's conviction. And that sensitivity is evidence of grace.

Satan loves to weaponize this passage to cause despair in the heart of a struggling believer. But this warning isn't meant to crush the repentant. It's intended to expose pride. This text isn't here to rob you of assurance. It's here to remind you of the seriousness of rejecting Christ. It's a call to respond while grace is available.

V. The Right Response to Jesus

This passage presents us with a contrast:

Jesus is crowded by those who want to touch Him.

His family dismisses him as crazy.

The scribes accuse him of being demonic.

So how should we respond?

With Faith. We must see Jesus for who He is: the One who binds the strong man—the One empowered by the Holy Spirit. The One sent by the Father to destroy the works of the devil and redeem sinners. You can call Him crazy. You can call Him a liar. Or you can call Him Lord. But you can't remain neutral. There's no middle ground with Jesus. You either see Him as sent by God or reject Him as dangerous. That's what this passage presses on us. The scribes knew the Scriptures. They knew theology. But they missed the heart of God standing right before them. May it not be so with us.

Reflection & Response

Why do you think Jesus was so misunderstood by His own family and the religious leaders?

What does it mean that the scribes attributed Jesus' power to Satan?

How does Jesus' parable of the "strong man" help clarify His mission?

What is your understanding of the "unforgivable sin"? Why is it so serious?

How can we guard our hearts from becoming hardened to the Spirit's witness about Jesus?

True Family

Mark 3:31–35

Jesus has been misunderstood by the crowds, accused by the scribes, and questioned by His family. Now, in the final scene of Mark 3, we are brought face to face with a radical redefinition of what it means to belong to the family of God. This passage is brief, but weighty. It challenges assumptions, and it draws a clear line between cultural belonging and kingdom belonging.

I. The Arrival of Jesus' Biological Family (v. 31)

"And his mother and his brothers came, and standing outside they sent to him and called him."

Mark sets the scene with just a few strokes: Jesus is inside, surrounded by people. His family is outside, trying to reach Him. It's essential to recall the context. Just a few verses earlier, in Mark 3:21, His family said, *"He is out of his mind."* Now they've arrived, likely to take Him home, perhaps to de-escalate a public scene or manage the rising tension. It's a well-meaning intervention, yet it's born of a misunderstanding. They think they're helping. They don't realize they're resisting the very mission of God.

Mary and Jesus' brothers are here. But they are "outside." That detail is more than geographic. It's theological. To be outside in Mark's gospel often symbolizes misunderstanding or unbelief. The insiders —the ones close to Jesus —are not always His relatives.

II. The Message Delivered (v. 32)

"And a crowd was sitting around him, and they said to him, 'Your mother and your brothers are outside, seeking you.'"

The crowd becomes the messengers. The implication is clear: "Jesus, your family wants to speak with you. You should probably stop what you're doing and go to them." In first-century Jewish culture, family honor was a big deal. To publicly ignore your family, especially your mother, would be seen as disgraceful. It's expected that Jesus will pause, step outside, and address them.

But what Jesus does next shocks everyone. Jesus doesn't dismiss His family out of disrespect. He reframes the conversation to redefine what true belonging looks like in His kingdom.

III. A Provocative Question (v. 33)

"And he answered them, 'Who are my mother and my brothers?'"

This isn't forgetfulness, nor is it rhetorical flair. It's a heart-level challenge. Who is genuinely close to Jesus? Who really belongs to Him? Who gets His time, His attention, His approval?

In a society where family ties were sacred, this question would sound almost rebellious. But Jesus isn't minimizing family, He's maximizing discipleship. He's redefining family through the lens of faith. Jesus is saying, "My truest relationships are not determined by blood, but by belief."

IV. The New Family of Faith (vv. 34–35)

"And looking about at those who sat around him, he said, 'Here are my mother and my brothers! For whoever does the will of God, he is my brother and sister and mother.'"

Jesus lifts His eyes and gestures to the group sitting at His feet —the crowd gathered around Him in obedience and hunger —and says, *"This is my family."* This is one of the most powerful moments in the gospel. Jesus declares that obedience, not biology, is the defining mark of family in God's kingdom.

The true family of Jesus is composed of those who hear and obey God's Word, not those of natural birth. This is good news for the outcast. For the one without family. For the one whose earthly home has been broken, strained, or lost. In Christ, you are not alone. You belong to a family —one that is eternal, global, and united by grace —the church.

But it's also a challenge. Cultural Christianity often assumes that church attendance or a Christian heritage equates to closeness with Jesus. This passage says otherwise. Proximity to Jesus is not the same as a relationship with Jesus. Spiritual belonging is marked by obedience.

V. Implications for the church today

This moment reshapes our understanding of community, discipleship, and identity.

The church is a Family.

We don't just attend a service. We belong to a people: Brothers and sisters, mothers and fathers in the faith.

Obedience Defines Relationship

Jesus doesn't say, "Whoever feels spiritual" or "Whoever believes in God." He says, *"Whoever does the will of God."*

Obedience doesn't earn salvation, but it proves spiritual family ties.

Earthly Family Must Be Held with Open Hands

Jesus loved His mother. Even on the cross, He cared for her (John 19:26–27). But he never allowed family ties to distract him from His divine mission.

We Must Prioritize the People of God

Many Christians treat church as optional, and family as ultimate. Jesus reverses that. He doesn't abandon His family, but He teaches us that faith and family are deeper than flesh and blood.

The church should be a kind of family where someone without earthly support can find belonging, help, and love. If Jesus redefined family around faith, we should too.

VI. A Word to Families

This passage also speaks to Christian households:

Parents: Do not assume your children are close to Jesus because they live in your home. Faith must be personal.

Spouses: Your partner's faith cannot cover your unbelief. You must follow Christ yourself.

Church leaders: Elevate spiritual family as a core identity marker for your people.

Jesus is not anti-family. He's pro-God's family. And that's an invitation for all.

Reflection & Response

What surprises you most about Jesus' response to His family?

How does this passage challenge cultural assumptions about religion and family?

In what ways are you prioritizing obedience to God's will?

How can you deepen your experience of the church as your true spiritual family?

Is there someone in your local church who needs to experience the welcome of God's family through you?

Chapter 4

The Word at Work: Kingdom Building
Mark 4:1–20

Jesus was not a mere moral teacher. He was a kingdom builder. And his primary tool for building the kingdom was his Word. That truth is powerfully on display in Mark 4, where Jesus begins to teach in parables. The crowds are massive, the anticipation is high, and Jesus opens His mouth not to impress, but to plant.

I. A Parable Proclaimed (vv. 1–9)

"Again, he began to teach beside the sea. And a very large crowd gathered about him..."

The scene is familiar: Jesus beside the sea, a growing crowd pressing in. But something shifts. To address them, Jesus steps into a boat and teaches from the water while the people listen from the shore. Then he tells a story—a parable—one of His most famous. This isn't just a nice farming illustration. It's a kingdom diagnostic—a spiritual mirror.

"Listen! Behold, a sower went out to sow..." (v. 3)

Jesus describes a farmer scattering seed. Some fall on the path, some on rocky ground, some among thorns, and some on good soil. The results vary drastically.

Path – birds snatch the seed

Rocky ground – sprouts quickly but withers in the sun

Thorns – choked by competing growth

Good soil – yields a bountiful harvest

Then Jesus says, *"He who has ears to hear, let him hear."*

That phrase signals something more profound than the surface story. This is not a farming lesson. It's a spiritual parable with eternal stakes. Every time God's Word is preached, hearts respond in one of these four ways. This isn't about agriculture, it's about you.

II. The Mystery of the Kingdom (vv. 10–12)

After the crowds disperse, the disciples and a few others ask Jesus to explain. Why the story? Why not just say what you mean?

Jesus answers with a striking statement:

"To you has been given the secret of the kingdom of God, but for those outside everything is in parables..." (v. 11)

Jesus isn't hiding the truth to be cruel. He's fulfilling prophecy (see Isaiah 6). Parables both reveal and conceal. They sift the hearers. Those with soft hearts lean in. Those with hardened hearts walk away confused. Parables are meant to expose, not entertain. They show who wants to understand, and who doesn't. This is important: Jesus isn't keeping people out of the kingdom. He's inviting them in, but they must come through faith, not mere curiosity.

III. The Parable Explained (vv. 13–20)

Now Jesus gives the meaning. The parable is about the Word, and the soil represents the hearts that hear it.

1. The Path (v. 15)

"Satan immediately comes and takes away the word that is sown in them."

This is the hard heart. The Word lands, but never sinks in. It sits on the surface, dismissed, ignored, rejected. And Satan snatches it away. Some people hear a faithful gospel sermon and forget it before they reach the parking lot. The enemy is always at work, stealing the seed. This reminds us that preaching is a form of spiritual warfare. The enemy doesn't fear eloquence; he fears the Word.

2. The Rocky Ground (vv. 16–17)

"They receive it with joy... but they have no root in themselves... when tribulation or persecution arises... they fall away."

This is the shallow heart. The Word is received with emotion, but not depth. There's enthusiasm, but no endurance. The gospel gets crowded out when life gets hard. These are the people who love Jesus at camp but walk away when school starts. Faith that flames up fast often burns out just as quickly. Jesus is warning us: not all joy is saving joy. True conversion lasts.

3. The Thorny Ground (v. 18–19)

"They are those who hear the word, but the cares of the world... the deceitfulness of riches... and the desires for other things enter in and choke the word."

This is the distracted heart. The Word takes root, but so do weeds. Competing loves suffocate faith. The pursuit of success, comfort, or pleasure overwhelms spiritual growth.

You can't grow a fruitful garden if you don't pull the weeds. If Jesus isn't first, He eventually gets choked out. This is especially relevant for our culture, where distraction is constant and idols are everywhere. The thorny soil warns us: divided hearts don't bear lasting fruit.

4. The Good Soil (v. 20)

"They hear the word and accept it and bear fruit, thirtyfold and sixtyfold and a hundredfold."

This is the responsive heart. The Word lands, sinks deep, and transforms. Obedience follows. Growth occurs. Fruit multiplies. The good soil shows what Jesus is after, not just hearing but responding. Not just proximity to the Word, but transformation by the Word. Fruit isn't optional. It's inevitable in the life of someone truly changed by grace.

IV. The Word and the Work

The central character in this parable isn't the soil, it's the sower. The power is in the seed. That's good news for every pastor, teacher, parent, and friend sowing the

Word. We're not responsible for the soil, but we are responsible for sowing.

You don't get to choose the harvest, but you do get to scatter the seed. This frees us from the performance anxiety that often accompanies ministry. The results are God's. The task is ours. And this parable also reminds us: the Word is at work. Even when we don't see immediate results, the seed is doing something under the surface.

V. What Kind of Soil Are You?

This parable isn't just about how *others* respond to the Word; it's a personal invitation to examine our own hearts.

Am I hard-hearted? Uninterested? Defensive?

Am I shallow? Quick to respond, but unwilling to endure?

Am I distracted? Crowded with cares and comforts?

Am I fruitful? Growing in love, obedience, and holiness?

Don't assume you're good soil just because you're in church. The fruit is the proof. This is a call to self-examination, but also to hope. The seed is powerful. The Spirit is active. God can break up hard ground, deepen shallow faith, and weed out distractions. He's still turning hearts into good soil.

Reflection & Response

Which of the four soils do you most identify with in this season of life?

What are some "thorns" that could be choking your spiritual growth right now?

How can you sow the Word more faithfully in the lives of others this week?

What does this passage teach you about how God builds His kingdom?

This Big Light of Mine

Mark 4:21–25

Jesus has just told His disciples the Parable of the Sower, teaching them how the Word lands in different hearts and produces various results. Now, in this next section, He offers a follow-up lesson: when the Word truly takes root, it cannot remain hidden. The truth of the kingdom is not just planted, it's meant to shine.

This often-overlooked passage is a powerful reminder that God's truth is meant to be visible, transformative, and shared. In Mark 4:21-25, Jesus uses everyday images —lamps, measures, and hearing — to call His disciples to live in the light of His truth and to spread that light boldly.

I. Light Was Made to Shine (v. 21)

"And he said to them, 'Is a lamp brought in to be put under a basket, or under a bed, and not on a stand?'"

63

Jesus begins with a question that would seem almost comical in its obviousness. Who lights a lamp and then hides it under a basket? The whole purpose of light is to illuminate. The moment you hide it, you've contradicted its nature. But Jesus isn't talking about home décor; He's talking about revelation. About truth. About the Word of God. Jesus is the light of the world, and when His Word is preached and received, that light isn't meant to be tucked away. It's meant to shine in public. This statement follows the parable of the sower for a reason.

Jesus has just described how the Word takes root in good soil. Now he's saying, "When that happens, don't hide it." Let it shine. It's a call to visible discipleship. The gospel is not a private possession. Kingdom truth is not meant to be hoarded; it's meant to be displayed. Some Christians live like secret agents. No one at work, school, or even their extended family knows they follow Jesus. But Jesus didn't call us to camouflage faith—He called us to shining witness.

II. Nothing Hidden Will Stay Hidden (v. 22)

"For nothing is hidden except to be made manifest; nor is anything secret except to come to light."

This verse has both encouragement and warning. Jesus tells His disciples that what is hidden now —His identity, the full meaning of His kingdom, and the truth about His mission —will be revealed. God doesn't whisper the gospel so that it remains buried. He plants it so it will break through the surface and shine. The gospel began in a manger and went all the way to the cross—but it didn't stay hidden. It exploded into history. That's the nature of God's truth—it refuses to be silenced."

There is also a subtle warning here. Every hidden thing will one day be exposed. Not just truth, but also hearts. God knows what's buried. One day, every secret thought, motive, and allegiance will come to light. For the faithful, this is a call to boldness. For the hypocrite, it's a call to repentance.

III. Pay Careful Attention (v. 23–24a)

"If anyone has ears to hear, let him hear. And he said to them, 'Pay attention to what you hear...'"

This is a familiar refrain from Jesus: "He who has ears to hear, let him hear." But here he intensifies it, *pay attention* to what you hear. The idea isn't just listening with your ears but receiving with your heart. In other words: Be intentional. Be alert. Be discerning.

We live in a world full of noise, social media, podcasts, news, and opinions. But how often do we truly listen to the Word of God with focused, humble attention? Spiritual growth is not automatic. It comes to those who actively engage in the Word. Discipleship requires attentiveness, leaning in, careful thought, and diligent application. This call to pay attention also reminds us that Jesus doesn't teach in parables to obscure truth from those who seek it. He invites everyone to press in, to ask, to learn, to grow.

IV. The Measure You Use (v. 24b–25)

"...with the measure you use, it will be measured to you, and still more will be added to you. For to the one who has,

more will be given, and from the one who has not, even what he has will be taken away."

These are striking words. Jesus is explaining a spiritual principle: the way you respond to the truth determines how much more truth you'll receive.

If you're hungry for God's Word, more will be given.

If you're careless or indifferent, even what you have will slip away.

This is one of the most sobering realities in the Christian life: You never stay neutral with God's Word. You're either growing deeper or drifting away. Jesus is teaching His disciples —and us —that stewardship matters. How we handle what we've been given determines what we'll receive next. This principle applies to more than just knowledge. It applies to opportunity, influence, growth, and fruitfulness. God delights to give more to those who are faithful with what they already have.

V. Let the Light Shine

This entire section is a challenge to faithful stewardship of the gospel:

Don't hide the truth—shine it.

Don't tune out the Word—listen carefully.

Don't waste your opportunities—use them well.

It also contains a hopeful promise: God isn't stingy with light. He delights to give more to those who seek

Him. If you're eager to grow in the knowledge of Christ, in the power of the Spirit, and in usefulness for the kingdom, then take heart, *still more will be added to you.*

Jesus isn't looking for perfect vessels; He's looking for open ones. And when we open our lives to His Word, the light grows brighter. This section should stir us to action. It's a call to shine the gospel in our homes, workplaces, and communities. The Word was never meant to be buried under fear, shame, or indifference. It was meant to be proclaimed.

VI. A Word for the Church

There's a corporate application here, too. This isn't just about individual obedience but about the collective witness of the church.

Is your church a lamp on a stand, or a lamp under a basket?

Are your gatherings saturated with God's Word and shaped by it?

Is the truth being proclaimed clearly and lived out boldly?

Churches don't die because they run out of money. They die because they stop shining the light. The call to shine applies to pulpits and pews. A Word-centered church is a light-bearing church. And a light-bearing church is a kingdom-advancing church.

Reflection & Response

Are there areas in your life where you've been hiding the light of Christ rather than displaying it?

What does it look like for you to "pay attention" to the Word this week?

How can your local church better embody the calling to shine the light of the gospel?

An Unshakable Kingdom

Mark 4:26–34

Jesus continues His teaching on the nature of the kingdom of God with two more parables, simple in form but profound in meaning. In both, He uses agricultural imagery to challenge our assumptions about how God works.

In a world that prizes power, control, and instant results, Jesus offers us images of slow, steady, and sovereign growth. The kingdom of God is not built by human ingenuity. It is sown by divine power and sustained by sovereign grace.

I. The Parable of the Growing Seed (vv. 26–29)

"And he said, 'The kingdom of God is as if a man should scatter seed on the ground. He sleeps and rises night and day, and the seed sprouts and grows; he knows not how.'" (vv. 26–27)

This parable is unique to Mark's gospel. A man scatters seed on the ground, and then life goes on; he sleeps and rises, day after day. Meanwhile, the seed

68

begins to grow. The farmer doesn't know how. He isn't doing the growing; he's simply watching the process unfold.

This is a humbling picture for pastors and preachers. You can sow the seed faithfully, but you can't force fruit. Growth belongs to God. This is true for all of us. Whether you're a parent teaching your children, a friend sharing the gospel, or a pastor proclaiming God's Word, you are not the source of power. Your job is to sow. God's job is to grow. That's both freeing and faith-building. It means we can labor faithfully without carrying the burden of outcomes. It also means we must be patient. Kingdom growth often happens gradually, invisibly, and mysteriously.

"The earth produces by itself, first the blade, then the ear, then the full grain in the ear." (v. 28)

This verse reminds us that spiritual growth is a gradual and ongoing process. It unfolds in stages, slowly, steadily, according to God's design. We don't get to skip steps. You can't microwave maturity. The kingdom doesn't work like fast food; it's more like farming. Plant, water, wait, repeat. And then comes the harvest.

"But when the grain is ripe, at once he puts in the sickle, because the harvest has come." (v. 29)

This is a reference to the final judgment, the plentiful harvest of souls. It's a reminder that the kingdom has an end goal. There will be a day when God gathers His people and brings all things to fulfillment.

So, what does this parable teach us?

The kingdom grows **mysteriously** – "he knows not how"

The kingdom grows **gradually** – "first the blade, then the ear..."

The kingdom grows **certainly** – "the harvest has come"

That's what makes it unshakable. We do not build it. God sustains it.

II. The Parable of the Mustard Seed (vv. 30–32)

"And he said, 'With what can we compare the kingdom of God...? It is like a grain of mustard seed, which... is the smallest of all the seeds on earth.'" (vv. 30–31)

This second parable builds on the first. It begins with a contrast: the kingdom starts *small*, mustard-seed small. Tiny. Insignificant. Seemingly unimpressive. That was true of Jesus' ministry—a poor rabbi from Nazareth, surrounded by fishermen and tax collectors. No army. No throne. No PR campaign. Just truth, love, and power. And yet...

"...when it is sown it grows up and becomes larger than all the garden plants and puts out large branches..." (v. 32)

That's the miracle of the mustard seed. It starts small, but it doesn't stay that way. It grows into something significant, substantial, and sheltering. Don't despise small beginnings. God loves to use the weak to shame the strong, and the small to surprise the proud. This is a parable of encouragement. For disciples discouraged by the slow progress of the gospel, or the humble state of the church, or the challenges of ministry, Jesus is saying: *Trust the seed. Watch it grow.*

There's also an allusion to Old Testament imagery here. The description of the tree with branches that provide shade for birds recalls passages such as Ezekiel 17:22–24 and Daniel 4, in which kingdoms are pictured as great trees. Jesus says, "This is the true kingdom." *It may start small, but it will outlast them all.*

III. God's Kingdom Strategy

Taken together, these two parables offer a compelling portrait of how God builds His kingdom:

Sow the Word – faithfully, prayerfully, consistently

Trust the process – spiritual growth is not always visible

Wait on God – He brings the harvest in His timing

Expect great things – what starts small can become mighty

If we build our churches like businesses, we'll get business results. But if we plant the Word and water it with prayer, we'll see kingdom fruit that lasts. Jesus was preparing His disciples for the long road ahead. He knew they would face rejection, persecution, and delay. But he also knew the seed would work. The kingdom would grow. And the harvest would come. This is why we must not lose heart. When gospel ministry feels small or slow, remember that's precisely how God designed it.

IV. Parables with a Purpose (vv. 33–34)

"With many such parables he spoke the word to them, as they were able to hear it." (v. 33)

Jesus didn't just teach truth; He tailored it to the listener's ability to receive it. He met people where they were. He used familiar language, relatable stories, and vivid images. But he also left room for reflection. Parables aren't just illustrations; they're invitations. They force the listener to lean in, ask questions, and wrestle with meaning.

"He did not speak to them without a parable, but privately to his own disciples he explained everything." (v. 34)

This final verse shows us something about discipleship. The crowds got parables; the disciples got explanations. Because Jesus was preparing them for kingdom-building ministry, if you want more light, stay near the lamp. If you want deeper truth, remain near the teacher. This verse invites us to do the same. Don't settle for surface-level understanding. Go deeper. Ask questions. Meditate on the Word. Follow Jesus closely, and He'll give you more.

V. Application: What This Means for Us

These parables may be short, but they have rich implications:

1. Be a faithful sower.

Don't obsess over results. Don't grow discouraged when growth is slow. Just keep sowing the Word, in your home, your church, your workplace, your community. Trust that the seed works.

2. Embrace small beginnings.

Kingdom work doesn't usually start big or loud. It begins with prayer, truth, service, and faithfulness. God grows mighty things out of mustard seeds.

3. Don't underestimate gospel power.

The Word may seem simple, but it is not weak. God's truth, planted in the heart, can change a life and change the world.

4. Stick close to Jesus.

If you want to understand more, walk with Him more. Press in. Ask questions. Listen carefully.

Reflection & Response

How do these parables challenge your view of spiritual growth and gospel ministry?

Are there places in your life where you're tempted to measure success by size or speed?

What are some "mustard seed" ministries or efforts you need to keep pursuing in faith?

How can you commit to sowing the Word more faithfully this week?

All Creation Submits

Mark 4:35–41

At the end of a long day of teaching, Jesus invites His disciples to cross the Sea of Galilee. What starts as a peaceful journey quickly transforms into a life-altering revelation. Mark 4:35–41 shows not only Jesus' authority over the natural world but also challenges how we respond to His power in our lives. It teaches us to trust the sovereign Lord who is with us in every storm.

I. A Storm That Shakes (vv. 35–37)

"On that day, when evening had come, he said to them, 'Let us go across to the other side.'"

It's evening. Jesus has been teaching large crowds beside the sea all day. Tired and weary, He instructs His disciples to sail across the Sea of Galilee. At first, everything seems normal, familiar waters, seasoned fishermen at the helm, a simple task. But in a moment, everything changes.

"And a great windstorm arose, and the waves were breaking into the boat, so that the boat was already filling."

The Sea of Galilee is notorious for sudden storms, and this one is fierce. Waves are crashing, winds are howling, and water is flooding in. Even experienced fishermen like Peter and Andrew are terrified. Sometimes, the most ferocious storms strike without warning. They shake our confidence, test our courage, and reveal our deepest fears.

This storm wasn't just a physical test; it was a spiritual revelation. Storms have a way of exposing what's truly in our hearts. The disciples were faithful followers, yet here they are frightened, overwhelmed, uncertain. It reminds us: faithfulness does not exempt us from storms. But the presence of a storm doesn't mean the absence of the Savior.

II. A Savior Who Sleeps (v. 38)

Amid this chaos, we find one of the most remarkable scenes in Scripture: *"But he was in the stern, asleep on the cushion."*

Jesus is sleeping and not pretending. Not indifferent. But genuinely resting. This picture of Jesus asleep is astonishing. It demonstrates His complete humanity— He is genuinely tired from ministry. Yet it also hints at His complete divinity—He's entirely confident and unafraid. Jesus isn't worried because He knows who controls the wind and waves. Even asleep, He remains fully sovereign.

However, to the disciples, His rest appears to be neglect. In desperation, they cry out, *"Teacher, do you not care that we are perishing?"* It's a question born of fear and misunderstanding. The disciples confuse Jesus' calmness with carelessness. Haven't we asked similar questions in our own trials? "God, don't you see me?" "Jesus, don't you care?" Moments of desperation can distort our view of God's goodness.

III. A Sovereign Who Speaks (v. 39)

"And he awoke and rebuked the wind and said to the sea, 'Peace! Be still!"

Notice the authority in Jesus' words. He doesn't perform a ritual or make a request; He issues a command. He rebukes the wind as easily as a parent calms a frightened child. Creation recognizes its Creator's voice, and it submits immediately.

"And the wind ceased, and there was a great calm."

Mark emphasizes immediacy, no gradual fading of the storm, instant calm, and perfect peace. This wasn't a coincidence; it was obedience. Creation recognized the voice of its Maker. All creation submits. Jesus' command reveals not only His power but His identity. Psalm 89:9 says about God, *"You rule the raging of the sea; when its waves rise, you still them."* In calming the storm, Jesus is doing what only God can do. He's showing Himself as the Lord over creation itself.

IV. A Question That Challenges (v. 40)

After calming the storm, Jesus turns to the disciples with two penetrating questions:

"Why are you so afraid?"

"Have you still no faith?"

These questions are deeply challenging. Jesus doesn't rebuke the disciples for waking Him up; He rebukes their fear, their panic, their lack of trust. Fear can blind us. It makes us forget who's in the boat. Jesus' question cuts to the heart: 'Do you trust Me?'

Remember, the disciples had already seen Jesus heal, cast out demons, and teach with unmatched authority. But this storm revealed something important: they still didn't fully grasp who was with them. Jesus' questions weren't harsh; they were loving. He was inviting His disciples deeper into faith, challenging them to trust Him not just in calm waters, but in the fiercest storms.

V. A Response of Awe (v. 41)

After Jesus' questions, Mark records the disciples' reaction: *"And they were filled with great fear and said to one another, 'Who then is this, that even the wind and the sea obey him?'"*

Notice the shift. Earlier, they feared the storm. Now, after seeing Jesus calm the waves, their fear changes; it deepens into awe and reverence. The storm was terrifying, but realizing who Jesus truly is, that's overwhelming. This is a holy fear and reverence before the majesty and power of Jesus. It's the fear that comes when you realize you're standing in the presence of God.

The disciples' question is crucial: *"Who then is this?"* That's the question Mark wants every reader to answer. Who is Jesus? He's not just a great teacher. He's not merely a healer. He's the sovereign Lord, the Creator, God incarnate. In other words, the storm's purpose was revelation. It wasn't random suffering; it was a divine appointment.

VI. Implications for Our Storms

This powerful account isn't just about what happened then; it's about how we face storms today. Consider three applications for our lives:

BEHOLD THE CHRIST

1. Storms Will Come—Even for Faithful Disciples

Jesus never promises a storm-free life. Instead, He promises His presence. When storms arise, remember: Jesus is in your boat.

2. Storms Reveal What We Truly Believe

Storms expose the reality of our faith. They ask: Do we trust Jesus only in calm seas, or do we trust Him in fierce storms as well?

3. Storms Point Us to a Sovereign Savior

Every storm you face is an invitation to know Christ more deeply. In trials, Jesus reveals Himself as sovereign, good, and faithful.

Don't waste your storms. Let them draw you closer to Christ, deepening your awe, trust, and obedience.

Reflection & Response

When storms come into your life, do you respond more like the panicked disciples or the sleeping Jesus?

How does this passage encourage you to trust Christ even when He seems silent or distant?

Why is it significant that creation submits immediately to Jesus' authority? How should that impact our own submission to Him?

How can you cultivate a deeper sense of awe and reverence for Jesus as you face trials in your life?

Chapter 5

An Unlikely Convert

Mark 5:1–20

In Mark 5, we encounter a stunning demonstration of Jesus' sovereign power and compassionate authority. After calming the raging sea, Jesus now confronts another chaotic storm, this time in the heart and life of one desperate man. This story of an unlikely convert reveals the astonishing reach of God's grace. No one is beyond hope. No one is too broken. No one is too far gone for Jesus Christ.

I. A Desperate Condition (vv. 1–5)

Mark begins by setting a vivid scene: *"They came to the other side of the sea, to the country of the Gerasenes."* Immediately, a man confronts them—a terrifying figure, tormented and isolated. Mark describes him in chilling detail:

Living among tombs.

Possessed by unclean spirits.

Uncontrollable and violent

Breaking chains and shackles

Screaming night and day, harming himself with stones

This is one of the saddest descriptions of human suffering in the Bible, a man utterly overwhelmed by darkness, abandoned by society, and plagued by many demons. It's hard to imagine a more hopeless picture. Here is a man totally isolated, trapped by spiritual oppression, abandoned, and feared. His people had no solution for him; their chains failed, their strength failed, their compassion failed.

This man's condition reminds us that spiritual bondage is real. A man beyond human help confronts us. Mark wants us to grasp clearly that no human intervention can free him from this deep spiritual captivity.

II. A Divine Confrontation (vv. 6–13)

But notice the astonishing reaction: when this tormented man sees Jesus from a distance, he runs, not to attack, but to fall at His feet.

"And crying out with a loud voice, he said, 'What have you to do with me, Jesus, Son of the Most High God?'" (v. 7)

Even demons recognize Jesus immediately. They're fully aware of who He is—"Son of the Most High God." They fear Him, begging not to be tormented. Demons know exactly who Jesus is. They're clearer in their theology than many people alive today. They immediately recognize His power and authority.

Jesus commands the evil spirits to leave, asking their name. They reply, "Legion," because there are many of them. The term "Legion" indicates thousands of soldiers in Roman military terms, signifying overwhelming power. Yet these spirits are helpless before Christ's authority. They pleaded not to be sent away, but into a nearby herd of pigs. Jesus allows it. Instantly, thousands of pigs rush off a cliff, drowning in the sea. This isn't a mere spectacle; it's evidence. It visibly demonstrates the reality of spiritual warfare, the destructive nature of evil, and the absolute authority of Jesus Christ.

III. An Astonishing Transformation (vv. 14–15)

When the townspeople arrive, they're shocked by what they see:

"They came to Jesus and saw the demon-possessed man... sitting there, clothed and in his right mind, and they were afraid." (v. 15)

This verse is powerful. Notice the complete reversal:

Once tormented, now calm.

Once naked and ashamed, now clothed with dignity.

Once out of his mind, now fully restored and rational.

Once isolated, now sitting peacefully at Jesus' feet.

This is the power of Jesus. He takes a life overwhelmed by chaos and restores peace. No sin, no darkness, no bondage is beyond the redeeming touch of Christ. This transformation is profound and undeniable. Jesus doesn't just reform behavior; He completely renews the man from the inside out. Jesus isn't interested in surface-level fixes. He brings comprehensive restoration through transformation.

IV. A Revealing Reaction (vv. 16–17)

How do the townspeople respond to this astonishing miracle? Do they celebrate? Do they worship? Unfortunately, no. Instead, Mark writes, *"And they began to beg Jesus to depart from their region."* (v. 17)

Why this reaction? Because the presence of Jesus disrupted their lives. It could have been the loss of the herd of pigs, but most likely it was a fearful reaction. Jesus disrupted the status quo. Many people prefer the comfort of what is familiar, even if the uncomfortable makes them better. Asking Jesus to leave reveals their priorities and heart. This shows an awkward truth: seeing a miracle doesn't always produce faith. Sometimes it exposes unbelief. The townspeople's response was fear, but the wrong kind. They feared change, disruption, and loss —not the Lord Himself.

V. A Gracious Commission (vv. 18–20)

But the story doesn't end there. The healed man wants to follow Jesus. He begs to join Him. Jesus, surprisingly, says no: *"Go home to your friends and tell them how much the Lord has done for you, and how he has had mercy on you."* (v. 19)

Jesus gives him a mission. Rather than leave the area, Jesus commissions him to stay and share the story of grace with his own people—the very people who had rejected Jesus.

Notice the emphasis:

"Go home"

"Tell them"

"How much the Lord has done"

"How He had mercy"

Jesus sends this unlikely convert as His first missionary to Gentile territory. He didn't have a theology degree; he had a testimony of mercy. He brought the gospel to the Gentiles even before the Apostle Paul. And the man obeyed immediately. He began proclaiming throughout the Decapolis (ten Greek cities), and Mark tells us, "everyone marveled." This unlikely convert, once rejected, isolated, and broken, is now a powerful messenger of grace. This is how God builds His kingdom, not with perfect people, but with redeemed ones.

VI. Lessons for Us

This passage is full of profound implications for our lives today:

1. No one is beyond the reach of Jesus.

No matter how far gone someone seems, Jesus can transform them. Never lose hope or stop praying for those you think are "too far."

2. Jesus' authority is absolute.

There's no darkness, no addiction, no spiritual oppression He can't break. Trust His power, call on Him in your struggles.

3. We must choose our response to Jesus.

Will we welcome His disruptive power or ask Him to leave? Let Christ disturb you. Let Him transform you, even when it's uncomfortable.

4. We are called to share our story.

The man had no training, just a testimony. If Jesus has transformed you, you have a powerful message. Share it with your community, your friends, your neighbors. You don't have to be impressive to be used by God; you have to be available and grateful.

Reflection & Response

Where in your life have you experienced the powerful transforming grace of Christ?

Are you currently resisting or welcoming Jesus' disruptive presence in your life?

Who in your life seems like an unlikely convert— and how can you trust God to reach them through you?

What holds you back from sharing your testimony of God's mercy with others? How can you take a step this week?

When Faith and Fear Collide

Mark 5:21–43

Mark's gospel repeatedly places us at the crossroads between faith and fear. Nowhere is this more vivid than in Mark 5:21–43, where two desperate lives intersect at the feet of Jesus. Here we see vividly what happens when human desperation meets divine compassion, and when our deepest fears collide with our faith.

I. Desperate Situations (vv. 21–26)

Mark's account opens with Jesus returning from healing the demon-possessed man. Immediately, He's engulfed by a large crowd. In this chaos, two desperate figures emerge: Jairus, a prominent synagogue leader, and an unnamed woman suffering from chronic illness.

Jairus' Crisis (vv. 22–23)

Jairus approaches first, falling at Jesus' feet: *"My little daughter is at the point of death. Come and lay your hands on her, so that she may be made well and live."*

Feel Jairus' urgency. He's powerful, influential, and respected, but none of that matters now. His daughter is fading fast. Only Jesus can help.

The Woman's Suffering (vv. 25–26)

Before Jesus can respond, we're introduced to another heartbreaking story—a woman plagued for twelve years by constant bleeding. Mark tells us:

She had suffered greatly.

Spent all she had on doctors who offered no help.

Only grew worse over time.

This woman's story is tragically familiar. Twelve years of chronic pain, isolation, and humiliation. Twelve years of unanswered prayers. Suffering doesn't discriminate; it strikes the powerful and the powerless alike. Both Jairus and this woman are helpless in different ways. And both come desperately to Jesus.

II. When Faith Breaks Through (vv. 27–34)

This woman, despite social stigma and religious impurity, takes a remarkable step of faith. She reaches out to Jesus, to touch His garment, believing that even a brief contact would bring healing. Mark emphasizes immediacy: *"Immediately...she felt in her body that she was healed."* One moment of faith changes everything. Twelve years of pain vanish in an instant. Faith isn't about the strength of our grip; it's about the object of our trust. This woman's faith was small, silent, hesitant, but her Savior was strong.

Jesus pauses the urgent mission to Jairus' house, turns around, and asks: *"Who touched me?"* His disciples are confused; many people were crowding Him. But Jesus knows this touch was different. He looks directly at her. The woman trembles, fearful of being exposed. But Jesus meets her fear with grace. Instead of rebuke, He gives her a new identity: *"Daughter, your faith has made you well; go in peace."*

This is the only instance in Scripture where Jesus addresses someone as "daughter." He speaks peace over her deepest fears, affirming her faith. Jesus never sees our interruptions as inconveniences. He sees them as opportunities to reveal His grace.

III. When Fear Threatens Faith (vv. 35–36)

As Jesus speaks peace to the woman, devastating news arrives from Jairus' home: *"Your daughter is dead. Why trouble the Teacher any further?"* (v. 35)

Feel the emotional whiplash Jairus experiences. He came to Jesus full of desperate hope, but now it seems too late. His greatest fear has become reality. But Jesus immediately speaks into Jairus' pain: *"Do not fear, only believe."* (v. 36) He's calling Jairus (and us) to trust His timing and purpose, even when things seem hopeless.

Fear always competes with faith. It screams that God is late, indifferent, or incapable. But Jesus' voice cuts through fear's lies, urging us to trust His plan even when it doesn't make sense.

IV. A Miracle at the Edge of Hope (vv. 37–43)

Jesus dismisses the skeptical crowd, allowing only Peter, James, John, Jairus, and his wife into the room. Jesus silences the noisy mourners: *"The child is not dead but sleeping."* They mock Him, but Jesus sees what they cannot. Human perspective sees defeat; Jesus sees victory. Faith trusts His perspective over our limited sight.

Jesus takes the girl's hand, saying gently, "Talitha cumi.""Little girl, arise." Instantly, life returns. She stands up immediately. Once again, Mark emphasizes immediacy. Death itself submits to Jesus' authority. The room fills with amazement, faith fulfilled, fear defeated.

V. Lessons from the Collision of Faith and Fear

This profound passage shows clearly what happens when faith and fear collide in the presence of Christ. Consider these essential lessons for our lives:

1. Jesus Welcomes Desperate People.

No matter who you are—an influential synagogue leader or a forgotten woman—Jesus welcomes you in your desperation. Don't hesitate to bring your deepest fears and needs to Him.

2. Faith Often Requires Waiting.

Jairus had to wait painfully while Jesus stopped to help another. Faith is trusting Christ's timing, even when it feels costly or confusing.

3. Jesus Turns Interruptions into Invitations.

What seemed like a delay became another opportunity to display His grace. Trust Jesus with your delays and interruptions—He has good purposes in them.

4. Your Faith is Powerful, Not Because of Its Size, but Because of Its Object.

It wasn't the strength of their faith but the power of their Savior that mattered. Even fragile, wavering faith finds strength when placed in Christ.

5. Faith is Trusting Jesus' Perspective Over Your Own.

When life falls apart, when circumstances scream "it's too late," listen closely to Jesus' words: "Do not fear, only believe." He sees what you cannot.

VI. Where Faith Wins Out Over Fear

This passage is more than a historical record; it's a personal challenge:

Will you trust Jesus when tragedy strikes?

Will you reach out boldly, even if your faith feels fragile?

Will you trust His timing when delays shake your confidence?

Genuine faith isn't the absence of fear. It's moving toward Jesus despite our fears. When faith and fear collide, faith wins, not because we have all the answers, but because we cling to the One who holds all things in His sovereign hands. This is the heart of the gospel: Christ enters our fear-filled world, speaks peace to our chaos, and overcomes even death itself. When faith and fear collide at the feet of Jesus, it's faith that emerges victorious.

Reflection & Response

Where are you currently experiencing a collision between faith and fear in your life?

How do these two stories encourage you to trust Jesus, even when His timing or methods don't make sense?

In what areas of your life do you need to step forward boldly, trusting Jesus despite your fear?

How does this passage reshape your view of Jesus' power, compassion, and timing?

Chapter 6

The Reality of Ministry: Facing and Embracing Rejection

Mark 6:1-13

When Jesus returned to His hometown in Mark 6:1–13, the response wasn't a parade or celebration—it was resistance and rejection. That moment reminds us of a crucial truth: faithful ministry does not guarantee universal acceptance. If the Son of God was rejected, then so will those who follow Him. This passage offers a sobering yet essential lesson in ministry: we must face rejection and embrace it —not with bitterness, but with faithfulness.

I. Jesus Was Rejected by Familiar People (vv. 1–6a)

Jesus arrives in Nazareth, the town where He grew up. He goes to the synagogue and begins teaching, just as He had in many other places. But here, something different happens. Instead of amazement that leads to faith, the people respond with *offense*.

"Where did this man get these things? What is the wisdom given to him? How are such mighty works done by his hands?" (v. 2)

They know His family: *"Is not this the carpenter, the son of Mary?"* In other words, "We watched Him grow up. Who does He think He is?" Their knowledge of Jesus in the flesh became a stumbling block. They were too familiar to have faith. Sometimes the hardest people to reach are the ones who know you best. Proximity doesn't equal receptivity.

This rejection isn't from skeptics in Jerusalem or hardened Pharisees; it's from neighbors, friends, and family. Mark tells us *"they took offense at him"* (v. 3). The word there is *scandalizó*—they were scandalized by Him. And then comes the heartbreaking line:

"He could do no mighty work there, except that he laid his hands on a few sick people and healed them." (v. 5)

It wasn't that Jesus lacked power, but that their unbelief blocked the blessing. Jesus marveled at their hardness. Rejection — even for Jesus — was real and painful.

II. Ministry Involves Multiplication and Mission (vv. 6b–7)

Rather than retreating or sulking, Jesus mobilizes. Mark says:

"And he went about among the villages teaching. And he called the twelve and began to send them out two by two." (vv. 6–7)

Jesus doesn't allow rejection to halt His mission. He sends out His disciples, multiplying the ministry. This is the first time the disciples are sent out on their own. Why two by two? For accountability, mutual encouragement, and validation (cf. Deut. 19:15), ministry is never meant to be done in isolation. We are not lone rangers in the kingdom. We are co-laborers, sent out with gospel authority, not personal ambition.

Jesus gives them authority, not their own, but His. Ministry is always derivative. We don't act on our own strength; we minister in His name and with His authority.

III. Ministry Requires Dependence, Not Self-Sufficiency (vv. 8–9)

"He charged them to take nothing for their journey except a staff, no bread, no bag, no money in their belts." (v. 8)

This is radical—no extra tunic. No money. No food. Why? To teach dependence. Ministry isn't about stockpiling resources; it's about walking by faith. Jesus wanted His disciples to learn that their provision would come as they went. He was training their trust. Sometimes God strips away what you think you need so you can learn to trust in what you really need—Him. This doesn't mean recklessness, but readiness. Gospel ministry requires us to hold loosely to earthly security and tightly to heavenly calling.

IV. Ministry Invites Both Hospitality and Hostility (vv. 10–11)

"Whenever you enter a house, stay there until you depart from there." (v. 10)

"And if any place will not receive you and they will not listen to you, when you leave, shake off the dust that is on your feet as a testimony against them." (v. 11)

Some people will welcome the message. Others will reject it. Jesus prepared them for both.

Hospitality is a blessing—but it's not always guaranteed.

Hostility is a reality, but it must not derail the mission.

Shaking the dust off wasn't bitterness; it was a symbolic act of judgment. It declared, "You heard the truth. You chose to reject it. We move on, entrusting you to God." Faithfulness doesn't mean everyone will respond. Our job is not to produce results but to proclaim the gospel.

V. Ministry Is Rooted in Preaching and Serving (vv. 12–13)

Mark closes the section by describing what happened:

"So they went out and proclaimed that people should repent. And they cast out many demons and anointed with oil many who were sick and healed them."

The disciples preached repentance, an unpopular message in any age. But it was accompanied by power. Their ministry mirrored Jesus'. It involved both word and deed, truth and compassion. If we only preach and never serve, we lack compassion. If we only help without proclaiming, we lack conviction. Ministry must have both.

Key Reflections for Ministry Today

This passage speaks especially to pastors, missionaries, teachers, and all believers engaged in Kingdom work. It reminds us:

1. You Will Be Rejected.

Even Jesus was. Don't let rejection surprise you or stop you. Expect it—and respond with grace and perseverance.

2. Familiarity Breeds Contempt.

Don't be discouraged when people close to you don't respond. Sometimes those who know you best are slowest to believe.

3. Multiply the Mission.

When doors close, find new ones. Train others. Raise leaders. Ministry is not about maintaining control but about multiplying the gospel.

4. Trust God for Provision.

Don't let fear of lack stop you from stepping out. He will provide what you need as you go.

5. Stay or Shake—Be Faithful Either Way.

Whether people welcome or reject you, be faithful. The results belong to God.

Conclusion: Keep Going

Ministry will break your heart. You will be misunderstood, rejected, and sometimes even mocked. But if Jesus experienced that, and kept going, so must we.

This passage doesn't just prepare us for rejection. It invites us to embrace it as part of the calling. Not every sermon will be received. Not every heart will be softened. But every step of faithfulness will be remembered by God. We cannot let rejection derail us from the mission. If Jesus kept going, so must we. So press on, preacher. Press on, servant of God. Proclaim the gospel with courage. Trust God for provision. Expect resistance, but don't retreat. Shake the dust and keep walking.

Reflection & Response

Where are you tempted to quit because of rejection or discouragement in ministry?

How does Jesus' example reframe your expectations?

What does dependence on God practically look like in your life or calling?

The Reality of Ministry: It Will Cost You Everything

Mark 6:14-29

In the middle of Jesus' growing public ministry, Mark pauses to tell us a story—not about Jesus directly, but about His forerunner, John the Baptist. It's a flashback, but not just to fill in details. It's a stark reminder: faithfulness to God may cost you your life.

This is not the ministry training most people expect. Mark 6:14–29 paints a grim picture of what it might mean to stand for truth in a world that rejects it. It shows us that gospel ministry will not only be rejected—it may cost you everything.

BEHOLD THE CHRIST

I. The Cost of Faithfulness (vv. 14–20)

The passage begins with confusion among the crowds and political leaders about who Jesus really is.

"King Herod heard of it, for Jesus' name had become known. Some said, 'John the Baptist has been raised from the dead.'" (v. 14)

Herod Antipas hears the rumors, and one sticks out: "This Jesus must be John the Baptist, raised from the dead." Why does this idea torment Herod so much? Because his conscience is haunted by what he did. Mark tells us how John had confronted Herod for his sin: *"It is not lawful for you to have your brother's wife."* (v. 18)

John didn't back down from confronting immorality. He wasn't intimidated by Herod's power or Herodias' pride. He called sin, sin. And it cost him. John was bold because he feared God more than man. He didn't soften the truth to gain influence. He spoke clearly, even when it put him in a prison cell.

Herodias held a grudge against John and wanted him dead, but Herod had a strange admiration for him. He feared John, knowing he was *"a righteous and holy man"* (v. 20). He even protected him, up to a point. This tension —conviction without repentance —still exists today. People may respect bold preachers. They may feel guilty when they hear the truth. But unless repentance follows, admiration won't save them. Herod liked to listen to John, but not enough to change. That's the danger of being entertained by the truth rather than being transformed by it.

II. The Seduction of Compromise (vv. 21–25)

Then, Mark writes chilling words:

"But an opportunity came..." (v. 21)

Herod throws himself a birthday party, which in Roman culture would have been a debauched, indulgent affair. All the critical men of Galilee are there: military commanders, nobles, and powerful guests. And then Herodias seizes her chance.

Her daughter, likely a young teen, comes in and dances for the men. The text implies this wasn't an innocent performance but a provocative display meant to please the crowd. Herod, drunk and enthralled, makes a foolish promise:

"Ask me for whatever you wish, and I will give it to you, up to half my kingdom." (v. 23)

It was a boast. An exaggerated oath to impress. But now he's trapped. The girl runs to her mother: *"What should I ask for?"* Without hesitation, Herodias answers: *"The head of John the Baptist."* When sin festers, it schemes. Herodias waited for her chance. And when it came, she struck with precision.

The request is grotesque. The girl returns and, shockingly, repeats it with detail: *"I want you to give me at once the head of John the Baptist on a platter."* It's not just execution, it's humiliation. And it's public.

III. The Weakness of People-Pleasing (vv. 26–29)

Herod is horrified. Mark says:

"The king was exceedingly sorry..." (v. 26)

That phrase is used only one other time in Mark, when Jesus is in Gethsemane. But Herod's sorrow is not godly sorrow. It's not repentance. It's grief over being trapped by his own pride. *"Because of his oaths and his guests, he did not want to break his word to her."* (v. 26)

Herod feared what people would think more than he feared doing evil. Herod feared losing face more than losing a prophet. His pride mattered more than a man's life. That's the tragedy of people-pleasing. It leads to cowardice, compromise, and, at times, catastrophic decisions. Herod valued his image over integrity. And he ordered John's execution.

The scene ends with a gruesome delivery: *"The head was brought on a platter and given to the girl, and she gave it to her mother."* (v. 28) But even in death, John remains a prophet. He's honored by his disciples, who take his body and lay it in a tomb. The world mocked him, but heaven welcomed him.

Key Lessons for the Church Today

Mark doesn't tell this story for shock value. He tells us to prepare ourselves.

1. Faithfulness May Cost You Everything

John didn't lose his head because he was reckless. He lost it because he was righteous. He spoke truth to power, and that power turned against him. Many will serve Christ until it costs them something, comfort, relationships, and reputation. But faithful ministry counts the cost and continues.

2. Don't Be Merely Convicted—Be Converted

John's words moved Herod, but he never repented. He listened often but never obeyed. His conscience was pricked but not changed. That's the danger of being around truth without ever submitting to it.

3. Beware the Fear of Man

Herod's downfall was not lust alone, but fear. He was afraid of what others would think. And so he chose sin over righteousness.

Proverbs 29:25:

"The fear of man lays a snare, but whoever trusts in the Lord is safe."

4. Bold Truth-Telling Is Still Needed

Our world is full of compromise, moral confusion, and hostility toward biblical truth. We don't need more polished voices; we need faithful ones. John is a model for ministers, missionaries, and every believer. He didn't adjust the message to the culture. He spoke the truth and left the consequences to God.

Conclusion

This scene isn't just about John; it foreshadows Jesus. Like John, Jesus would be arrested by a ruler who admired Him. Like John, He would be sentenced to death by someone who knew He was innocent. And like John, He would die not because He failed, but because He was faithful.

Ministry is not a game. It is a calling that may cost you everything. But it is worth it. If John was faithful to death, and Jesus was faithful to death, how can we expect an easier path? Let this sobering story strengthen your resolve. Following Christ may cost you everything. But in the end, you gain everything that matters.

Reflection & Response

Where are you tempted to compromise to please others instead of God?

Does truth merely convict you—or are you submitting to it?

What would it look like for you to live with courage and conviction in your current calling?

The Reality of Ministry: Caring for Others
Mark 6:30-44

The disciples were exhausted. After being sent out by Jesus to preach, heal, and cast out demons, they returned with hearts full and bodies empty. And Jesus, seeing their weariness, invites them to rest: *"Come away by yourselves to a desolate place and rest a while."* (v. 31) It's a rare moment of respite. But the ministry rarely waits. This well-known passage, *the feeding of the five thousand*, is not just about a miracle. It's about the heart of Jesus, the demands of discipleship, and the reality that ministry often calls us to pour out when we feel like we have nothing left to give.

I. The Need for Rest and the Call to Serve (vv. 30–34)

"The apostles returned to Jesus and told him all that they had done and taught." (v. 30)

You can almost hear the excitement in their voices. But they are also depleted. Ministry is draining. Jesus sees this and responds with compassion: *"Come away... and rest."*

Jesus is not a taskmaster. He cares for His servants. He knows the limitations of His followers, and He provides for rest. But when they arrive at their quiet place, the quiet is gone: *"Many saw them going and recognized them, and they ran there on foot from all the towns and got there ahead of them."* (v. 33)

By the time Jesus and the disciples step off the boat, thousands are waiting. If the disciples were looking for a break, they found a crowd. And how does Jesus respond? *"He had compassion on them, because they were like sheep without a shepherd."* (v. 34)

Jesus doesn't sigh or retreat. He teaches. He loves. His compassion is not passive—it moves Him to action. He doesn't ignore the disciples' need for rest, but He models a ministry that sacrifices comfort for others. Ministry is full of interruptions. But those interruptions often *are* the ministry. Jesus didn't resent the people; He loved them. And He expected the disciples to learn that too.

II. A Problem Too Big (vv. 35–37)

As the day stretches on, the disciples begin to worry. They're in a remote place, the hour is late, and people are hungry. Their solution is reasonable: *"Send them away... to buy themselves something to eat."* (v. 36)

In other words: "Let's close up shop and let them fend for themselves." But Jesus surprises them: *"You give them something to eat."* (v. 37) It's a stunning command. Jesus asks them to do what is clearly impossible. They respond with frustration: *"Shall we go and buy two hundred denarii worth of bread and give it to them to eat?"* That's over six months' wages. It's not a serious question—it's sarcasm. "Jesus, what do you expect from us?"

Jesus wasn't setting them up to fail. He was setting them up to *see*. To see that ministry isn't about what we can do, but about what He can do. How often do we face needs that exceed our strength? A grieving widow, a rebellious teen, a marriage on the rocks, a congregation full of burdens. The command to serve feels crushing—until we realize we were never meant to carry it alone.

III. Give What You Have (vv. 38–41)

Jesus asks a simple question: *"How many loaves do you have? Go and see."* (v. 38)

They find five loaves and two fish. It's a child's lunch. Laughably insufficient. But it's not about quantity, it's about obedience. *"Then he commanded them all to sit down in groups... And taking the five loaves and the two fish, he looked up to heaven and said a blessing and broke the loaves and gave them to the disciples to set before the people."* (vv. 39–41)

Jesus doesn't hand the food directly to the crowd. He gives it to the disciples—and they distribute it. The miracle flows through their hands. Jesus could have rained down manna from heaven. But instead, He worked through the tired, limited, unsure hands of His disciples. That's still how He works today. Your resources may feel meager. Your time is stretched. Your energy is drained. But Jesus asks, *"What do you have?"* Bring it to Him. Surrender it. And watch Him multiply it for His glory.

IV. More Than Enough (v. 42–43)

"And they all ate and were satisfied. And they took up twelve baskets full of broken pieces and of the fish." (v. 42–43)

Twelve baskets. One for each disciple. It's not just an overflow; it's a personal lesson. The disciples didn't just feed others; they were fed themselves. As they served, they were satisfied. Ministry wasn't their depletion; it was their provision. Don't believe the lie that serving others will always leave you empty. When you give in faith, God often fills you in the process.

Lessons for Today's Disciple

This miracle is about more than bread. It's a model for how Jesus continues to shepherd His church through tired, imperfect, dependent people. Here are a few truths to take to heart:

1. Jesus Cares About Your Rest

He sees your exhaustion. He invites you to rest. But He also calls you to hold your plans loosely and trust His timing.

2. The Need Will Always Exceed Your Ability

If you wait until you feel "ready," you'll never serve. Ministry always involves stepping out beyond your comfort zone and depending on Christ.

3. God Uses What You Offer

What do you have? A few hours? A humble word? A worn-out body and a willing heart? Jesus delights to use surrendered things.

4. When You Serve Others, God Often Feeds You Too

Twelve baskets. One for each tired disciple. God is faithful to care for those who care for others.

Conclusion: The Servant's Path

In this passage, the disciples learn that ministry isn't about heroic effort; it's about humble dependence. They know that people are not interruptions; they are the mission. And they learn that when they give all they have to Jesus, it's more than enough.

Ministry is hard. It's draining. But it's also beautiful. In it, we get to see the power of God displayed through our weakness. So don't hold back. Don't wait until you feel ready. Give what you have, and trust Jesus to do what only He can do.

Reflection & Response

What "loaves and fish" has Jesus given you to use for His kingdom?

Where is He calling you to serve—even when you feel tired or empty?

How can you trust Him to meet your needs as you meet the needs of others?

The Reality of Ministry: Being Patient With People

Mark 6:45-52

Ministry would be so much easier if people weren't so slow to grow.

If you've ever felt frustrated because someone didn't change fast enough, didn't listen clearly, didn't mature quickly, or didn't respond spiritually, you're not alone. Jesus knows that frustration. He experienced it firsthand. And yet, in this passage, we see that Jesus is patient with slow learners.

Mark 6:45–52 reminds us that the reality of ministry is not just the work we do but the people we walk with. And walking with people means waiting on them, enduring their misunderstandings, and continuing to love them even when they just don't get it.

I. Ministry Continues Even When You're Apart (v. 45–46)

"Immediately he made his disciples get into the boat and go before him to the other side, to Bethsaida, while he

dismissed the crowd. And after he had taken leave of them, he went up on the mountain to pray." (vv. 45–46)

Right after the miracle of feeding the five thousand, Jesus dismisses both the crowd and His disciples. He sends them away not because He's angry but because He's modeling something important. Jesus retreats to pray. He's not escaping ministry; He's engaging it at the deepest level. The disciples may have been physically distant from Him, but they were not spiritually disconnected. The disciples obeyed Jesus, yet they still faced the storm. Faithfulness doesn't guarantee ease. Ministry often involves rowing in the dark without seeing the whole picture.

II. Ministry Feels Like Rowing Against the Wind (v. 47–48a)

"And when evening came, the boat was out on the sea, and he was alone on the land. And he saw that they were making headway painfully, for the wind was against them." (vv. 47–48a)

This scene is full of irony. The disciples had just seen Jesus multiply bread and fish. They had watched Him meet needs with abundance. And now? They're straining, frustrated, making "painful headway." Ministry is like that sometimes. Progress is slow. The wind is against you. You feel like you're moving, but barely. Every decision, every counseling conversation, every discipleship effort feels like a battle.

And Jesus? He sees. From the mountain, He watches them struggle. And he doesn't immediately come to the rescue. Just because Jesus isn't stopping the storm doesn't mean He isn't watching. His delays are never disinterested. He waits, not to harm us, but to shape us. There's no promise in Scripture that ministry will be smooth sailing. But there *is* a promise that Christ sees, and He comes.

III. Jesus Shows Up in the struggle (v. 48b–50)

"And about the fourth watch of the night he came to them, walking on the sea. He meant to pass by them." (v. 48b)

The "fourth watch" means it was between 3 and 6 a.m. They've been rowing for hours. They're exhausted. And now, they see someone walking on the water, and they're terrified. *"But when they saw him walking on the sea they thought it was a ghost, and cried out, for they all saw him and were terrified."* (vv. 49–50)

Fear overtakes faith. They don't recognize Jesus. Their exhaustion has blurred their vision.

These were the same men who had just seen Jesus feed five thousand people with a boy's lunch. But now? They think He's a ghost. That's how quickly we forget.

Ministry demands patience not just for the people we serve, but also for ourselves. The disciples had front-row seats to God's power, yet they still didn't understand. That's what ministry is: walking with people who forget easily, fear quickly, and grow slowly.

And yet Jesus doesn't scold them. He speaks gently. *"But immediately he spoke to them and said, 'Take heart; it is I. Do not be afraid.'"* (v. 50) He reveals His presence. He reassures their hearts. His first words are not rebuke, but comfort.

IV. Jesus Enters the Boat (v. 51)

"And he got into the boat with them, and the wind ceased." (v. 51)

Jesus doesn't just calm the storm; He *enters* the struggle. He joins them where they are. And in that moment, peace returns. His presence stills the storm. Notice, the calming comes *after* His presence. Jesus doesn't always remove the struggle right away. But He always brings peace when He steps into our boat. The greatest gift Jesus offers in ministry is not a smoother path, but His presence in the midst of difficulty. He doesn't stand on the shore and shout instructions. He steps in.

V. Hearts That Are Still Hard (v. 52)

"For they did not understand about the loaves, but their hearts were hardened." (v. 52)

This verse stings a little. After all they'd seen, after the feeding of the five thousand, after Jesus walking on water, they still didn't *get it*. Their hearts were slow to believe. And Jesus? He doesn't fire them. He doesn't pick a new team. He stays with them. He teaches them. He loves them.

This is the reality of ministry: you will walk with people who just don't get it. You'll teach, and they won't apply. You'll warn, and they'll ignore. You'll counsel, and they'll return to their patterns. And your temptation will be to give up. But Jesus doesn't give up. If Jesus was patient with *these* disciples, then He's patient with me. And He's calling me to be patient with others. The path of ministry is littered with slow learners, and we're all one of them. Growth is gradual. Understanding comes in layers. And Jesus stays.

Lessons for Today's Disciple

This passage is more than a miracle story; it's a ministry manual. It teaches us how to view ourselves, others, and the God who walks on the waves.

1. Faithfulness Doesn't Mean ease

Just because you're obeying Christ doesn't mean the winds won't push against you. Expect resistance and row anyway.

2. Jesus Sees Your Struggles

Even when He seems distant, He's watching. He delays with purpose, not punishment.

3. People Grow Slowly

Ministry requires patience. Most growth is unseen. Don't be shocked when people don't "get it" right away.

4. Jesus Steps In

He doesn't stay at a distance. He enters our mess, calms our storms, and strengthens our hearts.

5. You Are a Slow Learner Too

Never forget Jesus is patient with *you*. Let that patience fuel your own toward others.

Conclusion

The disciples' hearts were hard, but Jesus stayed in the boat. He didn't jump out when they doubted. He didn't retreat when they misunderstood. He stayed. And that's what we're called to do. Stay in the boat with the people God has given us, even when they frustrate us, even when they forget everything we've said, even when we're tired.

Ministry is not about perfect people moving at an ideal speed. It's about broken people rowing together, being shaped by the presence of Christ. So, keep rowing. Keep loving. Keep being patient. Because Jesus hasn't left your boat and He never will.

Reflection & Response

Where do you feel like you're "rowing against the wind" in ministry right now?

Are you tempted to give up on someone who's growing slowly?

How can Christ's patience toward *you* fuel your patience toward others?

The Reality of Ministry: Bringing People to Jesus

Mark 6:53-56

If you summarize ministry in one sentence, it might be this: helping people get to Jesus. It's not about impressing them with our skills. It's not about fixing all their problems ourselves. It's not even about making them like us. Ministry, at its core, is about bringing people to the only One who can save, heal, and transform them.

In *Mark 6:53–56*, we see that clearly. Jesus and His disciples arrive in Gennesaret, and people immediately recognize Him. And what do they do? They start bringing sick people, hurting people, desperate people to Jesus.

I. Ministry Starts with Recognizing Jesus (v. 53–54)

"When they had crossed over, they came to land at Gennesaret and moored to the shore. And when they got out of the boat, the people immediately recognized him." Recognition leads to response. As soon as the people realize Jesus has arrived, they don't waste time. They know His reputation. They've heard what He can do. And now, here He is.

That's where ministry begins for us as well —not with our programs or strategies, but with a clear vision of who Jesus is. If we lose sight of Jesus, we'll start bringing people to ourselves instead of to Him. We'll make them dependent on us, not on Christ. But if our eyes are on Him, our ministry will always be about pointing others His way. This recognition wasn't just intellectual. It was urgent. They moved immediately because they believed Jesus was worth bringing people to.

II. Ministry Works Through Relationships (v. 55a)

"And ran about the whole region and began to bring the sick people on their beds to wherever they heard he was."

They didn't just send a note or wait for the sick to hear the news. They *ran* to get them. This was an active, personal, hands-on ministry. Bringing people to Jesus is rarely a passive thing. It's going to require us to move toward people, to meet them where they are, to take them by the hand and walk with them.

Think about it, every person brought to Jesus in this passage was carried there by someone else's effort. Someone saw their need, cared enough to act, and made the trip to get them to Christ. We will never bring people to Jesus if we are content to sit still. Ministry happens when we step into the lives of others, running toward them, not away from them. Relationships are the bridges God uses to carry people to Christ.

III. Ministry Brings People to Where Jesus Is (v. 55b–56a)

"...to wherever they heard he was. And wherever he came, in villages, cities, or countryside, they laid the sick in the marketplaces..."

The people didn't just gather the sick and stop there. They brought them to *where Jesus was*. That's the essential step, bringing people into contact with Him. In our context, this doesn't mean physically carrying them to the shore of Galilee. It means opening the word with them, bringing them into worship gatherings, praying with them, and speaking gospel truth into their lives. They laid the sick in the marketplaces, the most public place available. They weren't embarrassed or secretive. They wanted as many people as possible to encounter Jesus.

IV. Ministry Trusts in the Power of Christ (v. 56b)

"...and implored him that they might touch even the fringe of his garment. And as many as touched it were made well."

The people didn't come with demands or conditions. They came in faithfully believing that even touching the edge of His clothing could change everything. This is why we bring people to Jesus: we can't do for them what only He can. We can counsel, encourage, and serve, but we cannot forgive their sins, change their hearts, or give them eternal life. Only Jesus can do that. If we really believe Jesus can change lives, we will spend less time trying to be the hero and more time bringing people to Him.

V. Ministry Is for *All* Kinds of People

It's worth noticing the diversity in this scene, villages, cities, and the countryside. The sick weren't limited to one social class or background. Some were probably poor and overlooked; others may have been well-known in their communities. But every single one of them needed Jesus. And every single one who came to Him was welcomed. A ministry that reflects Christ's heart will resist favoritism. It will move toward whoever God puts in our path, whether they're easy to love or difficult, whether they have much to offer us or nothing at all.

Lessons for Today's Disciple

This short passage gives us a clear ministry blueprint.

1. See Jesus Clearly

Everything starts with recognizing Him for who He is—Lord, Savior, Redeemer.

2. Move Toward People

Don't wait for them to come to you. Go to them. Step into their world.

3. Bring Them to the Source

Lead them to where they can encounter Christ—His Word, His people, His presence.

4. Trust His Power, Not Yours

Believe that He can do far more than you can. Your role is to connect them to Him.

5. Welcome All

Ministry has no "preferred list." Christ's invitation is for everyone.

Conclusion

Bringing people to Jesus isn't glamorous. It's often inconvenient, messy, and exhausting. It requires patience, humility, and a willingness to put others ahead of yourself. But it's worth it because every step you take toward Jesus with someone else could change their eternity.

The most incredible privilege in ministry is not being known but making Him known. And that happens every time we carry someone to the feet of Jesus. So, keep carrying. Keep inviting. Keep moving people toward Christ. Because as long as He is present, there is hope for healing.

Reflection & Response

Who in your life needs to be brought to Jesus right now?

What step can you take this week to move toward them?

Do you trust Jesus to do the work you cannot?

Chapter 7

The Demise of True Religion, Part 1 – Legalism

Mark 7:1–8

Legalism is one of the greatest enemies of true religion. It cloaks itself in the language of holiness and reverence but robs God of glory by elevating human traditions above His Word. In *Mark 7:1–8*, Jesus confronts this counterfeit form of devotion head-on.

The setting is tense. The religious leaders have been watching Jesus closely, and they think they've found a flaw in His ministry, not in His teaching, not in His miracles, but in His disciples' failure to follow the ceremonial washing traditions. To them, this is proof that Jesus cannot be from God. To Jesus, it's proof that they have replaced God's commands with man-made rules.

I. The Accusation of the Pharisees (vv. 1–5)

"Now when the Pharisees gathered to him, with some of the scribes who had come from Jerusalem, they saw that some of his disciples ate with hands that were defiled, that is, unwashed. (For the Pharisees and all the Jews do not eat unless they wash their hands properly, holding to the tradition of the elders, and when they come from the marketplace, they do not eat unless they wash. And there are many other traditions that they observe, such as the washing of cups and

pots, copper vessels, and dining couches.) And the Pharisees and the scribes asked him, 'Why do your disciples not walk according to the tradition of the elders, but eat with defiled hands?'"

At first glance, this might seem like a conversation about hygiene. It's not. The Pharisees aren't worried about germs; they're concerned about ceremonial defilement. They had developed a system of ritual washings not commanded in Scripture, passed down orally as the "tradition of the elders." This tradition had grown into a complex code that went far beyond the law God gave through Moses.

Notice their question: *"Why do your disciples not walk according to the tradition of the elders?"* Not *"Why do they disobey God's law?"* but *"Why don't they follow our rules?"* This is the essence of legalism, judging righteousness by human standards rather than God's. The Pharisees were more concerned about keeping their hands clean than keeping their hearts clean. They mistook man's word for God's Word and elevated their tradition to the level of divine command.

II. The Rebuke of Jesus (vv. 6–7)

"And he said to them, 'Well did Isaiah prophesy of you hypocrites, as it is written,

"This people honors me with their lips,

but their heart is far from me;

in vain do they worship me,

teaching as doctrines the commandments of men."

117

Jesus doesn't respond with a mild clarification. He responds with a sharp rebuke. He calls them what they are: *hypocrites*. The word means "actors," people playing a role on a stage. They had all the right words. They honored God with their lips. But their hearts were miles away from Him.

Quoting Isaiah 29:13, Jesus highlights that this has always been the danger of outward religion that appears correct but is empty within. The problem with legalism is not that it aims too high but that it aims in the wrong direction. It substitutes external performance for internal devotion. When we teach human rules as if they were God's commands, our worship becomes empty. It's not just a little misguided; it's *vain*. It does not please God because it is not rooted in truth.

III. The Exposure of Their True Allegiance (v. 8)

"You leave the commandment of God and hold to the tradition of men."

Here's the heart of the matter. Legalism doesn't merely add to God's Word; it replaces God's Word. Jesus says they have *left* God's commandment. They have turned away from the very thing they claim to protect. This is what makes legalism so dangerous. It's not just a harmless over-enthusiasm for rules. It actively displaces God's authority with man's authority. It may look like devotion, but it's rebellion. The tragedy of legalism is that it convinces people they are close to God when, in fact, they are far from Him. They mistake compliance for communion.

IV. The Marks of Legalism

From this encounter, we can identify several marks of legalism:

Elevating Human Tradition to Divine Status

The Pharisees treated the "tradition of the elders" as equal to God's law. In practice, it was more important to them than Scripture.

Focusing on the Outward, Ignoring the Inward

They cared about ceremonial washings but neglected the heart.

Binding Consciences Where God Has Not

They made rules God never made, then judged others for not keeping them.

Replacing God's Commands with Man's

Over time, their rules pushed God's Word to the margins.

These marks can show up in our churches and our hearts today if we're not careful.

V. Guarding Against Legalism Today

Legalism is subtle because it often begins with good intentions—to avoid sin and encourage holiness. The problem comes when the fence we build around God's law becomes more important than the law itself.

We guard against legalism by:

Holding fast to Scripture as our sole authority (2 Tim. 3:16–17)

Examining our hearts as well as our actions (Ps. 139:23–24)

Refusing to judge others by our personal preferences (Rom. 14:1–4)

Remembering that righteousness is a gift of grace, not a human achievement (Phil. 3:9)

VI. True Religion: From the Heart

True religion begins with the heart. It flows from love for God, gratitude for His grace, and submission to His Word—outward obedience matters, but only when it springs from inward devotion. Jesus isn't calling us to care less about obedience—He's calling us to care more about the kind of obedience that comes from a transformed heart. God doesn't want your rituals if He doesn't have your heart. You can fool people with your traditions. You can even fool yourself. But you cannot fool Him.

Conclusion

The Pharisees thought they had true religion, but it was a counterfeit. It had the appearance of godliness but denied its power. Legalism still tempts us today because it offers a sense of control. It provides us with a checklist to manage. But God is not looking for managers of tradition; He is seeking worshipers in spirit and truth. Let's be people who love God's Word, submit to His authority, and refuse to add our own rules to His. Let's honor Him not only with our lips but with hearts that are near to Him.

Reflection & Response

Are there traditions or preferences in your life that you've elevated above God's Word?

Do your outward acts of worship reflect the actual state of your heart?

How can you help guard your church from drifting into legalism?

The Demise of True Religion, Part 2 – Traditionalism

Mark 7:9–13

In the previous section (vv. 1–8), Jesus exposed the Pharisees' legalism—elevating man-made rules above God's commands. Now, in *Mark 7:9–13*, He takes it a step further and shows where that path inevitably leads: traditionalism—clinging to religious customs so tightly that God's clear commands are set aside altogether. Legalism says, "My rules are equal to God's rules." Traditionalism says, "My rules are more important than God's rules." Both are deadly to true religion.

I. The Sharp Indictment (v. 9)

"And he said to them, 'You have a fine way of rejecting the commandment of God in order to establish your tradition!'"

Jesus is not complimenting them here. His words drip with holy sarcasm. "You're really skilled at this,"

He says. Skilled at *rejecting* God's commands. Proficient at *establishing* man's traditions. It's a tragic expertise.

Notice the progression from verse 8 to verse 9:

Verse 8: "You leave the commandment of God."

Verse 9: "You reject the commandment of God."

Leaving is drifting. Rejecting is deliberate. Traditionalism doesn't just wander away from God's Word; it pushes it aside with intention. When our traditions become untouchable, we will gladly set aside Scripture to keep them. And when we do, we are no longer worshiping God; we are worshiping our way of doing things.

II. The Example of Corban (vv. 10–12)

"For Moses said, 'Honor your father and your mother'; and, 'Whoever reviles father or mother must surely die.' But you say, 'If a man tells his father or his mother, "Whatever you would have gained from me is Corban"' (that is, given to God)—then you no longer permit him to do anything for his father or mother."

Here, Jesus gives a concrete example of how their tradition nullifies God's Word. The fifth commandment is clear: *Honor your father and mother.* This includes caring for them in their old age. In Jewish culture, this was both a sacred duty and a social necessity—there was no retirement system or government assistance.

But the Pharisees had developed a loophole. A person could declare their resources *Corban*—a gift dedicated to God. Once declared Corban, those resources could not be used for anything else, even caring for one's parents.

Here's the twisted part: many people still kept those resources for themselves until death, enjoying their use, and then transferring them to the temple. It became a way to appear deeply spiritual —"I've dedicated all my wealth to God" — while avoiding the costly responsibility of caring for one's parents. Jesus exposes this for what it is: disobedience masquerading as devotion.

III. The Heart of the Problem

What's going on here is more than just a bad policy; it's a heart problem. Traditionalism gives the illusion of honoring God while in reality dishonoring Him. It allows people to feel righteous without obeying God's commands. God says, "Honor your parents." The Pharisees say, "Here's a way to get around that, and we'll call it spiritual." This is what happens when human tradition is elevated above God's Word. Instead of serving as a fence to protect obedience, tradition becomes a detour around obedience.

IV. The Devastating Result (v. 13)

"...thus making void the word of God by your tradition that you have handed down. And many such things you do."

The word *void* means to invalidate, to cancel out. By their tradition, they had emptied God's Word of its authority in practice. It's possible to have the Bible in your hand, to quote it, even to defend it publicly, yet to nullify it in your life by holding to man-made traditions instead. And Jesus says this example is not isolated: *"And many such things you do."* Corban was just one of many ways their traditions undermined God's commands.

V. Warning Signs of Traditionalism

From this confrontation, we can identify warning signs that traditionalism is creeping in:

Sacrificing clear obedience for the sake of preference

If keeping a tradition requires disobeying God's Word, that tradition has become an idol.

Using spiritual language to mask disobedience

"It's for the Lord" can be a smokescreen for selfishness.

Allowing man-made rules to override God's priorities

In this case, the priority of honoring parents was replaced by the priority of enriching the temple.

Assuming past practice is equal to divine mandate

Just because we've always done something a certain way doesn't make it God's will.

VI. Guarding Against Traditionalism

How do we guard ourselves and our churches from falling into this trap?

Test every tradition by Scripture.

Traditions can be good if they help us obey God's Word. But if they contradict or overshadow His commands, they must be abandoned.

Value people over procedures

God's commands are often relational—love Him, love others. When traditions harm people in the name of honoring God, we've missed the point.

Stay humble and teachable.

We must be willing to change when confronted with Scripture, even if it means letting go of something cherished.

Remember the purpose of devotion.

The goal of worship is not to preserve our way but to glorify God by obeying His way.

VII. Tradition as a Servant, Not a Master

Tradition can be a servant to faith if it preserves truth, reinforces obedience, and points to Christ. But when tradition becomes a master, it demands loyalty at the expense of truth, obedience, and Christ Himself. The Pharisees had allowed their traditions to take the driver's seat, and the result was a head-on collision with the Son of God. Tradition is a terrible master. It makes you think you're honoring God while it slowly pulls you away from Him.

Conclusion

Jesus' words in this passage are a sobering reminder that it's not enough to avoid obvious sin. We must also avoid the subtle drift into traditionalism that renders the Word of God void. Let's love God's commands more than our customs. Let's hold our traditions with open hands and His Word with both hands. Let's ensure our devotion is measured by obedience to Him, not by adherence to our preferences.

Reflection & Response

Are there traditions in your life or church that have taken priority over God's clear commands?

How can you ensure that your devotion to God is rooted in obedience rather than custom?

What steps can you take to keep tradition as a servant to truth rather than a replacement for it?

You Aren't What You Eat

Mark 7:14–23

After confronting the Pharisees about legalism (vv. 1–8) and traditionalism (vv. 9–13), Jesus turns from sparring with the religious leaders to address the crowd. His words will be revolutionary for them not because He abolishes God's law, but because He reveals what truly defiles a person.

The religious leaders were obsessed with ceremonial washings and dietary laws. Jesus cuts through all of that with a single, radical statement: *"There is nothing outside a person that by going into him can defile him, but the things that come out of a person are what defile him."* This is the heart of the passage: Defilement comes from within, not from without.

126

I. A Public Declaration (vv. 14–15)

"And he called the people to him again and said to them, 'Hear me, all of you, and understand: There is nothing outside a person that by going into him can defile him, but the things that come out of a person are what defile him.'"

Notice the urgency: *"Hear me... and understand."* Jesus is not tossing out an interesting tidbit. He is announcing a truth that overturns generations of misunderstanding. For centuries, the Jewish people had observed strict food laws, not because eating pork or shellfish was morally wrong, but because God had set them apart as His people. The Pharisees took these ceremonial laws and piled layer upon layer of man-made regulations on top of them.

But Jesus is pointing to something more profound: you can follow every food law to the letter and still be utterly defiled in God's sight. Conversely, you could eat something ceremonially unclean and still be pure if your heart is pure. This is a staggering shift for His hearers. He's not erasing God's commands; He's revealing the purpose behind them.

II. A Private Explanation (vv. 17–19)

After dropping this spiritual bombshell in public, Jesus heads into a house with His disciples. Unsurprisingly, they have questions.

"And when he had entered the house and left the people, his disciples asked him about the parable. And he said to them, 'Then are you also without understanding? Do you not see that whatever goes into a person from outside cannot defile

him, since it enters not his heart but his stomach, and is expelled?' (Thus, he declared all foods clean.)"

Two key truths emerge here:

Defilement is a matter of the heart. Food bypasses the heart. It goes into the stomach and then out of the body. Spiritual purity is not determined by what's on your plate.

Jesus declared all foods clean. Mark adds this parenthetical note for his readers—especially Gentiles—making it clear that in Christ, the ceremonial food laws no longer apply. This would have been earth-shattering news for a Jewish audience.

III. The Real Source of Defilement (vv. 20–23)

"And he said, 'What comes out of a person is what defiles him. For from within, out of the heart of man, come evil thoughts, sexual immorality, theft, murder, adultery, coveting, wickedness, deceit, sensuality, envy, slander, pride, foolishness. All these evil things come from within, and they defile a person.'"

Jesus moves from the stomach to the heart, the control center of life. The problem is not external contamination but internal corruption.

He lists thirteen sins, and notice how broad the list is:

Thought sins: evil thoughts, coveting, envy, pride

Sexual sins: sexual immorality, adultery, sensuality

Social sins: theft, murder, slander

Religious/moral sins: wickedness, deceit, foolishness

This is not an exhaustive list, but it is comprehensive. It shows that sin is not just about immoral actions, it's about an evil heart.

IV. The Implications for Us

Jesus' teaching here has at least three significant implications for our lives:

1. External compliance cannot produce internal purity.

You can attend church, read your Bible, avoid certain behaviors, and still be far from God if your heart is not right.

2. The heart is the real battleground.

If defilement comes from within, then the battle against sin must be fought at the level of the heart, our desires, thoughts, and motives.

3. We need transformation, not just reformation.

We don't need better rules; we need new hearts. This is why the gospel is essential. Only Jesus can cleanse the heart and make us new.

V. Connecting to the Gospel

The bad news is that the source of our defilement is inside us. We can't escape it by changing environments or diets. The good news is that Jesus came to cleanse us from the inside out. Through His death and resurrection, He offers forgiveness for the guilt of sin and the gift of the Holy Spirit to transform our hearts. This is what the Old Testament anticipated: *"I will give you a new heart, and a new spirit I will put within you"* (Ezekiel 36:26).

VI. Guarding Against Modern Legalism

While most of us aren't tempted to measure holiness by dietary laws, we can still slip into our own versions of externalism:

Defining spirituality by political views, clothing styles, or music preferences

Assuming that avoiding certain "worldly" activities automatically makes us godly

Judging others based on cultural or personal standards rather than God's Word

Jesus' words call us to reject any system, ancient or modern, that locates holiness primarily in external conformity rather than in a transformed heart.

Conclusion

Defilement doesn't come from the outside in; it comes from the inside out. This means the only hope for true purity is the transforming work of Jesus Christ. Let's stop trying to manage appearances and instead run to the One who can cleanse the heart. Let's measure spirituality not by what's on the plate or in the closet, but by what's in the heart.

Reflection & Response

Where might you be tempted to measure your holiness by externals rather than the condition of your heart?

How does this passage shape the way you think about the sins you struggle with most?

What steps can you take this week to fight sin at the heart level through the power of the gospel?

Grace Beyond Borders

Mark 7:24–31

Miracles have marked the ministry of Jesus in Galilee, confrontations with religious leaders, and large crowds pressing in on Him. But in this passage, Mark takes us outside of Israel's familiar borders. Jesus withdraws to the region of Tyre and Sidon, Gentile territory. Here, He encounters a desperate mother whose faith would shock His disciples and illustrate a truth they had not yet fully grasped: God's grace extends beyond borders. This story reveals that the kingdom of God is not limited to one nation or people. It also shows us what genuine faith looks like: persistent, humble, and confident in Christ's mercy.

I. A Shocking Setting (v. 24)

"And from there he arose and went away to the region of Tyre and Sidon. And he entered a house and did not want anyone to know, yet he could not be hidden."

Tyre and Sidon were ancient cities with a long history of hostility toward Israel. They represented Gentile territory, outside the covenant promises given to Abraham. For Jesus to go there was unexpected, almost scandalous, for His Jewish followers. Mark says He entered a house and wanted to remain hidden, but His fame was too great. Even in Gentile territory, people had heard of Him. The fact that Jesus stepped into Gentile soil at all is proof that His mission was never meant to be boxed in by Israel's borders. His grace was always headed to the nations.

II. A Desperate Mother (vv. 25–26)

"But immediately a woman whose little daughter had an unclean spirit heard of him and came and fell at his feet. Now the woman was a Gentile, a Syrophoenician by birth. And she begged him to cast the demon out of her daughter."

This woman is desperate. An unclean spirit torments her daughter. She is powerless to help and runs to the only One who can. Mark highlights two things about her:

She was a Gentile. She had no claim to the covenant promises of Israel.

She was a woman. In that culture, women were often marginalized.

From a Jewish perspective, she had three strikes against her: a Gentile, a woman, and from a region known for paganism and hostility. Yet she comes boldly to Jesus, falls at His feet, and begs for help. Desperation is often the doorway to faith. When you've run out of your own resources, you realize He's your only hope.

III. A Testing Response (v. 27)

"And he said to her, 'Let the children be fed first, for it is not right to take the children's bread and throw it to the dogs.'"

At first, Jesus' words shock us. Did he really call her a dog? We need to understand the context. The Jews commonly referred to Gentiles as "dogs" in a derogatory sense. But the word Jesus uses here is softened—more like "little dogs" or "household dogs."

Still, the statement is testing. Jesus is affirming the priority of His mission: the gospel was to go first to Israel (cf. Rom. 1:16). The "children" are the people of Israel. The "bread" is the blessing of His ministry. The "dogs" are those outside. It's as if He is asking: "Do you understand the order of God's plan? Do you accept that I was sent first to the house of Israel?" This is not cruelty; it is a test of her understanding and faith.

IV. A Humble Reply (v. 28)

"But she answered him, 'Yes, Lord; yet even the dogs under the table eat the children's crumbs.'"

Her response is remarkable. She doesn't argue. She doesn't get offended. She accepts His statement, *"Yes, Lord."* But she sees an opening for grace: even the crumbs are enough.

What humility! What persistence! She acknowledges she has no rightful claim, but she believes there is more than enough mercy in Christ for her and her daughter. This woman understood what so many of Israel's leaders missed—that even a crumb of Jesus' power is enough to save. She didn't demand her rights. She pleaded for His mercy. This is faith coming to Jesus — not based on merit, but on His mercy.

V. A Gracious Answer (vv. 29–30)

"And he said to her, 'For this statement, you may go your way; the demon has left your daughter.' And she went home and found the child lying in bed and the demon gone."

Her faith moves Jesus. Her persistence and humility display the very essence of true faith. He grants her request immediately—her daughter is healed. Jesus doesn't even go with her. His word alone has authority over demons. When she returns home, her daughter is delivered. This is grace, grace that reaches beyond borders, beyond Israel, beyond all human distinctions.

VI. A Greater Lesson (v. 31)

"Then he returned from the region of Tyre and went through Sidon to the Sea of Galilee, in the region of the Decapolis."

The geography matters. Jesus goes deeper into Gentile territory before circling back. Mark is showing us that the gospel is not confined to Israel. This encounter is a foretaste of the Great Commission—that the gospel will go to all nations. The Syrophoenician woman is a preview of the Gentile mission. She reminds us that the kingdom of God is for all who come in humble faith.

VII. Lessons for Us

This encounter teaches us several lessons about faith and the nature of God's kingdom:

Faith Is Born of Desperation

Often, it's when we come to the end of ourselves that we honestly cry out to Jesus.

Faith Is Humble

True faith doesn't demand; it receives. It acknowledges unworthiness but clings to mercy.

Faith Is Persistent

She didn't walk away after the first obstacle. She pressed in, confident of Christ's compassion.

Grace Knows No Borders

The kingdom of God is for Jew and Gentile, for insider and outsider, for anyone who comes to Christ in faith.

Conclusion: Crumbs of Grace

The Syrophoenician woman's story is a beautiful reminder that Jesus' grace is abundant and overflowing. Even the crumbs from His table are enough to change a life. This woman wasn't too far or too unclean for Jesus. And neither are you. His mercy reaches further than your failures, further than your background, further than your borders. So come to Him with desperation. Come with humility. Come with persistence. And you will find that His grace knows no limits.

Reflection & Response

What areas of desperation in your life are driving you to Christ right now?

How does the humility of this woman challenge the way you approach God?

Who in your life might seem "outside the borders" of grace, and how can you help bring them to Christ?

Marvel Beyond Measure

Mark 7:31–37

Throughout Mark 7, we have seen Jesus breaking barriers. He confronted the Pharisees about their false religion, exposed the futility of legalism and traditionalism, and taught that true defilement comes from within. Then He stepped into Gentile territory, showing grace to a desperate mother whose faith astonished even His disciples.

Now, in verses 31–37, He continues His ministry in Gentile regions. This time, the focus is on a man who is deaf and has a speech impediment. The miracle that follows is unique in detail, deeply personal in tone, and climactic in effect. Those who witnessed it summed it up perfectly: *"He has done all things well. He even makes the deaf hear and the mute speak."* This passage reminds us that the work of Christ is marvelous beyond measure.

I. A Desperate Condition (vv. 31–32)

"Then he returned from the region of Tyre and went through Sidon to the Sea of Galilee, in the region of the

Decapolis. And they brought to him a man who was deaf and had a speech impediment, and they begged him to lay his hand on him."

The geography is striking. Jesus takes a long, winding route through Gentile territory, ending in the Decapolis, a predominantly non-Jewish region. His presence here is another reminder that His mission is not confined to Israel.

There, some people bring to Him a man who is both deaf and speech-impaired. His inability to hear left him unable to speak clearly. Imagine his isolation. He could not fully communicate or participate in his surroundings. The people begged Jesus to lay His hand on the man. They know His reputation. They've likely heard stories from when He healed another man possessed by demons in this very region (Mark 5). They believe His touch could make the difference.

II. A Tender Approach (vv. 33–34)

"And taking him aside from the crowd privately, he put his fingers into his ears, and after spitting, he touched his tongue. And looking up to heaven, he sighed and said to him, 'Ephphatha,' that is, 'Be opened.'"

Jesus takes the man aside privately. This is unusual, since many of His miracles happened in public. Why the privacy? Perhaps to spare the man embarrassment. Possibly to show that this moment was personal, not a spectacle. Then Jesus does something unique: He communicates in a way the man can understand. He puts His fingers in his ears. "Your ears are the problem." He touches his tongue. "Your speech will be restored."

He looks up to heaven, "The power is from God." He sighs—a groan that expresses both compassion for the man's suffering and anticipation of the cross, where He would bear the brokenness of this world.

Finally, He speaks: *"Ephphatha"*—*"Be opened."* With a single word, Jesus reverses years of disability. Jesus doesn't heal this man from a distance. He enters his world. He meets him at his point of need. That's the kind of Savior He is: personal, compassionate, and powerful.

III. A Complete Healing (v. 35)

"And his ears were opened, his tongue was released, and he spoke plainly."

The result is immediate and total. His ears are open; he can hear. His tongue is loosed; he can speak. And not haltingly or slowly, but plainly. Years of silence and struggle are undone in an instant. This is the nature of Jesus' power: complete, not partial; immediate, not gradual. He doesn't just improve people, He transforms them.

IV. A Curious Command (v. 36)

"And Jesus charged them to tell no one. But the more he charged them, the more zealously they proclaimed it."

Once again, Jesus tells people not to spread the news. Why? Likely because the crowds were eager to make Him a political deliverer or miracle worker rather than receiving Him as Savior and Lord. His mission was not about popularity but about the cross. Yet the more He charged them, the more they spread the news.

Their joy overflowed. Their amazement could not be contained.

V. A Marvelous Confession (v. 37)

"And they were astonished beyond measure, saying, 'He has done all things well. He even makes the deaf hear and the mute speak.'" Their response captures the wonder of Jesus' ministry: *"He has done all things well."*

This statement echoes the language of Genesis 1, where God looked at creation and declared it good. Now, here is the Creator at work again, restoring what sin has broken, making lives whole, and bringing about a new creation. Jesus never does anything halfway. He has never failed. Every act of His ministry is marked by excellence, compassion, and perfection. He has done all things well.

The people marvel because they see in Jesus what Isaiah prophesied of the Messiah: *"Then the eyes of the blind shall be opened, and the ears of the deaf unstopped; then shall the lame man leap like a deer, and the tongue of the mute sing for joy"* (Isaiah 35:5–6).

VI. Lessons for Us

This passage teaches us several truths about Christ and about our own lives of faith:

Jesus' grace reaches beyond borders.

He deliberately entered Gentile territory, showing that His mission was for the nations.

Jesus meets us personally.

He took the man aside, communicated in ways he could understand, and addressed his unique need.

Jesus' power is complete.

The healing was instant and total. What he does, He does well.

Jesus deserves our praise.

The crowd's confession should be ours: *"He has done all things well."*

Conclusion

Mark 7 ends with worship. After exposing false religion, after teaching about true defilement, after showing grace to outsiders, Jesus heals a man in a personal, powerful way. The result is amazement and praise: *"He has done all things well."* That's still true today. Look at creation, look at redemption, look at your own life, and you'll see that Jesus has never failed. His work is marvelous beyond measure. At the end of the day, when we look back at Jesus' work in our lives, we'll be able to say the same thing: He has done all things well.

Reflection & Response

How has Jesus personally met you in your moments of need?

Where do you need to trust that His work is complete, not partial?

How can you join the crowd in proclaiming, *"He has done all things well"* this week?

Chapter 8

Jesus Is Enough

Mark 8:1–10

The gospel of Mark moves quickly. Chapter 7 ended with astonishment as the crowd declared of Jesus, *"He has done all things well."* Now, at the beginning of chapter 8, Mark records another miracle that proves the same point: Jesus is enough.

Once again, we find ourselves with a hungry crowd in a desolate place. This time it's not five thousand but four thousand. Once again, the disciples face an impossible situation. And once again, Jesus provides, showing that He is more than sufficient for the needs of His people. The message of this passage is clear: Jesus is enough to satisfy both body and soul.

I. A Compassionate Savior (vv. 1–3)

"In those days, when again a great crowd had gathered, and they had nothing to eat, he called his disciples to him and said to them, 'I have compassion on the crowd, because they have been with me now three days and have nothing to eat. And if I send them away hungry to their homes, they will faint on the way. And some of them have come from far away.'"

The scene is familiar: a great crowd, a desolate place, no food. But notice what drives Jesus to act: His compassion. This is more than pity. The word describes

141

a deep gut-level stirring of mercy. He sees the crowd's hunger, their weariness, their need, and He cares.

They had been with Him three days. This wasn't a brief sermon stop; they lingered because they were captivated by His teaching. They wanted to be near Him. And He recognized their need. Jesus doesn't overlook human needs as though they don't matter. He cares for bodies as well as souls. He sees hunger, exhaustion, and frailty, and He responds with compassion. This is our Savior, aware of our weaknesses, attentive to our needs, moved by His mercy.

II. A Faithless Response (vv. 4–5)

"And his disciples answered him, 'How can one feed these people with bread here in this desolate place?' And he asked them, 'How many loaves do you have?' They said, 'Seven.'"

We might be tempted to roll our eyes at the disciples here. Didn't they just see Him feed five thousand with five loaves and two fish? Shouldn't they know what He can do? But before we judge too harshly, we should see ourselves. How often do we forget God's past provision when we face new problems? How often do we panic in the moment rather than trust His power?

The disciples look at the crowd and despair: "How can this be done?" Jesus looks at the same crowd and asks: "What do you have?" The difference between fear and faith is where you place your focus. The disciples saw the size of the problem. Jesus saw the sufficiency of God. They had seven loaves, hardly enough for four thousand men plus women and children. But in the hands of Jesus, little is always enough.

III. A Satisfying Provision (vv. 6–7)

"And he directed the crowd to sit down on the ground. And he took the seven loaves, and having given thanks, he broke them and gave them to his disciples to set before the people; and they set them before the crowd. And they had a few small fish. And having blessed them, he said that these also should be set before them."

The scene echoes the feeding of the five thousand, but with subtle differences. Jesus gives thanks, breaks the loaves, and gives them to the disciples to distribute. Then He blesses the fish. It is simple. No theatrics. No spectacle. Just quiet provision multiplied in His hands. And once again, Jesus involves His disciples. He could have made bread appear out of thin air, but instead, He gave it to them to set before the people. The miracle flows through their service. This is how He still works today. He provides, but He invites us to distribute. We are not the source; we are the servants.

IV. An Abundant Result (vv. 8–9)

"And they ate and were satisfied. And they took up the broken pieces left over, seven baskets full. And there were about four thousand people. And he sent them away."

Everyone ate. Everyone was satisfied. And there were leftovers, seven baskets full. This is abundance. Not only does Jesus meet the need, He exceeds it. He is not a stingy Savior. He gives more than enough.

The numbers are significant. At the feeding of the five thousand, there were twelve baskets left, likely symbolizing provision for the twelve tribes of Israel. Here, there are seven baskets, seven often representing completeness or universality. Many scholars see this as a picture of Jesus' sufficiency not just for Israel but for the nations. Whether Jew or Gentile, whoever comes to Him will be fed, whoever looks to Him will be satisfied. Jesus doesn't just barely get us by. He fills us. He satisfies us. He is more than enough.

V. A Clear Lesson (v. 10)

"And immediately he got into the boat with his disciples and went to the district of Dalmanutha."

The miracle is over. The crowd is satisfied. The disciples have once again witnessed His sufficiency. Soon they will face new challenges and wrestle with doubt again, but the lesson is clear: Jesus is enough. Mark doesn't dwell on the crowd's reactions this time. He moves the story forward. Why? Because the point is not the crowd's amazement but the disciples' education. They needed to learn what we need to learn: Jesus is enough.

VI. Lessons for Today

This passage teaches us truths that every disciple needs to remember:

Jesus cares for the whole person.

He is concerned not only with souls but with bodies, not only with eternity but with today.

Our resources are never the issue.

The disciples saw seven loaves and despaired. But Jesus doesn't ask us to provide what we don't have. He asks us to surrender what we do have and trust Him to multiply it.

Jesus satisfies fully.

The crowd was satisfied. There were leftovers. He doesn't give us crumbs; He provides us with abundance.

Jesus is enough for the nations.

This miracle in Gentile territory points to the global reach of His sufficiency. Whoever comes to Him will find more than enough.

Conclusion

The feeding of the four thousand reminds us that ministry is not about our resources but about His sufficiency. When we face overwhelming needs, we can either despair at the size of the problem or trust the size of our Savior. Jesus is enough for the weary. He is enough for the hungry. He is enough for Jew and Gentile, for the insider and the outsider, for you and for me. At the end of the day, the lesson is simple: Jesus is enough. Whatever your need, whatever your lack, whatever your fear—He is enough.

Reflection & Response

Where are you tempted to doubt that Jesus is enough for your situation?

What "loaves" has God placed in your hands that you need to surrender to Him?

How can you practically rest in His sufficiency this week?

Why Do You Doubt?

Mark 8:11–21

Mark 8 begins with the feeding of the four thousand, a powerful demonstration that Jesus is more than enough to meet the needs of His people. Yet immediately after this miracle, we encounter two very different responses: the Pharisees' demand for a sign and the disciples' struggle with forgetfulness. In both cases, the problem is unbelief. The Pharisees doubted because they refused to see what was right in front of them. The disciples doubted because they forgot what they had already experienced. And Jesus asks the piercing question: *"Why do you doubt?"*

I. The Pharisees Demand a Sign (vv. 11–13)

"The Pharisees came and began to argue with him, seeking from him a sign from heaven to test him. And he sighed deeply in his spirit and said, 'Why does this generation seek a sign? Truly, I say to you, no sign will be given to this generation.' And he left them, got into the boat again, and went to the other side."

The Pharisees were not seeking truth. They were seeking to test Jesus, to trap Him. Their request for a sign was not a genuine desire to believe—it was an excuse to continue in their unbelief. They had already seen signs. They had heard His teaching, witnessed His miracles, and still they hardened their hearts. They didn't need more evidence; they needed faith.

Notice Jesus' response: He sighed deeply in His spirit. This is not frustration alone—it's grief. Grief over their stubborn unbelief. Then he refuses to play their game. *"No sign will be given."* This reminds us that unbelief is not primarily an intellectual problem but a moral and spiritual one. It's not that the Pharisees lacked evidence—it's that they rejected the evidence they had.

When people say, 'If God would just give me a sign, then I'd believe,' they're missing the point. Faith is not born from seeing more miracles. Faith is born from hearing God's Word and submitting to it. Jesus departs, leaving them in their unbelief.

II. The Disciples Forget the Signs (vv. 14–16)

"Now they had forgotten to bring bread, and they had only one loaf with them in the boat. And he cautioned them, saying, 'Watch out; beware of the leaven of the Pharisees and the leaven of Herod.' And they began discussing with one another the fact that they had no bread."

Here, the scene shifts to the boat. The disciples realize they only have one loaf of bread. Their minds go immediately to physical lack: "What are we going to eat?" Jesus, however, is focused on something much more profound. He warns them about the leaven of the Pharisees and Herod, that is, the corrupting influence of unbelief and hypocrisy. Leaven works quietly but spreads everywhere. If they're not careful, the same unbelief they just witnessed in the Pharisees could infect them.

But the disciples miss the point. They start worrying about bread. Jesus speaks of spiritual danger, and they're talking about lunch. The disciples were in danger of being blinded by physical concerns to spiritual realities. They were so focused on what they didn't have that they forgot who was in the boat with them.

III. Jesus Confronts Their Doubt (vv. 17–21)

"And Jesus, aware of this, said to them, 'Why are you discussing the fact that you have no bread? Do you not yet perceive or understand? Are your hearts hardened? Having eyes do you not see, and having ears do you not hear? And do you not remember? When I broke the five loaves for the five thousand, how many baskets full of broken pieces did you take up?' They said to him, 'Twelve.' 'And the seven for the four thousand, how many baskets full of broken pieces did you take up?' And they said to him, 'Seven.' And he said to them, 'Do you not yet understand?'"

Jesus confronts their doubt with a series of questions. Why are you worried about bread? Don't you understand yet? Don't you remember? He reminds them of the feeding of the five thousand and the four thousand. In both cases, there was not only enough but an abundance left over. Twelve baskets, then seven baskets. Each miracle should have been a lasting reminder: Jesus is enough.

But they forgot. And forgetting led to doubting. The issue here is not bread—it's belief. Jesus is calling them to remember who He is and what He has done, and to trust Him in the present. Doubt often grows in the soil of forgetfulness. When we forget God's past faithfulness, we will doubt His present provision.

IV. Lessons for Us

This passage teaches us several vital lessons about faith and doubt.

1. Unbelief is not solved by more evidence.

The Pharisees had seen enough, but their hearts were hard. If someone refuses to believe God's Word, no amount of miraculous signs will convince them.

2. Beware the subtle influence of unbelief.

Leaven works quietly, but it spreads. Doubt and cynicism can infiltrate our hearts if we're not watchful.

3. Don't let physical concerns blind you to spiritual realities.

The disciples were worried about bread when the Bread of Life was in the boat with them. We, too, can become so preoccupied with daily concerns that we miss the spiritual lessons God is teaching us.

4. Remember God's past faithfulness.

One of the best ways to fight doubt is to remember. Recall the ways God has provided, guided, and sustained you. Let memory fuel faith.

V. The Call to Trust

At the heart of this passage is a simple but profound call: trust Jesus. He is enough. He has proven it again and again. The Pharisees rejected Him because of unbelief. The disciples doubted Him because of forgetfulness. But the correct response is faith. When we are tempted to doubt, we must remember. Remember His provision. Remember His promises. Remember His presence.

Conclusion

Jesus' question still echoes today: *"Do you not yet understand?"*

Faith is not about demanding more signs or obsessing over what we lack. Faith is about remembering who Jesus is and trusting that He is enough. So why do you doubt? Look at His past faithfulness, trust His present sufficiency, and rest in His future promises. He is enough. The disciples had one loaf in the boat. But what they failed to realize is that one loaf was enough, because Jesus was in the boat with them. And He is enough for us, too.

Reflection & Response

Where are you tempted to demand a "sign" from God rather than trust His Word?

How have you seen the "leaven" of unbelief creep into your thinking or actions?

What specific moments of God's past faithfulness can you recall to strengthen your faith today?

From Confusion to Clarity: Progressing in the Christian Life

Mark 8:22–26

The gospel of Mark is often fast-paced, but here we encounter a miracle that slows us down. In fact, it is the only miracle of Jesus recorded in stages. A blind man is brought to Jesus, and his healing comes not all at once, but in two steps.

Why? Certainly not because Jesus lacked power. He could heal instantly, as He had done many times before. Instead, this miracle is intentional—a living parable of how spiritual understanding comes gradually. The disciples, and we ourselves, don't always see everything clearly right away. Growth in Christ is often a journey from confusion to clarity.

I. A Brought Man (vv. 22–23a)

"And they came to Bethsaida. And some people brought to him a blind man and begged him to touch him. And he took the blind man by the hand and led him out of the village."

The story begins with others bringing this blind man to Jesus. He cannot get there on his own; he needs help. This is a beautiful reminder that part of our ministry is bringing others to Christ. Notice also the compassion of Jesus. He takes the man by the hand and leads him out of the village. The healing is not done as a public spectacle. It is private, personal, and tender. Jesus meets him in his weakness with gentleness.

The Christian life begins when someone brings you to Jesus. You may have thought you came on your own,

151

but behind your story is someone who prayed, someone who witnessed, someone who carried you to Christ.

II. A Partial Healing (vv. 23b–24)

"And when he had spit on his eyes and laid his hands on him, he asked him, 'Do you see anything?' And he looked up and said, 'I see people, but they look like trees, walking.'"

This is unusual. After Jesus' touch, the man is not fully healed. He can see, but only vaguely shapes without clarity. He sees people, but they look like trees walking.

Why would Jesus heal in stages? Not because His power was limited, but because He was teaching a lesson. Just as physical sight returned gradually to this man, spiritual sight often comes slowly to disciples.

The disciples themselves are the living illustration of this. They had seen Jesus' miracles, heard His teaching, and even confessed that He was the Christ (which comes in the following passage). Yet their understanding was blurry. They saw, but not clearly.

III. A Complete Healing (v. 25)

"Then Jesus laid his hands on his eyes again; and he opened his eyes, his sight was restored, and he saw everything clearly."

With a second touch, the man's sight is completely restored. Now he sees everything clearly. The two-stage miracle is complete. This is a picture of how Christ works with us. He doesn't just give partial sight; His goal is complete clarity. But He often brings us along gradually, patiently, step by step.

Some of you are discouraged because you don't feel like you see everything clearly yet. Take heart if Jesus has begun to open your eyes; He will finish the work. He is patient with our progress.

IV. A Private Command (v. 26)

"And he sent him to his home, saying, 'Do not even enter the village.'"

Jesus again keeps the miracle private. He doesn't want a crowd or commotion. He sends the man home, likely to protect Him from becoming a spectacle and to keep His mission focused. The emphasis here is not publicity but discipleship. The miracle is not for show—it is for teaching. The disciples are meant to see in this act a picture of their own journey of faith.

V. Lessons for the Christian Life

This unique miracle teaches us several important truths about the Christian life and spiritual growth.

1. Spiritual sight begins with being brought to Jesus.

No one comes to Christ on their own. God uses people to carry others through prayer, witness, and love.

2. Growth often comes gradually.

Like the blind man, we don't always see clearly at first. Our understanding of Christ deepens over time. Discipleship is a process, not an instant download.

3. Partial sight is not the goal.

It's possible to know Jesus partially, to see Him vaguely, to confess Him in part. But he desires that we see Him fully and clearly.

4. Jesus is patient with our progress.

He doesn't cast us aside when our vision is blurry. He touches us again, and again, until we see clearly.

5. Clarity comes through Christ's touch.

Only Jesus can open blind eyes. Our effort, discipline, and study matter, but ultimately it is His hand that grants true sight.

VI. From Confusion to Clarity

The placement of this miracle in Mark's gospel is deliberate. Immediately after this, Peter confesses Jesus as the Christ. But even then, the disciples don't fully understand. They see, but still dimly. The cross will bring fuller clarity. The resurrection will bring greater clarity still. And the Spirit at Pentecost will open their eyes fully.

This mirrors our own journey. We come to Christ with confusion. Over time, our sight grows clearer. The more we walk with Him, the more we see. One day, when He returns, we will see Him face to face with perfect clarity. The Christian life is a journey from blurred vision to clear vision. From confusion to clarity. From seeing people like trees walking to seeing Christ in all His glory.

Conclusion

The healing of the blind man at Bethsaida reminds us that growth in Christ is a process. Some see instantly; most of us grow gradually. But if Jesus has begun to open your eyes, He will finish what He started. Don't despair if your vision feels blurry today. Don't give up if your understanding feels incomplete. Trust the One who has touched you. He is patient. And in time, you will see everything clearly. Jesus doesn't leave His people half-healed, half-saved, half-changed. He brings His work to completion. If He's opened your eyes even a little, He will finish the job.

Reflection & Response

Who brought you to Jesus, and how can you get others to Him today?

Where do you feel like your spiritual sight is blurry?

How can you trust Jesus to bring you from confusion to clarity patiently?

Who Do You Say That He Is?

Mark 8:27–30

Every person must answer life's most important question: *Who is Jesus?*

Mark's gospel has been building to this very moment. We have seen Jesus calm storms, cast out demons, heal the sick, feed thousands, and even raise the dead. The crowds have marveled, the Pharisees have opposed Him, and the disciples have followed

Him in wonder and fear. But now, in this pivotal passage, Jesus looks at His disciples and asks the question that cuts through every other opinion: *"Who do you say that I am?"* Your answer to that question determines everything.

I. The Setting (v. 27)

"And Jesus went on with his disciples to the villages of Caesarea Philippi. And on the way he asked his disciples, 'Who do people say that I am?'"

The location matters. Caesarea Philippi was known for pagan worship, shrines to false gods, and devotion to Caesar himself. Against this backdrop of competing allegiances, Jesus raises the question of His own identity. He begins by asking, *"Who do people say that I am?"* He wants His disciples to articulate the various opinions circulating about Him.

Even today, the world is full of opinions about Jesus. Some call Him a great teacher, a prophet, a moral example, or a revolutionary. Few deny His influence, but many distort His identity. The setting of Caesarea Philippi is no accident. In the middle of a culture that worshiped many gods, Jesus was asking His disciples to make a clear distinction: Who am I compared to them?

II. The Opinions of the Crowd (v. 28)

"And they told him, 'John the Baptist; and others say, Elijah; and others, one of the prophets.'"

The disciples report the common views. Some thought Jesus was John the Baptist raised from the dead. Others said He was Elijah, the prophet expected

156

to return before the Messiah came (Malachi 4:5). Still others thought He was another prophet like those of old.

Notice that all of these opinions are respectful. No one is calling Him an ordinary man. They recognize something extraordinary about Him. Yet all of these opinions fall short. Respecting Jesus as a prophet is not the same as confessing Him as Lord.

Respect without faith is still rejection. It's not enough to admire Jesus as a moral teacher or a religious leader. The world is full of people who respect Jesus but do not worship Him. Respect is not the same as faith.

III. The Question to the Disciples (v. 29a)

"And he asked them, 'But who do you say that I am?'"

Here, the focus shifts. Jesus isn't content with public opinion. He presses the question home to His disciples personally. This is the question every person must answer—not what others say about Him, not what your parents believe, not what your culture thinks, but what *you* say. Faith is always personal. You cannot borrow someone else's confession. You must declare your own. This is why this moment is so significant. Everything in Mark's gospel has been leading here. Jesus has shown who He is through His works. Now, He calls for a response.

IV. The Confession of Peter (v. 29b)

"Peter answered him, 'You are the Christ.'"

Peter speaks on behalf of the disciples and gets it right: *"You are the Christ."* The word means "the Anointed One"—the promised Messiah, the king sent by God to deliver His people.

This is the first explicit confession of Jesus as the Christ in Mark's gospel. The demons had recognized Him earlier, but now His disciples openly confess it. This is the turning point. Up until now, the disciples have been struggling to understand. They have seen but not clearly, like the blind man in the previous passage. Now their vision sharpens. They confess Jesus as the Christ.

Yet their understanding is still incomplete. They imagine a conquering king, not a suffering servant. They confess rightly, but they do not yet grasp fully what it means. That fuller understanding will come through the cross. Peter's confession was both right and wrong. Right in who Jesus is—the Christ. Wrong in what he thought the Christ had come to do. It's possible to have the right words but the wrong meaning.

V. The Command of Silence (v. 30)

"And he strictly charged them to tell no one about him."

This seems strange. Why would Jesus tell them not to share this good news? Because their understanding was still incomplete. If they proclaimed Him as Messiah without understanding the cross, people would misunderstand His mission.

Jesus is not just the Christ who conquers, He is the Christ who suffers. The disciples must learn that the crown comes through the cross. Until they understand that, their proclamation would be premature.

VI. Lessons for Us

This passage calls us to wrestle with the same question the disciples faced: *Who do you say that He is?*

Public opinion cannot save you.

The world has many opinions about Jesus, but none of them are enough. Knowing what others believe is not the same as believing yourself.

Faith must be personal.

It's not enough to say, "My parents believe in Jesus," or "My church teaches this." What do *you* believe? Your confession must be your own.

Confession must be complete.

Peter confessed Jesus as the Christ, but his understanding was partial. True faith embraces not only His identity but His mission—to save through suffering and death.

Silence is sometimes strategic.

Jesus' command for silence reminds us that God's plan unfolds in His timing. Proclaiming Him as Messiah without the cross would distort the message.

VII. From Confession to Clarity

This passage is the hinge of Mark's gospel. Everything that has come before has been leading up to the question of who Jesus is. Everything after will explain what it means for Him to be the Christ.

Peter's confession marks the beginning of clarity, but more light is yet to come. Soon, Jesus will begin to teach plainly that He must suffer, die, and rise again. The disciples will struggle with this, but it is the heart of the gospel. It's not enough to say Jesus is the Christ if you don't understand the cross. The Christ without the cross is not the Savior of Scripture.

Conclusion

The question Jesus asked His disciples is the same question He asks you: *"Who do you say that I am?"* You cannot remain neutral. You cannot hide behind public opinion. You must answer for yourself. And there is only one correct answer: *"You are the Christ."* The promised Savior. The Son of God. The One who came not only to reign but to redeem. So who do you say that He is?

Reflection & Response

How does your confession of Christ compare with the opinions of the world around you?

Have you made a personal confession of Jesus as the Christ, or are you relying on someone else's faith?

How does understanding the cross deepen your confession that Jesus is the Christ?

It Will Cost You Everything

Mark 8:31–9:1

Peter has just confessed Jesus as the Christ (8:27–30). It was a high moment, the hinge of Mark's gospel. But immediately, Jesus begins to teach what kind of Messiah He is. He will not be the conquering king the disciples expected. He will be the suffering servant foretold in Scripture. This is the turning point. From here, Jesus sets His face toward Jerusalem and the cross. And He makes it clear that following Him will not be easy. It will cost everything.

I. Jesus Predicts His Suffering (v. 31)

"And he began to teach them that the Son of Man must suffer many things and be rejected by the elders and the chief priests and the scribes and be killed, and after three days rise again."

This is the first of three passion predictions in Mark's gospel. Notice the word *must*. This is not optional. This is divine necessity. The Son of Man *must* suffer. Why? Because this is God's plan for salvation. The cross is not an accident or a tragedy; it is the centerpiece of God's redemptive plan. Jesus lays out the path clearly: suffering, rejection, death, and resurrection. He is preparing His disciples for what is to come. But they cannot yet grasp it.

II. Peter Rebukes Jesus (v. 32)

"And he said this plainly. And Peter took him aside and began to rebuke him."

Jesus speaks plainly. No parables, no riddles. He tells them directly what will happen. But Peter cannot accept it. He has just confessed Jesus as the Christ, and now Jesus is talking about suffering and death? That doesn't fit Peter's expectations. So Peter takes Jesus aside and rebukes Him. Imagine rebuking the Son of God! Peter thought he was protecting Jesus, but in reality, he was opposing God's plan.

Peter had the right title but the wrong definition. He knew Jesus was the Christ, but he wanted a Christ without a cross. How often are we like Peter? We want salvation without suffering, glory without the cross, discipleship without denial.

III. Jesus Rebukes Peter (v. 33)

"But turning and seeing his disciples, he rebuked Peter and said, 'Get behind me, Satan! For you are not setting your mind on the things of God, but on the things of man.'"

Jesus' response is strong: *"Get behind me, Satan!"* Peter's words echoed the same temptation Satan offered in the wilderness, the crown without the cross. But Jesus will not be deterred. He sets His mind on the things of God, not the things of man. Here we see the danger of thinking we know better than God. Whenever we try to redefine Jesus or reshape His mission to fit our desires, we oppose Him.

IV. The Call to Discipleship (vv. 34–35)

"And calling the crowd to him with his disciples, he said to them, 'If anyone would come after me, let him deny himself and take up his cross and follow me. For whoever would save

his life will lose it, but whoever loses his life for my sake and the gospel's will save it.'"

Now Jesus expands the lesson. It's not just about Him—it's about us. To follow Jesus is to walk the same road He walked.

Three commands:

Deny yourself.

To deny oneself is more than denying things. It means saying no to self-rule, self-will, and self-centeredness. It is dethroning self and enthroning Christ.

Take up your cross.

The cross was not a religious symbol then—it was an instrument of execution. To take up your cross meant you were as good as dead. Following Jesus means dying to yourself daily.

Follow me.

Discipleship is not about a one-time decision but an ongoing journey. To follow Him is to walk His path, wherever it leads.

The paradox is evident: If you try to save your life, you will lose it. But if you lose your life for Christ and the gospel, you will save it.

V. The Value of a Soul (vv. 36–37)

"For what does it profit a man to gain the whole world and forfeit his soul? For what can a man give in return for his soul?"

Here, Jesus asks the most searching of questions. What good is it to gain everything the world offers if you lose your soul? Your soul is of infinite value. Nothing can replace it. No wealth, no success, no power can compensate for a lost soul. This is why following Jesus, though costly, is worth it. To cling to this world is to lose everything. To cling to Christ is to gain eternal life.

VI. The Warning of Shame (v. 38)

"For whoever is ashamed of me and of my words in this adulterous and sinful generation, of him will the Son of Man also be ashamed when he comes in the glory of his Father with the holy angels."

Jesus presses the cost further. If you are ashamed of Him now, He will be ashamed of you when He returns. This is sobering. Faith is not a private preference. Following Christ requires public allegiance. To deny Him before men is to face His denial before the Father. But the reverse is true as well. If you confess Him now, He will confess you then. If you stand with Him now, He will stand with you in glory.

VII. The Promise of Glory (9:1)

"And he said to them, 'Truly, I say to you, there are some standing here who will not taste death until they see the kingdom of God after it has come with power.'"

Jesus ends with a promise. Some standing there would not die before seeing the kingdom of God come with power. This likely points to the Transfiguration (which follows in 9:2–8), the resurrection, and the outpouring of the Spirit at Pentecost. The point is clear: though the path of discipleship is costly, the destination is glorious. The cross leads to the crown.

VIII. Lessons for Us

This passage teaches us what true discipleship looks like.

Jesus must suffer, and so must we.

The path of the Master is the path of the disciple. Suffering is not an accident; it is part of following Christ.

We cannot have Christ without the cross.

To try to redefine Jesus as someone who only brings comfort and never calls for sacrifice is to miss Him altogether.

Discipleship is costly, but worth it.

Losing your life for Christ is the way to save it. Gaining the world at the cost of your soul is the ultimate loss.

The future glory outweighs the present cost.

Whatever we give up now pales in comparison to the glory that will be revealed when Christ returns.

Conclusion

Jesus does not attempt to hide the cost of following Him. He doesn't lure us in with promises of ease. He tells us plainly: it will cost you everything. But He also promises that what we gain is infinitely greater. Eternal life. A soul saved. A share in His glory.

The question is not whether discipleship is costly; it is whether it is worth it. And the answer is yes. To follow Jesus is to lose your life and gain everything. Salvation is free, but following Jesus will cost you everything. And it is the best trade you will ever make.

Reflection & Response

Where are you tempted to seek Christ without the cross?

What does denying yourself and taking up your cross look like in your daily life?

How does the promise of future glory help you endure the cost of discipleship today?

Chapter 9

Jesus Christ, The Son of God

Mark 9:2–13

The question at the center of Mark's gospel is this: *Who is Jesus?* Peter confessed in chapter 8, *"You are the Christ."* Then Jesus explained that the Christ must suffer, die, and rise again, and that following Him means denying yourself and taking up your cross. But here, in the Transfiguration, we are given a glimpse of His glory. The disciples are reminded that the suffering Christ is also the glorious Son of God. The cross is real, but so is the crown. This passage calls us to behold Jesus Christ, the Son of God, and to listen to Him.

I. The Glory of the Son (vv. 2–3)

"And after six days Jesus took with him Peter and James and John, and led them up a high mountain by themselves. And he was transfigured before them, and his clothes became radiant, intensely white, as no one on earth could bleach them."

Jesus takes Peter, James, and John up a mountain. These three often serve as His inner circle. On the mountain, something remarkable happens. He is transfigured. The word means to be changed in form. His appearance radiates with divine glory. For a moment, the veil of His humanity is lifted, and His true majesty shines forth. His clothes become dazzling

167

white, beyond anything human effort could produce. This is the glory of the eternal Son of God breaking through. On the mountain, the disciples got a preview of what was coming. They saw not just a rabbi or a healer, but the radiant glory of the Son of God.

II. The Witness of the Law and the Prophets (v. 4)

"And there appeared to them Elijah with Moses, and they were talking with Jesus."

Suddenly, Moses and Elijah appear, representing the Law and the Prophets. Together, they testify to Jesus. Moses, the great lawgiver, and Elijah, the great prophet, point to the One who fulfills both. Their presence shows that the entire Old Testament finds its fulfillment in Christ. They are not the center of attention. They stand with Jesus, but all the focus is on Him.

III. The Confusion of the Disciples (vv. 5–6)

"And Peter said to Jesus, 'Rabbi, it is good that we are here. Let us make three tents, one for you and one for Moses and one for Elijah.' For he did not know what to say, for they were terrified."

Peter doesn't know what to say, so he blurts out an idea about building three tents. He wants to preserve the moment, to capture the glory. But in suggesting three tents, he unintentionally puts Jesus on the same level as Moses and Elijah.

Mark explains: Peter was terrified. His words come more from fear than understanding. We should not be too hard on Peter. When faced with the glory of God, we too are often overwhelmed and confused. But his response shows how easily we can miss the uniqueness of Jesus.

IV. The Testimony of the Father (v. 7)

"And a cloud overshadowed them, and a voice came out of the cloud, 'This is my beloved Son; listen to him.'"

The climax of the scene comes with the voice of God the Father. A cloud, often a symbol of God's presence, overshadows them, and the Father speaks.

Three things are declared:

"This is my beloved Son." Jesus is not just a prophet or teacher. He is the unique Son of God.

"Listen to him." Moses and Elijah fade into the background. Jesus is the final word. The disciples must listen to Him above all.

"Beloved." The Father affirms His love and approval of the Son.

This echoes the voice at Jesus' baptism (Mark 1:11) but is now directed to the disciples. They must hear and obey. The Father doesn't say, 'Listen to Moses. Listen to Elijah.' He says, 'Listen to Jesus.' He is the Son of God, the fulfillment of all Scripture. Our task is to hear Him.

V. The Supremacy of Christ (v. 8)

"And suddenly, looking around, they no longer saw anyone with them but Jesus only."

When the vision ends, Moses and Elijah are gone. Only Jesus remains. This is the point—He alone is supreme. The Law and the Prophets point to Him, but now that He has come, He is the focus. This reminds us that while we honor the saints and prophets of old, only Christ is worthy of worship. He is not one among many. He is the One and Only.

VI. The Mystery of Suffering (vv. 9–13)

"And as they were coming down the mountain, he charged them to tell no one what they had seen, until the Son of Man had risen from the dead. So they kept the matter to themselves, questioning what this rising from the dead might mean. And they asked him, 'Why do the scribes say that first Elijah must come?' And he said to them, 'Elijah does come first to restore all things. And how is it written of the Son of Man that he should suffer many things and be treated with contempt? But I tell you that Elijah has come, and they did to him whatever they pleased, as it is written of him.'"

As they come down the mountain, Jesus commands them to keep silent until after His resurrection. The disciples don't fully understand. They wrestle with the idea of rising from the dead and the prophecy about Elijah. Jesus explains that Elijah has already come in the ministry of John the Baptist. Just as John suffered, so too the Son of Man must suffer. The glory they witnessed on the mountain cannot be separated from the suffering that awaits them in Jerusalem. This is the great mystery of the gospel: the glorious Son of God came to suffer and die for sinners.

VII. Lessons for Us

This passage offers profound lessons for our faith today:

See the glory of Christ. The Transfiguration reminds us that Jesus is more than a man. He is the radiant Son of God, worthy of our worship.

Trust the testimony of Scripture. Moses and Elijah testify that all of God's Word points to Jesus.

Listen to Him. The Father's command is simple. Our task is to hear Christ and obey.

Don't separate glory from suffering. The path of the cross leads to the crown. Like the disciples, we must learn that suffering and glory are both part of God's plan.

Conclusion

The Transfiguration is a mountaintop moment in the gospel of Mark. It reveals the true identity of Jesus Christ, the Son of God. It reminds us that the cross is not the end of the story. The glory of the Son awaits. The Father's command still stands: *"This is my beloved Son; listen to him."* Not Moses, not Elijah, not the voices of the world, but Jesus. Listen to Him. When the cloud lifted, it was Jesus only. He is the Son of God, the center of our faith, the One to whom we must listen.

Reflection & Response

How does seeing the glory of Christ on the mountain strengthen your faith in Him?

In what ways do you need to obey the Father's command to *listen to Him*?

How does remembering both the suffering and the glory of Christ shape your discipleship?

Help My Unbelief

Mark 9:14-29

The Transfiguration was a mountaintop experience. Peter, James, and John saw the glory of Christ revealed. But immediately after, in stark contrast, they come down into the valley and encounter chaos, weakness, and unbelief. This passage reminds us that the Christian life is not lived on the mountaintop but in the valley. There we face spiritual battles, human frailty, and desperate need. But there too we meet the power of Christ, who responds to faith, even weak, struggling faith.

I. The Chaos in the Valley (vv. 14–18)

"And when they came to the disciples, they saw a great crowd around them, and scribes arguing with them. And immediately all the crowd, when they saw him, were greatly amazed and ran up to him and greeted him. And he asked them, 'What are you arguing about with them?' And someone from the crowd answered him, 'Teacher, I brought my Son to you, for he has a spirit that makes him mute. And whenever it seizes him, it throws him down, and he foams and grinds his teeth and becomes rigid. So I asked your disciples to cast it out, and they were not able.'"

The scene is one of conflict and failure. The disciples are surrounded by a crowd, locked in argument with the scribes. At the center of it all is a desperate father whose Son is tormented by a demon. He had brought his Son to the disciples, but they could not help him. Their failure became an opportunity for the scribes to criticize and the crowd to doubt.

This is often what happens when God's people fail to walk in His power: the world seizes the opportunity to mock and argue. The mountaintop was glorious, but the valley is messy. That's where we live most of our lives, in the struggle, the weakness, the need. And it's there we must learn to depend on Christ.

II. The Frustration of Jesus (vv. 19–20)

"And he answered them, 'O faithless generation, how long am I to be with you? How long am I to bear with you? Bring him to me.' And they brought the boy to him. And when the spirit saw him, immediately it convulsed the boy, and he fell on the ground and rolled about, foaming at the mouth."

Jesus expresses frustration: *"O faithless generation."* His words are not directed only at the disciples but at the entire scene, disciples who failed, scribes who argued, a crowd more interested in spectacle than faith. His lament reminds us of how patient He is with us, yet also how grieved He is when we fail to trust Him. Still, His compassion shines through: *"Bring him to me."* Where the disciples failed, Jesus calls the boy to Himself. The demon immediately reacts, showing its terror before the Son of God.

III. The Desperation of the Father (vv. 21–22)

"And Jesus asked his father, 'How long has this been happening to him?' And he said, 'From childhood. And it has

often cast him into fire and into water, to destroy him. But if you can do anything, have compassion on us and help us.'"

The Father describes the long agony of his Son's suffering. The boy has been tormented from childhood, often in life-threatening ways. The Father has lived in constant fear and grief. Finally, he pleads with Jesus: *"If you can do anything, have compassion on us and help us."* His words reveal both desperation and doubt. He is not sure Jesus can do it, but he is desperate enough to ask. This is often where we find ourselves caught between belief and doubt, between hope and despair.

IV. The Power of Faith (vv. 23–24)

"And Jesus said to him, 'If you can! All things are possible for one who believes.' Immediately the Father of the child cried out and said, 'I believe; help my unbelief!'"

Jesus seizes on the Father's words: *"If you can!"* The issue is not Christ's power but the man's faith. All things are possible for the one who believes, not because faith is powerful in itself, but because faith connects us to the One who is powerful. The Father responds with one of the most honest prayers in Scripture: *"I believe; help my unbelief!"*

This is not polished theology but raw honesty. He believes, but he also doubts. He trusts, but he also struggles. And he brings that mixture to Jesus. That's the prayer of every honest Christian. We believe, but we don't believe perfectly. We trust, but we struggle. And Jesus meets us in that place and answers even weak faith.

V. The Authority of Jesus (vv. 25–27)

"And when Jesus saw that a crowd came running together, he rebuked the unclean spirit, saying to it, 'You mute and deaf spirit, I command you, come out of him and never enter him again.' And after crying out and convulsing him terribly, it came out, and the boy was like a corpse, so that most of them said, 'He is dead.' But Jesus took him by the hand and lifted him up, and he arose."

Jesus acts with sovereign authority. He rebukes the spirit, commands it to leave, and forbids it to return. The spirit convulses the boy one last time, and he appears dead. But Jesus takes him by the hand and raises him. The imagery is striking, like a resurrection. Jesus not only delivers but restores. The boy is not only freed from torment but lifted to a new life.

VI. The Lesson for the Disciples (vv. 28–29)

"And when he had entered the house, his disciples asked him privately, 'Why could we not cast it out?' And he said to them, 'This kind cannot be driven out by anything but prayer.'"

In private, the disciples ask why they failed. Jesus' answer is simple: *"This kind cannot be driven out by anything but prayer."*

Their failure was not due to a lack of technique but a lack of dependence. They tried to act in their own strength instead of relying on God. Prayer is the posture of dependence. Without it, we have no power. This is a sobering reminder for us. Ministry cannot be done in our strength. Spiritual battles cannot be fought with human effort. We must depend on God through prayer.

VII. Lessons for Us

This passage teaches us profound lessons for our walk with Christ:

Life is lived in the valley. Mountaintop moments are rare. Most of life is lived in the valley, where faith is tested and Christ's power is needed.

Failure is an opportunity to learn dependence. The disciples' failure revealed their lack of prayer. Our failures remind us to depend more fully on Christ.

Faith, even weak faith, connects us to Christ. The Father's prayer, *"I believe; help my unbelief,"* shows that imperfect faith is still genuine faith when placed in Jesus.

Prayer is essential for spiritual power. Without prayer, we operate in our own strength and inevitably fail. With prayer, we depend on God's power.

Conclusion

The contrast between the mountaintop and the valley is striking. On the mountain, the disciples saw the glory of Christ. In the valley, they experienced their weakness and failure. But in both places, the answer is the same: Jesus.

When we face chaos, unbelief, and failure, we must bring it to Him. And even if our faith is weak, we can pray with the desperate Father: *"I believe; help my unbelief!"* Jesus is not looking for perfect faith. He's looking for genuine faith that clings to Him, even with trembling hands. And that kind of faith is enough, because He is enough."

Reflection & Response

Where in your life do you feel caught between belief and unbelief?

How can you cultivate greater dependence on God through prayer this week?

How does this passage encourage you when your faith feels weak?

Living in the Kingdom of Christ

Mark 9:30–41

Jesus has just healed a demon-possessed boy after the disciples failed in their own strength. That moment highlighted their weakness and His sufficiency. Now, as they continue their journey through Galilee, Jesus begins to teach them again about His coming suffering, death, and resurrection.

But the disciples are still slow to understand. Instead of grasping the weight of His mission, they fall into arguing about which of them is the greatest. Jesus takes this moment to teach what life in His kingdom looks like: humility, servanthood, and valuing even the smallest act done in His name.

I. Jesus Predicts His Death Again (vv. 30–32)

"They went on from there and passed through Galilee. And he did not want anyone to know, for he was teaching his

177

disciples, saying to them, 'The Son of Man is going to be delivered into the hands of men, and they will kill him. And when he is killed, after three days he will rise.' But they did not understand the saying, and were afraid to ask him."

This is the second time in Mark's gospel that Jesus explicitly predicts His suffering and death. Notice the detail: *"The Son of Man is going to be delivered."* The word suggests betrayal. He will be handed over, not by accident, but as part of God's sovereign plan.

Jesus is intentionally avoiding the crowds now. His focus is on teaching His disciples, preparing them for what is to come. Yet they do not understand. Worse, they are afraid to ask. Their silence reveals both confusion and fear. Here we see again the gap between Jesus' clarity and the disciples' blindness. He is focused on the cross; they are focused on themselves. The disciples didn't understand because they didn't want to. A suffering Messiah didn't fit their expectations. So instead of asking for clarity, they avoided the subject altogether.

II. The Argument About Greatness (vv. 33–34)

"And they came to Capernaum. And when he was in the house, he asked them, 'What were you discussing on the way?' But they kept silent, for on the way they had argued with one another about who was the greatest."

On the road, the disciples argued about greatness. While Jesus was teaching them about His impending death, they were debating rank and status.

When Jesus asks them about it, they fall silent. They know their argument was shameful. How often do we, too, fall into prideful comparison, measuring ourselves against others, even as we profess to follow a Savior who humbled Himself to the point of death?

This moment exposes the clash between human ambition and kingdom values. The world defines greatness in terms of power, position, and recognition. But in the kingdom of Christ, greatness looks very different.

III. The Redefinition of Greatness (vv. 35–37)

"And he sat down and called the twelve. And he said to them, 'If anyone would be first, he must be last of all and servant of all.' And he took a child and put him in the midst of them, and taking him in his arms, he said to them, 'Whoever receives one such child in my name receives me, and whoever receives me, receives not me but him who sent me.'"

Jesus sits down, the posture of a teacher. He calls the disciples close and redefines greatness: *"If anyone would be first, he must be last of all and servant of all."* In the kingdom of Christ, greatness is measured not by how many serve you but by how many you serve. To be first, you must choose to be last. To be great, you must become a servant.

Then He takes a child and places the child in their midst. Children in that culture had little status or importance. Yet Jesus embraces the child and says that to receive one such child in His name is to receive Him—and even the Father who sent Him. True greatness is seen in humble service, especially toward those who seem small and insignificant in the eyes of the world. Jesus flips the world's definition of greatness upside down. In His kingdom, greatness isn't about power or prestige—it's about humility, service, and receiving the least as though you were receiving Christ Himself.

IV. The Warning Against Prideful Exclusion (vv. 38–41)

"John said to him, 'Teacher, we saw someone casting out demons in your name, and we tried to stop him, because he was not following us.' But Jesus said, 'Do not stop him, for no one who does a mighty work in my name will be able soon afterward to speak evil of me. For the one who is not against us is for us. For truly, I say to you, whoever gives you a cup of water to drink because you belong to Christ will by no means lose his reward.'"

John raises an issue: they had seen someone casting out demons in Jesus' name, but since he was not part of their group, they tried to stop him. Notice the pride— *"he was not following us."* Jesus corrects them. His kingdom is bigger than their little circle. Anyone who acts in His name is not an enemy. The smallest act done in faith, even giving a cup of water, will not go unnoticed by God.

This is a warning against prideful exclusivity. The disciples were tempted to think they had a monopoly on Jesus' work. But Christ reminds them that His kingdom includes many servants beyond their small group. We must beware of narrowing the kingdom down to 'us' and excluding others who faithfully serve Christ. If they are for Him, they are not against Him. The kingdom is bigger than our little tribe.

V. Lessons for Us

This passage teaches us several vital lessons about life in the kingdom of Christ:

Christ's mission centers on the cross. We must never lose sight of the cross as the heart of His mission and ours.

True greatness is found in humble service. To be first, you must be last. To lead, you must serve.

Receiving the least is receiving Christ. How we treat the most overlooked and vulnerable reveals our heart toward Christ Himself.

The kingdom is bigger than us. We must resist prideful exclusivity and rejoice in anyone who faithfully serves Christ, even in small ways.

Conclusion

The disciples were slow to understand. While Jesus spoke of the cross, they argued about greatness. But Jesus redefined greatness and reminded them that His kingdom is marked by humility, service, and openness to others who serve in His name. Living in the kingdom of Christ means taking up the posture of a servant, welcoming the least, and valuing even the smallest act of faith. The world says, 'Be first, be great, be recognized.' Jesus says, 'Be last, be a servant, receive the least.' That is life in the kingdom of Christ.

Reflection & Response

Where in your life are you tempted to measure greatness by the world's standards rather than Christ's?

How can you take the posture of a servant in your home, church, or workplace this week?

Who are the "least" in your life whom you can receive and value in Jesus' name?

Salty, But Not Sinful

Mark 9:42–50

Jesus has just finished teaching His disciples about humility, servanthood, and valuing the least in His kingdom. Now, He turns to the seriousness of sin. The imagery is strong and sobering: better to be drowned, better to lose a hand or an eye, than to cause others—or yourself, to stumble into sin.

This passage reminds us that following Jesus is not casual. Sin is deadly serious. Holiness is not optional. And yet, at the same time, Jesus calls His disciples to live distinctly, salty, preserving, and influencing the world for Him.

I. A Warning About Causing Others to Stumble (v. 42)

"Whoever causes one of these little ones who believe in me to sin, it would be better for him if a great millstone were hung around his neck and he were thrown into the sea."

Jesus begins with a warning: do not cause others, especially "little ones who believe," to stumble. This could mean young believers, children, or anyone weak in faith. To mislead, tempt, or harm them spiritually is a grave offense. The imagery is shocking: a millstone, a massive stone used for grinding grain, tied around the neck, and thrown into the sea. Jesus says this fate would be preferable to facing God's judgment for leading others into sin.

This underscores the weight of our influence. Our words, actions, and example matter. How we treat the weak, the vulnerable, the impressionable, matters deeply to Christ. You may not think of yourself as a leader, but someone is watching you. Someone is following your example. That's why Jesus warns so strongly here because our sin doesn't just affect us. It can drag others down with us.

II. A Warning About Personal Sin (vv. 43–48)

"And if your hand causes you to sin, cut it off. It is better for you to enter life crippled than with two hands to go to hell, to the unquenchable fire. And if your foot causes you to sin, cut it off. It is better for you to enter life lame than with two feet to be thrown into hell. And if your eye causes you to sin, tear it out. It is better for you to enter the kingdom of God with one eye than with two eyes to be thrown into hell, 'where their worm does not die and the fire is not quenched.'"

Jesus moves from warning about harming others to warning about harming ourselves through sin. The language is extreme: cut off your hand, cut off your foot, tear out your eye. He is not advocating literal mutilation but using powerful imagery to make the point: deal radically with sin. Do not coddle it, excuse it, or play with it. Sin must be killed before it kills you.

It is better to lose something precious now and enter life than to keep it and be thrown into hell. Jesus is teaching the eternal seriousness of sin and the reality of judgment. Hell is described here with terrifying language: unquenchable fire, undying worm. It is not temporary or symbolic; it is real, eternal punishment.

This is a call to holiness, to radical repentance. It is better to lose what feels essential than to lose your soul. Jesus isn't calling us to self-harm. He's calling us to do spiritual surgery. You don't tolerate cancer; you cut it out. That's how we must deal with sin.

III. Everyone Will Be Salted With Fire (v. 49)

"For everyone will be salted with fire."

This is a difficult phrase, but it likely means that everyone will experience refining or testing. Fire in Scripture often symbolizes both judgment and purification. For unbelievers, fire implies judgment. For believers, fire means refining. God allows trials, hardships, and even suffering to purify our faith and make us holy.

The imagery of salt and fire also connects to Old Testament sacrifices, which were offered with salt as a sign of covenant faithfulness (Leviticus 2:13). Jesus may be pointing to the fact that His followers are called to live as living sacrifices, purified and preserved by God's refining work.

IV. The Call to Remain Salty (vv. 50)

"Salt is good, but if the salt has lost its saltiness, how will you make it salty again? Have salt in yourselves, and be at peace with one another."

Jesus ends with an exhortation: remain salty. Salt in the ancient world preserved food, purified it, and added flavor. For His disciples, being salty means living distinctly, preserving truth, resisting corruption, and influencing the world for good. But if salt loses its distinctiveness, it becomes useless. A disciple who compromises with sin or blends in with the world loses the very quality that makes him effective.

Jesus adds, *"Be at peace with one another."* The call to holiness and distinctiveness must not lead to pride or division. Instead, disciples are to live in unity, marked by both purity and peace. The world doesn't need more bland Christians. It needs salty ones, believers who live distinctly, who resist sin, who preserve truth, who bring the flavor of Christ wherever they go.

V. Lessons for Us

This passage gives us three clear lessons for following Christ today:

Take responsibility for your influence. Do not cause others to stumble. Your example matters.

Deal radically with your own sin. Don't toy with it. Don't justify it. Kill it before it kills you.

Live distinctly as salt. Be different from the world. Preserve truth. Resist corruption. Pursue peace with others.

Conclusion

Jesus' words here are sobering. Sin is serious. Hell is real. Holiness is necessary. But He also calls His disciples to be salty—to live distinctly, preserving truth and influencing the world for Him. To follow Christ means we must be both ruthless with sin and radiant with holiness. We must not be bland, but salty. Not sinful, but distinct. If you are in Christ, you are called to be different. Don't lose your saltiness. Don't let sin rob you of your distinctiveness. Be salty, but not sinful.

Reflection & Response

Who in your life is watching your example? How can you avoid causing them to stumble?

What sin do you need to deal with radically, not excusing it but cutting it off?

In what ways can you live more distinctly as salt in the world this week?

Chapter 10

The Truth About Divorce, Marriage, and Remarriage

Mark 10:1-12

Few topics are as personal and painful as divorce. Many families bear scars from broken marriages. Even in the church, the realities of divorce and remarriage bring questions, confusion, and heartache.

In this passage, the Pharisees confront Jesus with a divorce question. Their aim is not to learn but to trap Him. Yet Jesus, as always, cuts through their schemes and points them back to the authority of Scripture. He exposes their hardness of heart and upholds God's good design for marriage from the very beginning.

This text challenges us to see marriage not as a human contract that can be broken at will, but as a divine covenant designed by God.

I. The Pharisees' Trap (vv. 1–2)

"And he left there and went to the region of Judea and beyond the Jordan, and crowds gathered to him again. And again, as was his custom, he taught them. And Pharisees came up and in order to test him asked, 'Is it lawful for a man to divorce his wife?'"

Jesus moves into the region of Judea, where crowds gather to hear His teaching. The Pharisees approached with a question: *"Is it lawful for a man to divorce his wife?"*

Their motive is clear, Mark says they asked "to test him." They were not genuinely seeking the truth. They wanted to trap Jesus in a controversial debate.

At that time, Jewish teachers were divided on the issue. Some, following Rabbi Shammai, allowed divorce only for serious sexual immorality. Others, following Rabbi Hillel, permitted divorce for nearly any reason, even trivial matters like a burnt meal. By raising the question, the Pharisees hoped to force Jesus into one camp or the other and discredit Him. But Jesus refuses to be trapped by their shallow debate. Instead, He directs them back to Scripture.

II. The Law of Moses (vv. 3–5)

"He answered them, 'What did Moses command you?' They said, 'Moses allowed a man to write a certificate of divorce and to send her away.' And Jesus said to them, 'Because of your hardness of heart he wrote you this commandment.'"

Jesus asks them what Moses commanded. They reference Deuteronomy 24, where Moses permitted a certificate of divorce. But notice what Jesus highlights: this was not God's ideal; it was a concession. Moses permitted divorce, not because it was good, but because of the hardness of people's hearts. It was damage control, regulating a practice that already existed because of sin.

Divorce was never the design. It was a reluctant allowance because of human sinfulness. Jesus wants the Pharisees and us to see that the objective standard is not found in Moses' concession but in God's creation. The Pharisees were content to argue about the boundaries of divorce. Jesus points them back to the beauty of marriage. They want to know how to get out; He shows them God's plan for staying in.

III. God's Design in Creation (vv. 6–9)

"But from the beginning of creation, 'God made them male and female.' 'Therefore a man shall leave his father and mother and hold fast to his wife, and the two shall become one flesh.' So they are no longer two but one flesh. What therefore God has joined together, let not man separate."

Jesus takes them back to Genesis 1 and 2. Before sin entered the world, God designed marriage.

Created order: *"God made them male and female."* Marriage is rooted in creation, not culture. It is the covenant union of one man and one woman.

Leaving and cleaving: *"A man shall leave his father and mother and hold fast to his wife."* Marriage creates a new, primary family bond.

One flesh union: *"The two shall become one flesh."* Husband and wife are joined in the most profound intimacy and unity—physical, emotional, spiritual.

Jesus concludes: *"What therefore God has joined together, let not man separate."* Marriage is God's doing. It is not ultimately a human contract to be dissolved at will but a divine covenant joined by God Himself. This is the heart of Jesus' teaching. Marriage is sacred. It is meant to be lifelong. Divorce was never part of God's design.

IV. The Disciples' Question (vv. 10–12)

"And in the house, the disciples asked him again about this matter. And he said to them, 'Whoever divorces his wife and marries another commits adultery against her, and if she divorces her husband and marries another, she commits adultery.'"

Later, in private, the disciples press Jesus further. His answer is even stronger: remarriage after divorce is adultery. In Jewish culture, adultery was generally framed as a sin against the husband. But Jesus frames it as a sin against the spouse, elevating the dignity of women. He makes clear that both men and women are accountable before God.

The point is unmistakable: divorce does not dissolve the marriage bond in God's eyes. To marry another while your spouse is still living is to commit adultery. Matthew's gospel includes an exception clause (*"except for sexual immorality"*), which we must take seriously. But Mark's account emphasizes the norm: God's design is lifelong, covenantal marriage. Divorce and remarriage are not to be taken lightly.

V. Lessons for Us

This passage teaches us several crucial lessons about marriage, divorce, and remarriage:

God's design is creation, not concession. The Pharisees wanted to focus on Moses' allowance. Jesus points us back to Genesis, marriage as a covenantal, lifelong union of one man and one woman.

Divorce flows from hardness of heart. Moses permitted it because of sin. Where hearts are hardened, marriages break. But this is not God's desire.

Marriage is a covenant joined by God. What God has joined, we must not separate. This calls us to honor marriage, fight for faithfulness, and pursue reconciliation whenever possible.

Remarriage after divorce is adultery—except where Scripture gives an exception. We must handle this truth with both conviction and compassion, upholding God's standard while caring for those who have failed or been sinned against.

VI. Pastoral Application

This teaching is weighty. Many have been wounded by divorce. Some carry guilt or regret. Others have been abandoned against their will. The church must uphold God's design for marriage while also extending grace and hope to those who have fallen short. The gospel is good news for sinners, including those who have sinned or been sinned against in marriage.

Through Christ, there is forgiveness, healing, and new life. No one is beyond the reach of His redeeming grace. If you've been through the pain of divorce, know this: the gospel is for you. Christ offers forgiveness, hope, and restoration. And if you're married now, fight for your marriage. Lean on His grace, and don't give up.

Conclusion

The Pharisees wanted to trap Jesus with a debate about divorce. But Jesus pointed them back to God's design for marriage in creation. He calls us to see marriage as sacred, covenantal, and lifelong.

Divorce was permitted because of the hardness of heart, but it was never the plan. What God has joined together, let not man separate. As followers of Christ, we are called to honor marriage, guard against sin, and display the covenant love of Christ and His church in our relationships.

Reflection & Response

How does Jesus' teaching on marriage challenge the way our culture views divorce?

What steps can you take to guard your own marriage—or prepare for a future marriage—in light of God's design?

How can you support and encourage those in your church who are hurting from divorce?

Jesus Loves the Little Children

Mark 10:13–16

Children hold a special place in God's heart. Yet in the ancient world, they were often considered insignificant. They had no social standing, no legal rights, and no cultural clout. Against this backdrop, Mark records a decisive moment when Jesus not only welcomes children but holds them up as examples of how to receive the kingdom of God. This short passage carries a profound message: Jesus values children, rebukes those who hinder them, and calls all of us to embrace Him with childlike faith.

I. The Disciples' Wrong Attitude (v. 13)

"And they were bringing children to him that he might touch them, and the disciples rebuked them."

Parents were bringing their children to Jesus to be blessed. This was a common Jewish practice, rooted in the belief that a godly man's blessing could shape a child's future. The parents likely wanted Jesus to lay His hands on their children and pray for them.

But the disciples rebuked the parents. Why? Likely because they thought children were not worth Jesus' time. In their eyes, children were a distraction from His more important ministry to adults.

This reveals the disciples' wrong attitude. They underestimated the value of children and misunderstood the heart of Jesus. They treated the ministry to children as less significant, when in reality it is central to the kingdom. The disciples thought children were a waste of Jesus' time. But Jesus doesn't see children as a distraction. He sees them as a priority.

II. Jesus' Indignant Response (v. 14)

"But when Jesus saw it, he was indignant and said to them, 'Let the children come to me; do not hinder them, for to such belongs the kingdom of God.'"

Mark rarely records Jesus' emotions, but here he tells us Jesus was "indignant." That word means deeply grieved, stirred to anger. Jesus is not mildly disappointed; He is righteously upset.

Why? Because His disciples were misrepresenting His heart. They were putting up barriers to those He came to welcome. Jesus issues a command: *"Let the children come to me; do not hinder them."* Children are not distractions. They are not unworthy. They are welcome in His presence.

Then He makes a stunning statement: *"For to such belongs the kingdom of God."* Not only are children welcome, they are examples of what it means to belong to God's kingdom. Their humility, dependence, and trust illustrate the posture every disciple must have before God.

III. The Lesson of Childlike Faith (v. 15)

"Truly, I say to you, whoever does not receive the kingdom of God like a child shall not enter it."

Jesus presses the lesson home. Children do not earn, achieve, or contribute to receive love. They simply receive. They are helpless, dependent, and trusting. That is the posture Jesus says is necessary to enter His kingdom. You cannot come with pride, self-sufficiency, or a résumé of accomplishments. You must come empty-handed, with the simple trust of a child.

This turns the world's values upside down. We esteem independence, strength, and achievement. But Jesus values humility, dependence, and faith. You don't strut into the kingdom. You crawl in like a child. The kingdom is for the weak, the needy, the dependent, those who trust in Christ."

IV. Jesus' Tender Action (v. 16)

"And he took them in his arms and blessed them, laying his hands on them."

Jesus not only spoke words of welcome, but He also showed it with His actions. He took the children in His arms. This is a picture of His tenderness, love, and compassion. Then He blessed them. This was not a perfunctory act. The word for "blessed" here suggests a fervent, heartfelt prayer of blessing. Jesus valued these children enough to stop, embrace them, and commend them to God's care. This is the heart of our Savior. He does not push away the weak or the small. He draws them close and pours out His blessing.

V. Lessons for Us

This passage gives us several important lessons for our lives and our churches today:

Value children as Jesus does. They are not distractions from real ministry—they are the heart of it. Parents, invest in discipling your children. Churches, prioritize children's ministry.

Do not hinder children from coming to Christ. This includes obvious obstacles, like neglecting their spiritual training, as well as subtle ones, like hypocrisy that drives them away. We must remove barriers and point them clearly to Jesus.

Learn from children how to receive the kingdom.
Their humility, dependence, and trust are exactly what
God requires of us. We must put away pride and self-
sufficiency and come to Him like children.

Embrace the tender heart of Jesus. He delights to
bless the weak, the overlooked, and the dependent.
That includes not only children but also all who come
to Him in faith.

Conclusion

The disciples thought children were beneath Jesus'
notice. But Jesus was indignant at their attitude. He
welcomed the children, embraced them, and blessed
them. Then He taught that the kingdom belongs to
those who come like children, helpless, dependent, and
trusting.

To follow Christ means we must value children as
He does, guard against hindering them, and embrace
the childlike faith He requires. The kingdom of God
doesn't belong to the proud or the self-reliant. It
belongs to the childlike, those who come empty-
handed and trust Him completely.

Reflection & Response

Do you see children as distractions or as central to
God's kingdom work?

What barriers, intentional or unintentional, might
you be putting up that keep children from Christ?

How can you cultivate a more childlike faith in your
own walk with God?

The Great Exchange

Mark 10:17–31

What does it take to inherit eternal life? That is the most important question anyone can ask. In Mark 10, a wealthy young man comes running to Jesus with that very question. His sincerity and zeal are evident, but when confronted with the cost of discipleship, he walks away sorrowful.

This passage confronts us with the radical demands of following Christ. Eternal life is not gained by keeping commandments or holding on to wealth, but by surrendering all to Jesus. In return, He promises eternal treasure and life in the age to come.

I. The Ruler's Question (vv. 17–20)

"And as he was setting out on his journey, a man ran up and knelt before him and asked him, 'Good Teacher, what must I do to inherit eternal life?' And Jesus said to him, 'Why do you call me good? No one is good except God alone. You know the commandments: "Do not murder, Do not commit adultery, Do not steal, Do not bear false witness, Do not defraud, Honor your father and mother."' And he said to him, 'Teacher, all these I have kept from my youth.'"

The young man runs to Jesus and kneels before Him. He is earnest and respectful. He asks the right question: *"What must I do to inherit eternal life?"* But notice the subtle problem: he assumes eternal life can be achieved by something he must *do*. He thinks salvation is a matter of performance. Jesus responds by pointing him to the commandments. He lists the second table of the law, commands about how we treat others. The man replies with confidence: *"All these I have kept from my youth."*

Here is a man, moral, religious, and outwardly upright. Yet he still lacks assurance. Something is missing. His question reveals that, despite his morality, he knows he does not have eternal life. This man is the kind of church member every pastor would want. He's earnest, he's moral, he's respectful. But Jesus reveals that beneath his religious résumé, his heart clings to an idol.

II. Jesus' Radical Demand (vv. 21–22)

"And Jesus, looking at him, loved him, and said to him, 'You lack one thing: go, sell all that you have and give to the poor, and you will have treasure in heaven; and come, follow me.' Disheartened by the saying, he went away sorrowful, for he had great possessions."

Mark tells us Jesus looked at the man and *loved him.* This demand was not harsh; it was spoken in love. Jesus saw the idol that enslaved him and called him to surrender it. The demand is radical: sell all you have, give to the poor, and follow Me. Jesus was not giving a universal requirement for all believers to sell everything, but He was exposing this man's particular idol: his wealth.

The man's response is heartbreaking. Instead of joyfully receiving eternal treasure, he walks away sorrowful. His wealth was too precious to release. He wanted eternal life, but not enough to let go of his idol. Here is the tragedy: he stood before the only One who could give him eternal life, yet he clung to temporary riches.

III. The Danger of Riches (vv. 23–27)

"And Jesus looked around and said to his disciples, 'How difficult it will be for those who have wealth to enter the kingdom of God!' And the disciples were amazed at his words. But Jesus said to them again, 'Children, how difficult it is to enter the kingdom of God! It is easier for a camel to go through the eye of a needle than for a rich person to enter the kingdom of God.' And they were exceedingly astonished, and said to him, 'Then who can be saved?' Jesus looked at them and said, 'With man it is impossible, but not with God. For all things are possible with God.'"

Jesus uses this moment to teach His disciples about the danger of riches. Wealth can create a false sense of security, self-sufficiency, and independence from God. The disciples are stunned. In their culture, wealth was seen as a sign of God's blessing. But Jesus declares it is actually a barrier. He uses vivid imagery: a camel going through the eye of a needle. Humanly speaking, it is impossible.

The disciples despair: *"Then who can be saved?"* That is precisely the point. Salvation is not something we can achieve. With man, it is impossible. Only God can save. This is the heart of the gospel. Eternal life is not earned by law-keeping or good works. It is a miracle of God's grace.

IV. The Promise of Eternal Reward (vv. 28–31)

"Peter began to say to him, 'See, we have left everything and followed you.' Jesus said, 'Truly, I say to you, there is no

one who has left house or brothers or sisters or mother or father or children or lands, for my sake and for the gospel, who will not receive a hundredfold now in this time, houses and brothers and sisters and mothers and children and lands, with persecutions, and in the age to come eternal life. But many who are first will be last, and the last first.'"

Peter, ever the spokesman, points out that the disciples had left everything to follow Jesus. Jesus responds with a promise. Those who sacrifice for Him will not ultimately lose. Whatever we give up for the sake of Christ and the gospel will be repaid a hundredfold. This is not a health-and-wealth guarantee, but a promise of the spiritual family and blessings believers experience in the church.

Jesus is honest: these blessings come *with persecutions*. Following Him brings reward, but also suffering. Yet the ultimate promise is eternal life in the age to come. Jesus ends with a warning: *"Many who are first will be last, and the last first."* In God's kingdom, worldly status is overturned. The rich young ruler, who seemed first, walked away last. The humble disciples, who appeared last, will be honored first.

V. Lessons for Us

This passage teaches us several vital lessons about salvation and discipleship:

Religious morality cannot save. The rich young ruler kept the commandments outwardly, but his heart was far from God. Salvation is not about performance but faith in Christ.

Jesus calls us to surrender idols. For this man, it was wealth. For us, it may be money, reputation, comfort, or control. To follow Jesus, we must be willing to release whatever competes with Him.

Salvation is impossible apart from God. We cannot earn or achieve eternal life. It is a miracle of God's grace.

Following Jesus brings both cost and reward. We may lose comfort, relationships, or possessions, but we gain Christ, His people, and eternal life.

Conclusion

The rich young ruler asked the right question: *"What must I do to inherit eternal life?"* But he left with the wrong answer, because he was unwilling to let go of his idol.

Jesus calls us to the great exchange: give up what cannot last to receive what cannot be lost. Eternal life is not found in wealth, morality, or self-effort. It is found only in surrendering all to Christ and receiving His gift of grace. The question isn't whether you'll give something up to follow Jesus. The question is: will you give up what cannot last to gain what cannot be lost?

Reflection & Response

What idols in your life are competing with your devotion to Christ?

How does this passage challenge your view of wealth, possessions, and security?

What sacrifices might Jesus be calling you to make to follow Him more fully?

The Prophets' Prediction: The gospel According to Jesus

Mark 10:32–34

The gospel is not a human invention. It is not something the apostles dreamed up to explain Jesus' death. It is the message Jesus Himself proclaimed in advance.

In Mark 10:32–34, we find the third and most detailed prediction of His suffering, death, and resurrection. Here, Jesus lays out the gospel before it happens, showing that every detail is part of God's sovereign plan. This passage is the gospel according to Jesus: He will be betrayed, condemned, mocked, flogged, crucified, and raised.

I. The Road to Jerusalem (v. 32)

"And they were on the road, going up to Jerusalem, and Jesus was walking ahead of them. And they were amazed, and those who followed were afraid. And taking the twelve again, he began to tell them what was to happen to him."

The scene is vivid. Jesus is on the road to Jerusalem, walking ahead of His disciples. He is resolute, determined, striding toward the very place where He will be killed. The disciples are amazed and afraid. They sense the gravity of the moment. Jesus is not being dragged to His death; He is marching toward it. Then He takes the twelve aside once again. Patiently, for the third time, He tells them what is going to happen.

II. The Prophets Fulfilled (v. 33a)

"'See, we are going up to Jerusalem, and the Son of Man will be delivered over to the chief priests and the scribes, and they will condemn him to death and deliver him over to the Gentiles.'"

Jesus begins with betrayal: *"The Son of Man will be delivered."* This echoes the prophecies of Isaiah's Suffering Servant, who was "despised and rejected by men" and "cut off for the transgression of my people" (Isa. 53:3, 8). The religious leaders, chief priests, and scribes will condemn Him to death. Then He will be handed over to the Gentiles. Both Jew and Gentile will participate in His rejection.

This is precisely what the prophets foretold: the Messiah would suffer at the hands of His own people and the nations. None of this is accidental. It is the fulfillment of God's plan written centuries before. The gospel was not plan B. It was plan A from before the foundation of the world. The prophets pointed to it, and Jesus walked toward it.

III. The Passion Predicted (v. 34a)

"'And they will mock him and spit on him, and flog him and kill him.'"

Jesus gives chilling detail: mockery, spitting, flogging, death. Each of these would come true in Jerusalem.

Mockery: Soldiers would ridicule Him, dressing Him in a purple robe and a crown of thorns.

Spitting: A sign of utter contempt.

Flogging: The brutal Roman scourging that often killed its victims before crucifixion.

Killing: Death by crucifixion, the most shameful and excruciating form of execution.

Jesus knew every detail in advance. He walked toward Jerusalem with eyes wide open. He embraced the cup of suffering for our salvation.

IV. The Resurrection Promised (v. 34b)

"'And after three days he will rise.'"

The prediction ends not with death but with life. After three days, He will rise. This is the heart of the gospel: Christ died for our sins, was buried, and rose again on the third day, just as He said. The cross is not the end. The grave is not the final word. resurrection triumphs over death.

V. Lessons for Us

This short but powerful passage teaches us several vital truths:

Jesus is sovereign over His suffering. He was not a victim caught in events beyond His control. He went willingly to the cross, knowing every detail.

The gospel is rooted in prophecy. The events of Good Friday and Easter Sunday were foretold by the prophets and fulfilled by Christ. Our faith rests on God's eternal plan.

The cross shows the depth of our sin and the greatness of His love. He endured mockery, abuse, and death because our sin demanded judgment.

The resurrection secures our hope. The story does not end in death. Because He rose, we who believe in Him will rise also.

Conclusion

The disciples were amazed and afraid as Jesus marched toward Jerusalem. They did not yet grasp what He was saying. But we, looking back, see the beauty of His words. The gospel is not wishful thinking or human theory. It is the plan of God, predicted by the prophets and proclaimed by Jesus Himself.

He was delivered, condemned, mocked, flogged, killed, and on the third day, He rose. This is the gospel according to Jesus. Jesus knew every detail of what awaited Him in Jerusalem. And He went anyway, for you, for me, for our salvation."

Reflection & Response

How does Jesus' determination to go to Jerusalem encourage your faith in His love and commitment to you?

What does this passage teach you about God's sovereignty in salvation?

How can you live more boldly in light of the certainty of the resurrection?

Greatness in Service, Not Status

Mark 10:35–45

Ambition is not always evil. God calls us to desire greatness—but greatness as He defines it, not as the world defines it. The problem is that our ambitions are often selfish, rooted in pride and a thirst for recognition. In this passage, James and John ask Jesus for positions of honor. Their request reveals a worldly mindset, but Jesus seizes the opportunity to redefine greatness. In His kingdom, greatness is not about status or position but about service. And the ultimate example is Jesus Himself, who gave His life as a ransom for many.

I. The Request for Greatness (vv. 35–37)

"And James and John, the sons of Zebedee, came up to him and said to him, 'Teacher, we want you to do for us whatever we ask of you.' And he said to them, 'What do you want me to do for you?' And they said to him, 'Grant us to sit, one at your right hand and one at your left, in your glory.'"

James and John approach Jesus with boldness, even presumption: *"We want you to do for us whatever we ask."* They want the places of highest honor, at His right and left hand in glory. Their timing is shocking. Jesus has just predicted His suffering, death, and resurrection. While he speaks of a cross, they are dreaming of thrones.

Their request reflects a worldly vision of greatness: power, prestige, and position. They believe following Jesus will bring them recognition and glory. It's easy to shake our heads at James and John, but how often do we come to Jesus the same way, wanting Him to rubber-stamp our desires instead of surrendering to His?

II. The Cup and the Baptism (vv. 38–39)

"Jesus said to them, 'You do not know what you are asking. Are you able to drink the cup that I drink, or to be baptized with the baptism with which I am baptized?' And they said to him, 'We are able.' And Jesus said to them, 'The cup that I drink you will drink, and with the baptism with which I am baptized, you will be baptized.'"

Jesus responds with sobering words: *"You do not know what you are asking."* The places of honor in His kingdom are not gained by ambition but by suffering. He uses two images: the cup and the baptism. In Scripture, the cup often symbolizes suffering and judgment. Baptism here refers not to water but to being overwhelmed or plunged into suffering.

James and John confidently reply, *"We are able."* They still don't understand. But Jesus tells them they will indeed share in His sufferings. James would later be martyred (Acts 12:2). John would endure exile and persecution. The lesson is clear: following Jesus means sharing His suffering before sharing His glory.

III. The Sovereignty of God (v. 40)

"But to sit at my right hand or at my left is not mine to grant, but it is for those for whom it has been prepared."

Jesus reminds them that the Father determines positions of honor in His kingdom. They are not rewards for ambition but gifts of God's sovereign plan.

This corrects our pride. Greatness is not seized but granted. It is not achieved through manipulation or politics but received through God's gracious will.

IV. The Indignation of the Disciples (v. 41)

"And when the ten heard it, they began to be indignant at James and John."

The other disciples hear of James and John's request and are indignant—not because they are more spiritual, but because they wanted the same thing. Their pride is exposed as well. Pride breeds competition, jealousy, and division. Ambition for status always disrupts unity. This moment reveals how deeply the disciples misunderstood Jesus' teaching. Even after three predictions of His death, they are still clinging to worldly ideas of greatness.

V. The Redefinition of Greatness (vv. 42–44)

"And Jesus called them to him and said to them, 'You know that those who are considered rulers of the Gentiles lord it over them, and their great ones exercise authority over them. But it shall not be so among you. But whoever would be great among you must be your servant, and whoever would be first among you must be slave of all.'"

Jesus calls the disciples together and redefines greatness. He contrasts worldly rulers with the greatness of the kingdom. In the world, rulers "lord it over" others. Power is about control, dominance, and authority. But Jesus says, *"It shall not be so among you."*

In His kingdom, greatness is measured by service. To be great, you must be a servant. To be first, you must be a slave of all. This is radical. A servant had no rights, no status, no recognition. Yet Jesus says this is the path to true greatness. Greatness in the world is measured by how many people serve you. Greatness in God's kingdom is measured by how many people you serve.

VI. The Ransom of Christ (v. 45)

"For even the Son of Man came not to be served but to serve, and to give his life as a ransom for many."

Here is the ultimate example. Jesus, the Son of Man, the King of glory, did not come to be served but to serve. His entire mission was one of humble service. And the climax of that service is the cross: *"to give his life as a ransom for many."* The word ransom refers to the price paid to secure a slave's freedom. Jesus' death is the substitutionary payment that frees us from sin and judgment.

This is the heart of the gospel. Greatness is not grabbing power but giving your life. And Jesus is the supreme model.

VII. Lessons for Us

This passage gives us several crucial lessons for following Christ:

Check your ambitions. Are you seeking greatness as the world defines it, or as Christ defines it?

Expect suffering before glory. To follow Jesus is to share His cup and baptism. The cross comes before the crown.

Pursue servanthood. Greatness is measured not by status but by service. Look for ways to serve, not to be served.

Rest in God's sovereignty. Positions of honor are not seized but given by God's plan. Our call is to be faithful servants.

Look to Christ's ransom. Our salvation rests not on our service but on His. He gave His life for us. Now we live for Him.

Conclusion

James and John wanted seats of honor. The other disciples were jealous. But Jesus redefined greatness: it is not about status but service. The Son of Man Himself came not to be served but to serve, and to give His life as a ransom for many. That is true greatness.

In God's kingdom, greatness is not about climbing higher; it's about stooping lower. The way up is down. The path to glory is the path of the cross.

Reflection & Response

How does your view of greatness line up with Jesus' teaching in this passage?

In what ways can you intentionally serve others this week rather than seeking recognition?

How does Jesus' ransom on the cross shape your identity and motivation as His disciple?

The Making of a Disciple of Jesus Christ

Mark 10:46–52

What does it mean to be a disciple of Jesus Christ?
Mark's gospel has shown us both the failures and the
growth of the twelve. Now, as Jesus approaches
Jerusalem, Mark closes this section with the healing of
blind Bartimaeus.

This story is more than just a miracle; it is a portrait
of discipleship. Bartimaeus, though physically blind,
sees more clearly than many. He recognizes Jesus as the
Son of David, cries out for mercy, perseveres in the
face of opposition, and follows Jesus "on the way." Here
we see what true discipleship looks like.

I. A Blind Beggar by the Road (v. 46)

*"And they came to Jericho. And as he was leaving Jericho
with his disciples and a great crowd, Bartimaeus, a blind
beggar, the son of Timaeus, was sitting by the roadside."*

Jesus and His disciples are passing through Jericho,
joined by a large crowd on their way to Jerusalem for
Passover. By the roadside sits Bartimaeus, a blind
beggar. In that culture, blindness meant poverty,
helplessness, and marginalization. He was dependent
on others for survival. His situation pictures our
spiritual condition apart from Christ: blind, helpless,
and in need of mercy. Mark names him, Bartimaeus—
suggesting that he became known in the early church.
His story was remembered because it illustrated the
essence of following Jesus.

211

II. A Persistent Cry for Mercy (vv. 47–48)

"And when he heard that it was Jesus of Nazareth, he began to cry out and say, 'Jesus, Son of David, have mercy on me!' And many rebuked him, telling him to be silent. But he cried out all the more, 'Son of David, have mercy on me!'"

Hearing that Jesus is passing by, Bartimaeus cries out: *"Jesus, Son of David, have mercy on me!"*

Notice two things:

He recognizes Jesus' identity. Calling Him "Son of David" is a messianic confession. Though blind, Bartimaeus sees what many sighted people miss—that Jesus is the promised King.

He cries for mercy. He knows he cannot earn or demand. He pleads for grace. This is the heart of true discipleship: recognizing who Jesus is and crying out for mercy.

The crowd rebukes him, trying to silence him. But Bartimaeus persists, crying out all the more. True faith perseveres even in the face of opposition. The crowd told him to shut up, but Bartimaeus knew this was his one chance. And so he cried louder. That's faith—it refuses to be silenced.

III. The Compassionate Call of Jesus (vv. 49–50)

"And Jesus stopped and said, 'Call him.' And they called the blind man, saying to him, 'Take heart. Get up; he is calling you.' And throwing off his cloak, he sprang up and came to Jesus."

Jesus stops. Amid the noise of the crowd, He hears the cry of one blind beggar. That is the compassion of Christ; He is never too busy to respond to those who cry for mercy. He calls Bartimaeus, and the same crowd that tried to silence him now encourages him: *"Take heart. Get up; he is calling you."*

Bartimaeus throws aside his cloak, leaps up, and comes to Jesus. That cloak was likely his most valuable possession, essential for warmth and survival. Casting it aside symbolizes leaving everything to come to Christ.

IV. The Honest Request (v. 51)

"And Jesus said to him, 'What do you want me to do for you?' And the blind man said to him, 'Rabbi, let me recover my sight.'"

Jesus asks a simple question: *"What do you want me to do for you?"* He invites Bartimaeus to express his need. Notice the contrast: just a few verses earlier, James and John had asked Jesus, *"Teacher, we want you to do for us whatever we ask of you"* (v. 35). They wanted glory and power. Bartimaeus asks for mercy and sight. This is the difference between selfish ambition and faithful discipleship. Bartimaeus does not demand status—he asks Jesus to meet his most profound need.

V. The Gift of Faith (v. 52a)

"And Jesus said to him, 'Go your way; your faith has made you well.' And immediately he recovered his sight..."

Jesus grants his request. His sight is restored immediately. But notice Jesus' words: *"Your faith has made you well."* Faith here is not mere belief in healing;

it is trust in Jesus as the Son of David, the merciful King. His faith connects him to the saving power of Christ. This is not just physical healing but a picture of spiritual salvation. Bartimaeus received mercy because he trusted in Christ.

VI. The Path of Discipleship (v. 52b)

"...and followed him on the way."

Bartimaeus does not simply receive his sight and return to his old life. He follows Jesus "on the way." This phrase is significant. The "way" in Mark's gospel points to the way of the cross. True discipleship is not just about receiving blessings from Jesus but about following Him wherever He leads, even to suffering and death. Bartimaeus becomes the model disciple: he sees who Jesus is, cries out for mercy, receives salvation, and follows on the way of the cross.

VII. Lessons for Us

This passage gives us a vivid picture of discipleship, with lessons for our own walk with Christ:

Recognize your need. Like Bartimaeus, we are blind beggars in need of mercy. Discipleship begins with humility.

Cry out to Jesus. Do not let the crowd silence you. True faith perseveres in seeking Christ.

Respond to His call. When Jesus calls, throw aside whatever hinders and come to Him.

Ask honestly. Bring your real needs before Christ. He delights to show mercy.

Follow on the way. Salvation is not the end but the beginning. True discipleship means walking with Jesus on the way of the cross.

Conclusion

Bartimaeus was a blind beggar, but he saw more clearly than many. He recognized Jesus as the Son of David, cried out for mercy, and received his sight. Then he followed Jesus on the way.

This is the making of a disciple: seeing Christ for who He is, trusting Him for mercy, and walking with Him in obedience. Bartimaeus wasn't content to get his sight and go home. He followed Jesus on the way. That's what a true disciple does: he receives mercy and then walks with Christ wherever He leads.

Reflection & Response

Where do you need to cry out to Jesus for mercy today?

What "cloak" might you need to throw aside to follow Him fully?

How is Christ calling you to follow Him more closely "on the way?

Chapter 11

The Messiah's Royal Procession

Mark 11:1–11

Jesus has been moving steadily toward Jerusalem. Now, at the beginning of Mark 11, the moment arrives. This is the Triumphal Entry, also known as Palm Sunday. But it is far more than a parade.

Here, Jesus presents Himself publicly as Israel's Messiah and King. Yet His procession is unlike that of earthly rulers. He comes not with military might or political power, but in humility, fulfilling prophecy, and pointing to the cross that awaits Him. This scene is both a coronation and a revelation: the King has come, but He will reign by laying down His life.

I. The Preparation of the King (vv. 1–6)

"Now when they drew near to Jerusalem, to Bethphage and Bethany, at the Mount of Olives, Jesus sent two of his disciples and said to them, 'Go into the village in front of you, and immediately as you enter it, you will find a colt tied, on which no one has ever sat. Untie it and bring it. If anyone says to you, "Why are you doing this?" say, "The Lord has need of it and will send it back here immediately."' And they went away and found a colt tied at a door outside in the street, and they untied it. And some of those standing there said to them, 'What are you doing, untying the colt?' And they told them what Jesus had said, and they let them go."

Jesus's entrance is carefully prepared. He sends two disciples to fetch a colt. His detailed instructions show His sovereign control. He knows precisely where the colt is and what will happen when they untie it. The fact that it is a colt "on which no one has ever sat" points to its sacred purpose. In the Old Testament, animals set apart for holy use were to be unused by others. Jesus will ride this colt as part of His royal procession.

Notice the authority of His words: *"The Lord has need of it."* Even here, we see His kingly authority. All is unfolding according to His plan. Jesus doesn't stumble into Jerusalem. He orchestrates every detail. Even the colt is part of God's sovereign plan.

II. The Prophecy Fulfilled (vv. 7–8)

"And they brought the colt to Jesus and threw their cloaks on it, and he sat on it. And many spread their cloaks on the road, and others spread leafy branches that they had cut from the fields."

Jesus mounts the colt, and the people spread cloaks and branches before Him. This act recalls royal processions in Israel's history. Cloaks were laid under kings as a sign of submission (2 Kings 9:13). Branches symbolized victory and celebration.

Most significantly, this fulfills Zechariah 9:9: *"Behold, your king is coming to you; righteous and having salvation is he, humble and mounted on a donkey, on a colt, the foal of a donkey."* The King is coming—but not on a warhorse. He comes in humility and peace, not in conquest. His kingdom will not be established by force of arms but by the sacrifice of His life.

217

III. The Praise of the Crowd (vv. 9–10)

"And those who went before and those who followed were shouting, 'Hosanna! Blessed is he who comes in the name of the Lord! Blessed is the coming kingdom of our father David! Hosanna in the highest!'"

The crowd erupts in praise, quoting from Psalm 118, a psalm of salvation and victory. *"Hosanna"* means "save us now." They welcome Jesus as the one who comes in the name of the Lord, the one bringing the promised kingdom of David. Their words are valid, but their expectations are shallow. Many in the crowd envision a political Messiah who will overthrow Rome and restore Israel's glory. They do not yet grasp that His kingdom will come through the cross, not the sword.

Still, their cries of "Hosanna" echo the longing of every human heart, for salvation, for deliverance, for a king who will make things right. The crowd wanted a kingdom of power. Jesus came to bring a kingdom of peace. They wanted a throne without a cross. But Jesus knew the only way to the crown was through Calvary.

IV. The Pause at the Temple (v. 11)

"And he entered Jerusalem and went into the temple. And when he had looked around at everything, as it was already late, he went out to Bethany with the twelve."

The scene ends quietly. After all the excitement, Jesus enters the temple, looks around, and leaves. There is no immediate action, no dramatic confrontation. Judgment and cleansing are coming—but not yet. The next day, He will drive out the money changers. For now, He surveys the temple, taking it all in. His kingly authority is evident even in this pause.

This moment reminds us that Jesus operates on God's timetable. He enters Jerusalem as King, but His mission will unfold step by step, according to the father's plan.

V. Lessons for Us

This passage teaches us several vital truths about Jesus and His kingdom:

Jesus is the sovereign King. Every detail of His entry was planned. Nothing happens outside His control.

Jesus fulfills prophecy. He came as the humble King, just as Zechariah foretold. God's Word can be trusted.

Jesus' kingdom is not of this world. He came not with force but with humility, not to conquer Rome but to conquer sin and death.

We must respond to the King. The crowd cried "Hosanna," but many would later cry "Crucify Him." The question for us is whether we will submit to Him as King on His terms.

Conclusion

The Triumphal Entry is both a royal procession and a revelation. Jesus enters Jerusalem as the promised Messiah, the Son of David, the sovereign King. But He comes not on a warhorse, wielding power, but on a donkey, bringing peace. The crowd cries out, *"Hosanna!"*—save us now. And that is precisely what He has come to do. But the salvation He brings is deeper than they imagined. It will come not by overthrowing Rome but by dying on a cross. The King has come. But He rules by serving, He conquers by dying, and He saves by laying down His life.

Reflection & Response

What expectations do you bring to Jesus? Do you want Him to serve your agenda, or are you willing to follow Him as the humble King?

How does Jesus' fulfillment of prophecy strengthen your trust in God's Word?

Where in your life do you need to submit afresh to Jesus as King?

A Phony or a Follower?

Mark 11:12–25

Appearances can be deceiving. Some things look healthy on the outside but are hollow within. The same can be true spiritually. Jesus uses a simple image—a fruitless fig tree—to expose empty religion that looks alive but bears no fruit.

This passage is both sobering and instructive. It challenges us to examine our hearts: Are we genuine followers of Jesus, or are we merely putting on a show? Mark weaves together two scenes —the cursing of the fig tree and the cleansing of the temple —to reveal one central truth: God desires genuine faith that bears fruit, not lifeless ritual that merely looks the part.

I. The Barren Tree (vv. 12–14)

"On the following day, when they came from Bethany, he was hungry. And seeing in the distance a fig tree in leaf, he went to see if he could find anything on it. When he came to it, he found nothing but leaves, for it was not the season for figs. And he said to it, 'May no one ever eat fruit from you again.' And his disciples heard it."

As Jesus and His disciples travel from Bethany to Jerusalem, He sees a fig tree covered in leaves. The leaves create the expectation of fruit. But when Jesus inspects it, there is nothing but leaves. Even though it wasn't the primary fig season, early figs often appeared with the leaves. The tree gave the impression of life, but was barren.

Jesus's action seems harsh at first —cursing a tree — but it's symbolic. The fig tree represents Israel, especially her religious life centered in the temple. Outwardly impressive, but inwardly fruitless. This is not about Jesus being hangry. It's about hypocrisy. The fig tree looked alive, but there was no fruit. It's a living parable of Israel's spiritual barrenness.

II. The Corrupted Temple (vv. 15–17)

"And they came to Jerusalem. And he entered the temple and began to drive out those who sold and those who bought in the temple, and he overturned the tables of the money-changers and the seats of those who sold pigeons. And he would not allow anyone to carry anything through the temple. And he was teaching them and saying to them, 'Is it not written, "My house shall be called a house of prayer for all the nations"? But you have made it a den of robbers.'"

Jesus goes straight to the temple. What he finds there confirms the message of the fig tree: great activity, but no actual fruit. The outer court, the Court of the Gentiles, had been turned into a marketplace. Instead of being a place of prayer and worship for all nations, it had become a place of profit and exploitation.

Jesus' response is fierce and righteous. He overturns the tables, drives out the merchants, and stops people from using the temple as a shortcut through town. His words thunder with prophetic authority:

"My house shall be called a house of prayer for all the nations, but you have made it a den of robbers."

The temple had become a place where religious leaders took advantage of worshipers rather than leading them to God. Their rituals were flourishing, but their hearts were far from Him. The temple was supposed to be a place where sinners met God, but it had become a place where sinners were manipulated. Religion without repentance is just robbery with stained glass.

III. The Corruption Confronted (vv. 18–19)

"And the chief priests and the scribes heard it and were seeking a way to destroy him, for they feared him, because all the crowd was astonished at his teaching. And when evening came, they went out of the city."

Instead of repentance, the religious leaders respond with rage. They fear Jesus because the people are amazed at His teaching. Their power is threatened, and their hearts are hardened. It's another picture of fruitless religion, outwardly zealous, inwardly corrupt. They care more about preserving their position than pursuing holiness.

IV. The Withered Tree (vv. 20–21)

"As they passed by in the morning, they saw the fig tree withered away to its roots. And Peter remembered and said to him, 'Rabbi, look! The fig tree that you cursed has withered.'"

The next morning, the disciples see the fig tree shriveled from the roots up. What Jesus had spoken had come to pass. The fig tree's withering is a vivid picture of judgment. Just as the tree was destroyed for its barrenness, so too would Israel's religious system face judgment. Within a generation, the temple would be destroyed in AD 70.

God takes hypocrisy seriously. He desires authentic faith that bears fruit, not lifeless ritual. The fig tree withered because it was all show and no substance. That's what happens to every religion, every church, and every person that has leaves but no life.

V. The Lesson on Faith and Forgiveness (vv. 22–25)

"And Jesus answered them, 'Have faith in God. Truly, I say to you, whoever says to this mountain, "Be taken up and thrown into the sea," and does not doubt in his heart, but believes that what he says will come to pass, it will be done for him. Therefore I tell you, whatever you ask in prayer, believe that you have received it, and it will be yours. And whenever you stand praying, forgive, if you have anything against anyone, so that your father also who is in heaven may forgive you your trespasses.'"

After the disciples marvel at the withered tree, Jesus turns the moment into a lesson on faith. The problem isn't that God withholds power; it's that His people often lack faith. The command to "have faith in God" reminds us that spiritual fruit flows from dependence on Him. Fruitless religion is the result of self-reliance. True disciples trust God fully and pray expectantly.

The promise about moving mountains isn't a blank check—it's a call to believe God can accomplish what seems impossible when our desires align with His will. And Jesus adds a vital condition: *"Whenever you stand praying, forgive."* Genuine faith expresses itself in forgiveness. Fruitful disciples are not bitter disciples.

Faith and forgiveness are the fruits that mark genuine followers of Jesus. You can't claim to walk by faith if you refuse to walk in forgiveness. The same faith that moves mountains must also move your heart toward mercy.

VI. Lessons for Us

Fruitless religion invites judgment. God is not impressed by activity without authenticity.

Faith that bears fruit depends on God. True disciples trust, pray, and obey.

Forgiveness is evidence of genuine faith. Those who have received mercy extend mercy.

Jesus still examines His people. Just as He inspected the tree and the temple, He inspects our hearts. Does he find fruit, or only leaves?

Conclusion

Jesus' actions in this passage are not random; they are a powerful warning against hypocrisy and a call to authentic faith. The fig tree was full of leaves but bore no fruit. The temple was full of people but lacked prayer. Both faced the judgment of God.

But there is hope. Jesus invites us to turn from fruitless religion and live by faith, to pray, forgive, and bear fruit that lasts. Don't be a phony with leaves but no life. Be a follower who bears fruit for the glory of God.

Reflection & Response

Does your life show spiritual fruit or just religious activity?

What "tables" might Jesus need to overturn in your heart today?

How can you express genuine faith and forgiveness this week?

Faith Seeking Understanding
Mark 11:27–33

Jesus' ministry has reached a critical point. He has entered Jerusalem as King, cleansed the temple, and condemned fruitless religion. Now the religious leaders confront Him directly. They want to know by what authority He does these things.

But this is not an honest question. They are not seeking truth—they are seeking a reason to reject Him. In contrast, true faith doesn't demand proof before belief; it believes and then seeks understanding. This passage contrasts faith that seeks understanding with unbelief that hides behind questions.

I. The Confrontation of Authority (v. 27)

"And they came again to Jerusalem. And as he was walking in the temple, the chief priests and the scribes and the elders came to him."

Jesus returns to the temple the day after cleansing it. He's walking openly among the people, teaching and ministering. Then the religious leaders approach, the chief priests, scribes, and elders. This trio forms the Sanhedrin, the ruling council of Israel. They represent the highest human authority in Judaism.

Their confrontation is not casual. It's an official challenge. They come to trap Him in His words, to discredit Him publicly. They didn't come to learn. When people reject Jesus, it's not usually because of a lack of evidence but because they don't want to submit to His authority.

II. The Question of Authority (v. 28)

"And they said to him, 'By what authority are you doing these things, or who gave you this authority to do them?'"

Their question sounds legitimate: *"By what authority?"* But their motive is clear. They are challenging His right to cleanse the temple, to teach, to heal, and to act as though He is the Lord of the place. Their words drip with sarcasm: "Who gave you permission?"

Ironically, the question itself reveals their blindness. The temple belongs to Jesus; it is His Father's house. He doesn't need their permission. His authority comes directly from heaven. This same question echoes through history: *"Who gives Jesus the right to rule over my life?"* True disciples answer gladly: "He is Lord." But the heart of unbelief always resists His authority.

III. The Counter-Question (vv. 29–30)

"Jesus said to them, 'I will ask you one question; answer me, and I will tell you by what authority I do these things. Was the baptism of John from heaven or from man? Answer me.'"

Jesus doesn't evade their question; He exposes it. His counter-question is brilliant. By asking about John the Baptist, Jesus forces them to reveal their hearts. If they acknowledged that John's ministry was from God, they would have to admit that Jesus, whom John proclaimed as the Messiah, was also from God.

But if they denied John's authority, they would lose credibility with the people who revered him as a prophet. Jesus' question is not a trick; it's a test of sincerity. If they are genuinely seeking the truth, they will have to face the evidence.

IV. The Cowardice of Unbelief (vv. 31–32)

"And they discussed it with one another, saying, 'If we say, "From heaven," he will say, "Why then did you not believe him?" But shall we say, "From man"?'—they were afraid of the people, for they all held that John really was a prophet."

Instead of answering honestly, the leaders huddle together and calculate their response. Their goal is not to find the truth but to protect their reputation. If they say "from heaven," they condemn themselves for rejecting John. If they say "from man," they risk losing the crowd. So they are trapped, not by Jesus' cunning, but by their own hypocrisy.

Unbelief always fears man more than God. The fear of man keeps them from confessing what they know to be true. Unbelief doesn't ask questions because it wants answers; it asks questions to justify rebellion.

V. The Consequence of Evasion (v. 33a)

"So they answered Jesus, 'We do not know.'"

Their answer is not honest ignorance; it's willful evasion. They knew what they believed; they just refused to say it. When people continually reject the truth, God allows their hearts to harden. The religious leaders, who should have led the nation in repentance, instead hide behind false humility. Their "we do not know" is not an admission of confusion; it's a confession of unbelief.

VI. The Silence of Judgment (v. 33b)

"And Jesus said to them, 'Neither will I tell you by what authority I do these things.'"

Jesus' response is both gracious and just. He refuses to cast pearls before swine. When hearts are hard and motives are corrupt, more revelation only increases guilt. This silence is an act of judgment. Jesus withholds further truth because they have rejected the truth already given.

There's a sobering principle here: persistent unbelief leads to divine silence. When people refuse to respond to the light they've received, that light begins to fade. God is not obligated to answer questions that come from rebellion. When we reject the truth we have, we forfeit the truth we might have received."

VII. Lessons for Us

This short exchange offers profound lessons about faith and unbelief:

Faith seeks understanding. True faith does not demand proof before belief—it believes and then grows in understanding.

Unbelief hides behind questions. The religious leaders weren't seeking truth; they were avoiding submission.

The fear of man leads to compromise. Like the leaders, many today care more about public opinion than divine truth.

Rejecting light brings darkness. When we resist God's revelation, He sometimes allows us to remain in silence.

Jesus' authority demands our submission. The real issue is not what we understand, but whether we will obey.

VIII. Faith That Seeks, Not Tests

There's a kind of questioning that honors God. It's the cry of a believer who says, "Lord, I believe; help my unbelief." It's faith that longs to understand more deeply, not faith that sets conditions.

The difference is the heart behind the question. The religious leaders asked to test. Disciples ask to trust. When faith seeks understanding, it grows. When unbelief demands explanation, it hardens. The difference between a skeptic and a seeker is humility. The seeker bows the knee even before all the answers come.

IX. Jesus' Authority and Our Response

Throughout Mark's gospel, the question of authority has been central. Jesus commands demons, heals the sick, forgives sins, and even calms storms. Every act displays divine authority. Now that same authority confronts the human heart. We cannot remain neutral. We will either bow or resist, believe or reject, follow or flee. The issue is not whether Jesus has authority; He does. The issue is whether we will submit to it.

Conclusion

The religious leaders came to trap Jesus, but their own words condemned them. They asked about authority yet refused to recognize the One who possessed all authority in heaven and on earth. Jesus does not cater to unbelief. He reveals Himself to those who trust Him and hides Himself from those who mock Him.

True disciples don't have all the answers, but they know the One who does. Faith doesn't demand to see everything clearly; it believes in the light that has already been given. Faith is not the absence of questions; it's the refusal to let those questions keep you from trusting Christ."

Reflection & Response

Do you ask questions to learn or to resist?

Where in your life might you be withholding submission to Christ's authority?

How can you cultivate a faith that seeks understanding rather than demands control?

Chapter 12

Love's Final Call

Mark 12:1–12

Throughout His ministry, Jesus has confronted the religious leaders of Israel with truth and grace. Now, in this parable, He tells a story that exposes their rejection of God's messengers and their coming rejection of Him.

The Parable of the Tenants is one of Jesus' most direct and convicting teachings. It summarizes the history of God's dealings with His people: His gracious provision, their rebellion, His patient pursuit, and His final act of love in sending His Son. This parable reveals both the severity of judgment and the depth of divine love—a love that continues to call even those who have rejected it.

I. The Vineyard and Its Owner (v. 1)

"And he began to speak to them in parables. 'A man planted a vineyard and put a fence around it and dug a pit for the winepress and built a tower, and leased it to tenants and went into another country.'"

Jesus begins with a familiar image, a vineyard. For His Jewish audience, this immediately recalled Isaiah 5, where Israel is described as the vineyard God planted with care. The details are deliberate: the owner plants, fences, digs, and builds. Nothing is neglected. He provides everything needed for fruitfulness.

Then he leases the vineyard to tenants and goes away. The arrangement implies trust—these tenants are stewards of what belongs to another. In this parable, the **owner** represents God, the **vineyard** represents Israel, and the **tenants** represent her leaders. God entrusted them with His truth, His worship, and His people. God had done everything necessary for Israel to bear fruit. They didn't need more provisions; they needed repentance.

II. The Servants and Their Rejection (vv. 2–5)

"When the season came, he sent a servant to the tenants to get from them some of the fruit of the vineyard. And they took him and beat him and sent him away empty-handed. Again he sent to them another servant, and they struck him on the head and treated him shamefully. And he sent another, and him they killed. And so with many others: some they beat, and some they killed."

When harvest time comes, the owner sends servants to collect his share of the fruit. Instead of honoring their agreement, the tenants violently reject them. One is beaten, another is shamed, and others are killed. The violence escalates with each messenger.

This is a vivid summary of Israel's history. God sent prophets again and again to call His people to repentance. Instead of receiving them, they were persecuted and murdered—men like Isaiah, Jeremiah, and Zechariah. Yet the owner keeps sending servants. This is the astonishing patience of God. He does not immediately bring judgment; He continues to call His people to bear fruit. If you want to see the patience of God, look at how many times He sends someone to warn before He judges. His love is relentless, even toward those who despise Him.

III. The Sending of the Beloved Son (vv. 6–8)

"He had still one other, a beloved son. Finally he sent him to them, saying, 'They will respect my son.' But those tenants said to one another, 'This is the heir. Come, let us kill him, and the inheritance will be ours.' And they took him and killed him and threw him out of the vineyard."

At last, the owner sends his beloved son. This is not another servant; it is his heir, the one who represents his very person. Surely, the tenants will respect him. But they don't. They see an opportunity to seize the vineyard for themselves. Their reasoning is wicked and absurd: *"If we kill the son, we can claim the inheritance."*

This act represents Israel's ultimate rejection of God, their rejection of His Son. Within days of speaking this parable, Jesus will be seized, condemned, and killed outside the city, the son thrown out of the vineyard.

This is love's final call, God sending His beloved Son, knowing He will be rejected, but still offering mercy one last time. This is the heart of the gospel: God sent His Son to people who would hate Him, reject Him, and kill Him, all so He could save them. That's love beyond comprehension.

IV. The Judgment of the Tenants (v. 9)

"What will the owner of the vineyard do? He will come and destroy the tenants and give the vineyard to others."

The question now shifts to judgment. What should the owner do? Justice demands that he act. Jesus answers His own question: *"He will come and destroy the tenants."* The judgment is severe but righteous. This was partially fulfilled when Jerusalem and the temple were destroyed in AD 70. But it also points to a broader reality: God will judge all who reject His Son.

Then comes a surprising statement: *"He will give the vineyard to others."* The privilege of representing God's kingdom will pass from Israel's corrupt leaders to a new people, the church, made up of Jews and Gentiles united by faith in Christ. If you reject the son, you lose the vineyard. God will not let His work die; He'll raise new people who bear fruit for His glory.

V. The Rejected Stone (vv. 10–11)

"Have you not read this Scripture: 'The stone that the builders rejected has become the cornerstone; this was the Lord's doing, and it is marvelous in our eyes'?"

Jesus ends the parable by quoting Psalm 118:22-23, the same psalm the crowds shouted during His triumphal entry. The imagery shifts from a vineyard to a building. The builders (Israel's leaders) reject a stone, deeming it unfit. But that very stone becomes the cornerstone—the foundation of a new structure.

Jesus is that stone. Rejected by men, chosen by God. What they discard, God exalts. This is the mystery of redemption: rejection leads to resurrection; death gives way to life. The crucified son becomes the cornerstone of God's eternal kingdom. They thought killing the son would end His claim. But it only fulfilled His mission. What they rejected became the very thing God used to save.

VI. The Response of Rebellion (v. 12)

"And they were seeking to arrest him but feared the people, for they perceived that he had told the parable against them. So they left him and went away."

The meaning is not lost on them. The religious leaders know this parable is about them. But instead of repenting, they harden their hearts further. They want to arrest Him, but fear the crowd. Their fear of man outweighs their fear of God.

This is tragic. The story Jesus told was a final call, a plea to turn from rebellion before it's too late. Yet their hearts remain unmoved. They knew exactly what Jesus meant. The parable wasn't confusing; it was convicting. But conviction without repentance only hardens the heart.

VII. Lessons for Us

This parable isn't just history; it's a mirror. It calls us to examine how we respond to God's Word and His Son.

God is patient, but His patience is not endless.

He sends messenger after messenger, giving every opportunity to repent. But eventually, judgment comes.

Rejecting God's messengers leads to dismissing His Son.

The same heart that resists correction will eventually resist Christ Himself.

The gospel is love's final call.

In sending Jesus, God made His ultimate appeal. There is no greater expression of His mercy than the cross.

What man rejects, God redeems.

The rejected stone becomes the cornerstone. Our most extraordinary rebellion became God's greatest act of salvation.

Conclusion

The Parable of the Tenants is a sobering picture of divine patience and human rebellion—but it is also a story of hope. The same God who sent servant after servant, and finally His Son, still calls people today. His love continues to reach out through the message of the gospel.

We must each decide how we will respond. Will we reject the son and face judgment? Or will we receive Him as Savior and become part of His vineyard, bearing fruit for His glory? Love keeps calling. But one day, the call will end. Don't wait until it's too late to respond to the Son.

Reflection & Response

How has God patiently pursued you through His Word, His Spirit, or others?

Are there areas of your life where you've resisted His authority?

How can you respond to God's love today by bearing fruit for His kingdom?

Dual Citizenship: When Kingdoms Collide

Mark 12:13–17

Jesus' confrontation with the religious leaders continues. After exposing their hypocrisy through the parable of the tenants, they regroup and send another delegation to trap Him this time with a political question.

Their goal is simple: force Jesus to choose sides. If he supports paying taxes to Rome, He'll alienate the Jewish people. If he opposes it, they can report Him to the Roman authorities as a rebel.

But Jesus' answer slices through their trap with divine wisdom. In a single statement, He defines how His followers are to live in a world of competing loyalties—citizens of both an earthly kingdom and a heavenly one.

I. The Trap Is Set (vv. 13–14a)

"And they sent to him some of the Pharisees and some of the Herodians, to trap him in his talk. And they came and said to him, 'Teacher, we know that you are true and do not

care about anyone's opinion. For you are not swayed by appearances, but truly teach the way of God."'

The Pharisees and the Herodians were strange allies. The Pharisees despised Rome's pagan rule; the Herodians supported it. The only thing they shared was a hatred for Jesus. Mark says they came "to trap him." The word means to catch or ensnare, like trapping an animal. Their praise is flattery—meant to disguise their deceit. They call Him "Teacher," pretending respect, but their goal is manipulation.

Their description of Jesus is, ironically, true: He speaks the truth and isn't swayed by men. But they use truth as bait for deceit. Flattery is hypocrisy's disguise. They buttered Jesus up, hoping He'd let His guard down, but truth never needs to flatter.

II. The Loaded Question (v. 14b)

"Is it lawful to pay taxes to Caesar, or not? Should we pay them, or should we not?"

Here's the trap. The tax in question was the *poll tax*, a head tax imposed by Rome that every adult had to pay. For Jews, it was especially offensive because it symbolized their subjection to Gentile rule.

If Jesus says *yes*, the Pharisees can accuse Him of betraying His people. If He says *no*, the Herodians can accuse Him of rebellion against Rome. Either way, they win, or so they think. It's the perfect setup for a lose-lose answer.

III. The Hypocrisy Exposed (v. 15a)

"But, knowing their hypocrisy, he said to them, 'Why put me to the test? Bring me a denarius and let me look at it.'"

Jesus sees through their scheme immediately. He calls out their hypocrisy—literally, their play-acting. They appear concerned about the truth but are only interested in trapping Him. Then he asks for a denarius, the Roman coin used to pay the tax. It bore the image of Emperor Tiberius, inscribed: *"Tiberius Caesar, son of the divine Augustus."* To pious Jews, this was idolatrous.

Notice something subtle: Jesus doesn't have a denarius. They do. The very men who object to Roman taxes carry Caesar's coin in their pockets. Their hypocrisy runs deep. They hated Rome's rule but loved Rome's money. They condemned compromise while living comfortably in it.

IV. The Brilliant Response (vv. 15b–17a)

"And they brought one. And he said to them, 'Whose likeness and inscription is this?' They said to him, 'Caesar's.' Jesus said to them, 'Render to Caesar the things that are Caesar's, and to God the things that are God's.'"

Here is one of the most profound statements ever made about the relationship between faith and government. Jesus first asks a simple question: *"Whose likeness and inscription is this?"* The answer is obvious— Caesar's image is on the coin. Then comes His divine wisdom: *"Render to Caesar the things that are Caesar's, and to God the things that are God's."*

The word *render* means "to give back." Jesus acknowledges legitimate human authority. Since the coin bears Caesar's image, paying taxes is giving back what belongs to him. But the statement doesn't end there. The second half is the key: *"and to God the things that are God's."* Humans bear God's image, not Caesar's. Therefore, our ultimate allegiance belongs to God alone.

Jesus simultaneously affirms and limits government authority. We are to respect earthly rulers, but we worship only the heavenly King. The coin had Caesar's image, but you have God's image. Give the coin to Caesar, but give yourself to God.

V. The Wonder of His Wisdom (v. 17b)

"And they marveled at him."

The trap fails. His answer leaves them speechless. He avoids their snare, exposes their hypocrisy, and delivers a timeless truth that transcends politics. They wanted to talk about Rome's authority; Jesus makes them face God's authority. Their question about taxes becomes a question of the heart.

VI. Lessons for Us

This brief exchange carries profound implications for how followers of Christ live as citizens of two kingdoms.

1. We are called to honor legitimate authority.

Government is part of God's design for maintaining order and justice (Romans 13:1–7). Paying taxes, obeying laws, and respecting leaders are part of living under His providence.

Christians should be the best citizens, obedient, respectful, and prayerful, because we trust in a sovereign God who rules over rulers.

2. We must never give Caesar what belongs to God.

While we render taxes and respect, we do not render worship or ultimate loyalty. When the government demands what only God deserves, we must obey God rather than men (Acts 5:29).

There will always be tension between earthly citizenship and heavenly allegiance. True disciples live in both worlds but belong ultimately to one.

3. God's image defines our allegiance.

The coin bears Caesar's image, but you bear God's. Everything you are, your mind, body, and soul, belongs to Him. Paying taxes may be a civic duty, but giving yourself to God is a sacred one.

4. Jesus' wisdom still speaks today.

In a polarized world where politics easily divide, Jesus reminds us that our mission transcends earthly kingdoms. The church's hope is not in legislation but in the Lord. Our King reigns, and His kingdom will never pass away. Christians should engage the world but never be owned by it. Our loyalty to Christ must shape how we live under Caesar.

VII. When Kingdoms Collide

Jesus' words, profound yet straightforward, show how to live when kingdoms collide. We live in the tension between heaven and earth, between the already and the not yet. We work, pay taxes, and participate in civic life, but our hearts belong to another realm.

The challenge is not to withdraw from the world, nor to blend into it, but to live faithfully within it. We honor human authority while proclaiming divine sovereignty. This means living with humility and courage, submitting to rulers when we can, standing firm when we must, and always remembering that Christ's authority is absolute. Caesar's rule is temporary. Christ's reign is eternal. So give Caesar his coin, but give Christ your life.

Conclusion

The Pharisees and Herodians came with a political trap, but Jesus gave them a spiritual truth that still echoes through the centuries:

"Render to Caesar the things that are Caesar's, and to God the things that are God's."

It's not a clever evasion; it's a declaration of the kingdom of God. Jesus claims authority over every area of life: politics, money, morality, and the human heart. Our dual citizenship calls us to live wisely and faithfully, rooted in heaven while walking on earth. Give your taxes to Caesar, but give your heart to God. One day, every kingdom will fall, but the kingdom of Christ will stand forever.

Reflection & Response

In what areas of life do you feel the tension between earthly and heavenly citizenship?

How can you demonstrate godly submission to authority while keeping your ultimate allegiance to Christ?

What does it look like, practically, to "give to God what is God's" in your daily life?

Relationships and Resurrection in the Life to Come

Mark 12:18–27

The question of life after death has always stirred curiosity, hope, and skepticism. In Jesus' day, it sparked sharp theological debates, especially between the Pharisees and the Sadducees.

The Pharisees believed in angels, spirits, and the resurrection of the dead. The Sadducees, however, denied it all. They accepted only the first five books of Moses and rejected any notion of resurrection because they thought it couldn't be proven from the Pentateuch.

In this passage, the Sadducees attempt to trap Jesus with a contrived question. But their hypothetical reveals not only their disbelief, but also their ignorance of Scripture and the power of God.

I. The Setup by the Sadducees (vv. 18–23)

"And Sadducees came to him, who say that there is no resurrection. And they asked him a question, saying, 'Teacher, Moses wrote for us that if a man's brother dies and leaves a wife, but leaves no child, the man must take the widow and raise offspring for his brother. There were seven brothers; the first took a wife, and when he died left no offspring. And the second took her, and died, leaving no offspring. And the third likewise. And the seven left no offspring. Last of all the woman also died. In the resurrection, when they rise again, whose wife will she be? For the seven had her as wife.'"

The Sadducees approach with mock reverence, "Teacher," but their goal is ridicule, not understanding. They quote from the law of Moses (Deut. 25:5–10) about *levirate marriage,* a custom designed to preserve family lines in Israel. Then they spin an absurd scenario: seven brothers all marrying the same woman in sequence, each dying childless. Finally, they pose their punchline question: *"In the resurrection, whose wife will she be?"*

It's meant to make belief in resurrection look ridiculous. They imagine heaven as a mere extension of earth, governed by the same laws and relationships. But their question exposes a fatal misunderstanding: they think of eternity in earthly terms. The Sadducees weren't curious; they were condescending. They thought their clever logic could make the faith in resurrection look foolish. But their logic only revealed how small their view of God really was.

II. The Rebuke of Ignorance (v. 24)

"Jesus said to them, 'Is this not the reason you are wrong, because you know neither the Scriptures nor the power of God?'"

Jesus' response is sharp and direct. He gives two reasons for their error: they misunderstand both Scripture and God's power. They prided themselves on knowledge, yet the very Scriptures they claimed to honor testified to resurrection life. Their problem was not a lack of intellect but a lack of faith.

They denied the supernatural because they underestimated God. They assumed what was impossible for man was impossible for God. Jesus confronts us with a timeless truth: all theological error begins when we either distort God's Word or diminish His power. If your God can't raise the dead, He's not the God of the Bible. The Sadducees had a small view of Scripture and an even smaller view of God.

III. The Reality of the Resurrection (v. 25)

"For when they rise from the dead, they neither marry nor are given in marriage, but are like angels in heaven."

Jesus moves from correction to revelation. He affirms resurrection as a fact—*"when they rise,"* not *"if."* Then he explains that resurrected life is fundamentally different from earthly life.

In heaven, people are not married or given in marriage. This does not diminish marriage; rather, it fulfills its purpose. Earthly marriage points to the greater reality of eternal union with Christ.

246

Resurrection life is not an improved version of this life; it's an entirely new order of existence.

Jesus adds, "They are like angels in heaven." He's not saying we become angels, but that, like them, we will live in a glorified, immortal state no longer subject to death, decay, or earthly institutions. Marriage is a shadow; Christ is the substance. The intimacy, love, and joy we taste in marriage now will be fully realized in our eternal relationship with Him.

IV. The Revelation of Scripture (vv. 26–27a)

"And as for the dead being raised, have you not read in the book of Moses, in the passage about the bush, how God spoke to him, saying, 'I am the God of Abraham, and the God of Isaac, and the God of Jacob'? He is not God of the dead, but of the living."

Knowing the Sadducees accept only the books of Moses, Jesus proves resurrection from Exodus 3. When God spoke to Moses at the burning bush, He said, *"I am the God of Abraham, Isaac, and Jacob."* Notice the tense: *"I am,"* not *"I was."* Centuries after their deaths, God still identifies Himself with them. The covenant relationship He established was not temporary but eternal.

If God is truly their God, then Abraham, Isaac, and Jacob must still live. The living God cannot be the God of the dead. Jesus uses their own Scripture to affirm the truth they deny. The patriarchs are not gone; they are alive in the presence of God, awaiting the final resurrection. God's covenant promises don't end at the grave. When He says, 'I am your God,' it means death can't break that relationship.

V. The Power of God Displayed

Jesus' answer not only silences the Sadducees but also reveals the breathtaking power of God.

The resurrection is not wishful thinking; it is the ultimate demonstration of God's power to redeem, restore, and renew. The same voice that spoke to Moses from the bush will one day call every believer from the grave. Resurrection means that every injustice will be set right, every sorrow healed, every loss reversed. Death will not have the last word; God will.

The God who spoke life into existence will speak life into our graves. The empty tomb of Jesus is the down payment on every believer's resurrection.

VI. The Hope of Resurrection Life

The Sadducees viewed death as the end. Jesus reveals it as the beginning of unending joy in the presence of God. Heaven is not static; it is life in its fullest expression. No sin, no sorrow, no separation, only worship, joy, and the unbroken fellowship of the redeemed with their Savior.

Relationships will not be lost but transformed. Every holy affection will be purified and perfected. We will know and love one another more deeply because we will know and love Christ completely. This is the hope that sustains believers through grief and loss, the promise that death is not final. If you are in Christ, death is not the end of your story; it's the doorway into glory.

VII. The Final Rebuke (v. 27b)

"You are quite wrong."

Jesus ends where He began, with unmistakable clarity. The Sadducees are not just mistaken; they are entirely wrong. Their unbelief is moral, not intellectual. They reject what they do not want to believe. But truth stands firm. God's word is true, His power is real, and the resurrection is certain. Jesus doesn't adjust the truth to fit their theology; He adjusts their theology to fit the truth."

VIII. Lessons for Us

Faith must rest on both Scripture and the power of God.

The Word of God defines what we believe; the power of God makes it a reality.

Heaven is not an extension of earth—it's perfection beyond imagination.

Every good thing here is only a glimpse of the glory to come.

God's promises outlast death.

If He is your God now, He will be your God forever.

Resurrection hope shapes how we live now.

We face suffering and loss not with despair but with confidence that the best is yet to come.

Conclusion

The Sadducees came with skepticism; Jesus answered with Scripture and power. Their question was meant to humiliate, but it became an opportunity for revelation. God is not the God of the dead but of the living. Every believer who has died in Christ is alive with Him, awaiting the day when our mortal bodies will be raised in glory.

Resurrection hope changes everything; it frees us from fear, fuels our faith, and fills us with joy. The question isn't whether there's life after death. The question is whether you have life before death, life in Christ, who is the resurrection and the life.

Reflection & Response

How does your view of heaven affect the way you live today?

What does it mean for you that God is "not the God of the dead, but of the living"?

How can resurrection hope reshape your outlook on loss, suffering, or fear?

Above All, Love

Mark 12:28–34

The religious leaders had spent much of Jesus' time in Jerusalem trying to trap Him with questions about politics, theology, and authority. But in this passage, something different happens. One scribe approaches not to attack, but to inquire.

He has seen Jesus' wisdom, heard His teaching, and recognizes truth when he hears it. His question cuts to the heart of the law, and Jesus' answer cuts to the heart of true religion: love for God and love for others. This is more than a summary of commandments; it is the very essence of Christianity.

I. The Sincere Question (v. 28)

"And one of the scribes came up and heard them disputing with one another, and seeing that he answered them well, asked him, 'Which commandment is the most important of all?'"

Unlike the Pharisees and Sadducees before him, this scribe is not hostile. He's curious. The rabbis had counted 613 commandments in the Old Testament — 248 positive and 365 negative — and debated endlessly about which was the greatest. Some said ceremonial laws were supreme; others pointed to moral ones. This scribe wants to know: *What's at the center of it all? What matters most to God?*

It's an important question, one we still need to ask. In a world obsessed with rules, systems, and performance, Jesus points to something greater than mere external obedience. This scribe wasn't trying to trap Jesus; he was trying to understand Him. And Jesus rewards sincere seekers with simple, powerful truth."

II. The Supreme Commandment (vv. 29–30)

"Jesus answered, 'The most important is, "Hear, O Israel: The Lord our God, the Lord is one. And you shall love the Lord your God with all your heart and with all your soul and with all your mind and with all your strength."

251

Jesus begins by quoting the Shema (Deuteronomy 6:4-5), the daily confession of Israel's faith. It starts with theology, *"The Lord our God, the Lord is one."* There is one God, and He alone deserves our total devotion.

Then comes the command: *"You shall love the Lord your God with all your heart, soul, mind, and strength."* This love is not sentimental; it's comprehensive. It calls for every part of who we are—our emotions, will, intellect, and energy.

Heart: the center of affections and desires.

Soul: the seat of identity and devotion.

Mind: the faculty of thought and understanding.

Strength: the sum of one's abilities and resources.

To love God "with all" means nothing is held back. This is love expressed through worship, obedience, and delight in Him above all else. The greatest commandment is not 'Do more,' but 'Love more.' Religion without love is empty, but love for God fuels everything else in the Christian life.

III. The Second Commandment (v. 31)

"The second is this: 'You shall love your neighbor as yourself.' There is no other commandment greater than these."

Jesus adds a second command from Leviticus 19:18, connecting love for God with love for people. The two are inseparable; one flows from the other. If you genuinely love God, you will love those made in His image. The vertical and horizontal cannot be divided.

Loving your neighbor means more than avoiding harm; it means seeking their good. It is active, self-giving, and sacrificial. Jesus doesn't say we must first learn to love ourselves before loving others. The assumption is that we naturally care for ourselves. The command is to extend that same care, concern, and compassion toward others. If you claim to love God but despise people, you're deceived. True love for God always spills over into love for others.

IV. The Unity of Love (v. 31b)

"There is no other commandment greater than these."

Notice that Jesus speaks of these two as one commandment, *"There is no other commandment greater than these."* They are distinct but inseparable. Love for God is the root; love for neighbor is the fruit. You cannot have one without the other.

This unity of love fulfills the entire law. Every command in Scripture can be traced back to one of these two principles. As Paul later writes, *"Love is the fulfilling of the law"* (Romans 13:10). When you love God supremely, you'll obey Him willingly. When you love others sincerely, you'll serve them joyfully.

V. The Scribe's Insight (vv. 32–33)

"And the scribe said to him, 'You are right, Teacher. You have truly said that he is one, and there is no other besides him. And to love him with all the heart and with all the understanding and with all the strength, and to love one's neighbor as oneself, is much more than all whole burnt offerings and sacrifices.'"

BEHOLD THE CHRIST

This scribe gets it. He agrees with Jesus and even expands on His answer. He recognizes that love for God and others is greater than ritual sacrifices. This is remarkable, coming from a man steeped in the temple system. He understands that external religion without inward devotion is worthless. God doesn't just want your ritual; He wants your heart.

This scribe understood what many churchgoers miss: you can attend worship, give generously, and serve faithfully—but if love for God and people is missing, you've missed the point.

VI. The Commendation of Jesus (v. 34)

"And when Jesus saw that he answered wisely, he said to him, 'You are not far from the kingdom of God.' And after that no one dared to ask him any more questions."

Jesus commends the scribe: *"You are not far from the kingdom of God."*

He's close, closer than the Pharisees and Sadducees who had tried to trap Jesus, but he's not yet in. Understanding truth is not the same as embracing it. Many are "not far" from the kingdom; they know what's true, they agree with it, they even admire Jesus, but they haven't surrendered to Him.

The scribe had the correct theology and the right priorities. What he needed was the right relationship, faith in Christ Himself. It's possible to know the correct answer and still miss the kingdom. The question is not just, 'Do I understand what God requires?' but, 'Do I love Him as He deserves?'

254

VII. Lessons for Us

Love is the essence of obedience.

Every command of God flows from the command to love Him and others.

Doctrine and devotion belong together.

The Shema begins with theology and ends with love. Sound doctrine should produce a warm heart, not a cold spirit.

True religion is relational, not ritual.

God desires hearts that love Him, not hands that merely perform for Him.

We need divine love to fulfill divine law.

We cannot love God or others rightly apart from the Spirit's work in our hearts (Romans 5:5).

VIII. Love That Flows from the Gospel

It's worth remembering that Jesus spoke these words on His way to the cross. Soon, He would demonstrate the greatest love the world has ever seen. The commands to love God and neighbor are impossible without the grace of Christ. Only when we experience His love can we reflect it.

1 John 4:19 says, *"We love because he first loved us."* The gospel transforms the heart so that love becomes not duty but delight. You can't manufacture this kind of love. It's born in the heart of those whom God has loved through the cross of Christ.

Conclusion

The scribe asked, *"Which commandment is the most important?"* Jesus answered, *"Love."*

That's the center of Christianity, love for God that consumes every part of us, and love for people that reflects the heart of God. This love fulfills the law, displays the gospel, and proves the reality of our faith. You can have all the correct answers, but if you don't have love, you're still far from the kingdom. Love is the language of heaven, and only those who speak it belong there.

Reflection & Response

Is your relationship with God marked more by love or by performance?

Who is one person God is calling you to love in action this week?

How can you cultivate deeper love for God through worship, obedience, and gratitude?

Beware of Pastors and Preachers

Mark 12:35–40

After a long series of confrontations with the religious leaders, Jesus now turns the tables. He has answered their traps and silenced their questions. Now, standing in the temple courts before the watching crowds, He issues a public warning, a sobering indictment against the scribes, the spiritual leaders of Israel.

They were supposed to shepherd God's people, but instead, they used their position for pride and personal gain. Jesus exposes the danger of self-exalting religion and calls His followers to something radically different: humble, Christ-centered service. Jesus isn't just warning about ancient scribes, He's warning about a spirit that still creeps into the church today: pride in ministry, a hunger for attention, and using the things of God to elevate self.

I. The Exaltation of Christ (vv. 35–37)

"And as Jesus taught in the temple, he said, 'How can the scribes say that the Christ is the son of David? David himself, in the Holy Spirit, declared, "The Lord said to my Lord, 'Sit at my right hand, until I put your enemies under your feet.'" David himself calls him Lord. So how is he his son?' And the great throng heard him gladly."

Before warning about the scribes, Jesus reveals their most significant error: they failed to understand who the Messiah truly is. The scribes correctly taught that the Christ would come from David's line, but they missed that He would also be David's Lord. They saw the Messiah as a political figure, not a divine one. Jesus quotes Psalm 110:1 to expose their shallow theology. David calls the coming Messiah "Lord," showing that the Christ is more than a mere descendant.

Jesus is both the Son of David and the Son of God, fully human and fully divine. Their failure to recognize this truth revealed their spiritual blindness. They could teach Scripture, quote verses, and lead prayers, but they didn't know the Lord those Scriptures proclaimed.

You can know theology and still miss Jesus. The scribes studied the word but never bowed before the One the Word was about. The crowd, however, "heard Him gladly." Ordinary people who were weary of religious hypocrisy found hope in the authority and authenticity of Jesus.

II. The Exposure of Hypocrisy (vv. 38–40a)

"And in his teaching he said, 'Beware of the scribes, who like to walk around in long robes and like greetings in the marketplaces and have the best seats in the synagogues and the places of honor at feasts, who devour widows' houses and for a pretense make long prayers.'"

Jesus now exposes the scribes' spiritual rot. He doesn't tell the crowd to hate them, but to beware —to be on guard. Their danger wasn't simply false teaching but false living.

1. They loved appearance more than substance.

"They like to walk around in long robes..."

These robes were long, flowing garments that signified status. The scribes wore them not for modesty but for attention. They wanted to be seen as holy and set apart. Their religion was a show, not a surrender. They looked the part but lacked the heart. They wanted to look spiritual without being spiritual. They wore religion like a costume.

2. They loved recognition more than humility.

"...and greetings in the marketplaces and the best seats in the synagogues and places of honor at feasts."

They craved titles, status, and applause. In the synagogue, they sat up front facing the congregation. At banquets, they took the highest seats. Their ministry became about being admired rather than serving others. This is a warning to every generation of church leaders: beware the subtle pull of pride. It's possible to preach Christ while secretly seeking your own glory.

3. They loved gain more than God.

"...who devour widows' houses..."

Here, the mask falls off completely. Their greed exploited the vulnerable. They manipulated widows into supporting them financially under the guise of religious duty. Their supposed "ministry" became a means of enrichment. Instead of caring for those in need, they consumed them. This is the opposite of true shepherding. Jesus said, *"The good shepherd lays down his life for the sheep"* (John 10:11). These men used the sheep to fatten themselves. A wolf in a robe is still a wolf. It doesn't matter how religious they sound; if they use people for gain, they're devouring God's flock.

4. They loved performance more than prayer.

"...and for a pretense make long prayers."

They prayed not to commune with God but to impress men. Their prayers were performances designed to display piety. Jesus isn't condemning long prayers—He's condemning empty ones. Real prayer flows from humility; false prayer seeks attention.

III. The Sentence of Judgment (v. 40b)

"They will receive the greater condemnation."

Jesus ends with chilling words. Those who use religion for self-gain, who abuse their position of trust, will face greater judgment. Scripture teaches that spiritual leadership carries weighty accountability (James 3:1). To teach truth while living in hypocrisy is not a small sin—it's a great one.

Their condemnation is "greater" because their responsibility was greater. They had access to the truth, yet they used it to exalt themselves rather than glorify God. The same word that saves the humble will condemn the proud. It's a fearful thing to speak for God while serving self. Jesus' warning reminds us that outward success in ministry means nothing if the heart is proud. God does not measure greatness by platform or applause but by faithfulness and humility.

IV. The Marks of True Ministry

In contrast to the scribes, Jesus embodies what faithful ministry looks like.

Humility over honor.

Jesus came "not to be served but to serve" (Mark 10:45). He took the lowest place so that others might be lifted up.

Sincerity over showmanship.

His prayers were not for pretense but for communion. His life was marked by authenticity.

Compassion over exploitation.

Where the scribes devoured widows, Jesus defended them. His ministry brought healing and hope to the overlooked.

Submission over self-promotion.

He sought the Father's will, even to the point of death. True leaders follow His example, living for the glory of God, not the applause of men.

If the ministry ever becomes about building your name instead of magnifying His, you've already lost your way.

V. Lessons for Today

This passage may sound like a warning for pastors only, but its principles apply to all believers. Every Christian is called to serve, and every servant must guard their heart.

1. Beware of pride disguised as spirituality.

Pride is subtle—it hides behind religious language and "good intentions." Examine whether your service is about God's glory or your recognition.

2. Beware of using people instead of loving them.

True ministry gives; false ministry takes. The test of leadership is not how many follow you, but how many are strengthened because of you.

3. Beware of performance without devotion.

Public ministry means nothing without private worship. What you do for God must flow from who you are before God.

4. Beware of hypocrisy that begins in small compromises.

The scribes didn't start corrupt. Pride grows slowly. Guard your heart before ministry becomes a platform for ego instead of grace.

VI. The Call to Watchfulness

Jesus says, *"Beware."* That word implies vigilance. We must constantly watch our motives and measure them by the standard of Christ. It's easy to point fingers at corrupt leaders, but Jesus' warning invites self-examination. Are we more concerned with appearance or authenticity? More eager for honor or holiness?

The antidote to pride is proximity to Jesus. When we stay close to Him, His humility transforms ours. The closer you walk with Christ, the smaller you'll think of yourself. Pride shrinks in the shadow of His cross.

VII. The Ultimate Example

Jesus closes this section not with another warning but with a contrast. The very next passage, the widow's offering, shows a humble woman giving her all to God in faith. The scribes took from widows; this widow gives to God. That's not an accident. Mark places these stories side by side to show the difference between false and true devotion. Proud religion robs; humble faith gives. The kingdom of God doesn't advance through impressive men but through faithful servants who love God more than themselves.

Conclusion

Jesus' words are both warning and invitation. They remind us that spiritual pride is deadly, but humility leads to blessing. The scribes loved attention, applause, and admiration. But the faithful servant loves Christ—and that's enough. So Jesus says, *"Beware."* Not to make us suspicious of every leader, but to make us mindful of our own hearts. May every pastor, every servant, and every believer hear this warning and respond with humility:

"He must increase, but I must decrease." (John 3:30)

Reflection & Response

In what ways can pride subtly creep into your service to God?

How can you cultivate humility and sincerity in ministry or daily life?

What would it look like to serve others this week with the heart of Christ, not for recognition but for love?

Giving to the Glory of God
Mark 12:41–44

After warning the crowds about the pride and hypocrisy of the scribes, Jesus shifts His focus from the

263

teachers of Israel to the temple treasury. He moves from *the proud who take* to *the humble who give.*

This moment is a masterclass in quiet worship: no stage, no announcement, no applause, just a widow and her God. And Jesus, watching. He sees not the size of her gift but the sacrifice behind it. In this simple act, the Lord reveals a truth that cuts across every age: God measures giving not by portion but by proportion, not by what we give but by what we keep. God is not impressed by the amount we give; He's moved by the heart that gives. The measure of our generosity is not in dollars and cents, it's in devotion and surrender.

I. The Setting of the Scene (v. 41)

"And he sat down opposite the treasury and watched the people putting money into the offering box. Many rich people put in large sums."

The temple treasury was located in the Court of Women, an area accessible to all worshipers. Against the wall stood thirteen trumpet-shaped chests where people deposited their offerings. Each chest had an inscription marking its purpose, some for the temple tax, others for freewill offerings. Jesus takes a seat opposite the treasury. He doesn't lecture or announce, He *watches.*

That word is worth pausing over. Jesus is watching how people give. He's not interested in amounts but in motives. He sees beyond the clang of coins into the condition of hearts. The rich come first. Their gifts are impressive, large sums given publicly. There's no indication their giving was wrong. But Jesus doesn't commend them, because He sees something missing: sacrifice. We might measure generosity by how much goes out of our hands; Jesus measures it by how much is left in our hands.

II. The Sacrifice of the Widow (v. 42)

"And a poor widow came and put in two small copper coins, which make a penny."

Then she appears, a poor widow. In the ancient world, widows were among the most vulnerable people. Without a husband or inheritance, many lived on the edge of survival. Her gift? Two *lepta*, the smallest coins in circulation, are together worth about one sixty-fourth of a day's wage. In our terms, a few pennies. To everyone else, it was nothing. But to Jesus, it was everything.

The rich gave large sums out of abundance; she gave a small sum out of poverty. Yet hers was the greater gift because it was born out of devotion, not display. The widow's coins made barely a sound in the offering box, but they thundered in heaven. God heard her faith. She didn't give what she could spare; she gave what she couldn't afford to lose. And she did it quietly, without fanfare, because her offering wasn't for others to see; it was for God.

III. The Savior's Evaluation (vv. 43–44a)

"And he called his disciples to him and said to them, 'Truly, I say to you, this poor widow has put in more than all those who are contributing to the offering box. For they all contributed out of their abundance, but she, out of her poverty, has put in everything she had...'"

Jesus calls His disciples close; it's a teaching moment. He begins with "Truly," signaling that what follows is both authoritative and astonishing. The widow's offering, He says, is *more* than all the others combined, not in amount, but in meaning.

They gave out of abundance what they could easily part with. She gave out of poverty, what she could not replace. They gave their leftovers; she gave her livelihood. This flips our entire understanding of generosity upside down. In God's economy, the value of a gift is determined by the sacrifice it requires and the heart that offers it.

Jesus doesn't need our money; He desires our trust. Giving is not just about funding God's work—it's about forming our faith. When she gave her two coins, she was saying, *"Lord, I trust You with everything I have left."* That's worship. That's faith.

IV. The Significance of Her Sacrifice (v. 44b)

"...everything she had, all she had to live on."

This is the climax of the story. She didn't just give generously, she gave completely. The phrase "all she had to live on" literally means "her whole life." Her offering symbolized total surrender. She held nothing back.

It's important to note: Jesus doesn't stop her. He doesn't say, "She's poor, someone give it back to her." Instead, He honors her act of worship because it reflects His own. Soon, He too will give *all He has*, His very life, for the glory of God and the salvation of sinners.

This widow foreshadows the cross. She gives her livelihood; He will give His life. She offers all she has to live on; He offers His life so that we might live. The widow gave her all to God, and Jesus would soon give His all for her. Her sacrifice pointed to His.

V. The Lesson for Disciples

This passage is not primarily about money; it's about worship. Giving reveals what we treasure most. The widow's offering teaches us several timeless lessons about life in the kingdom of God.

1. God sees what others overlook.

No one in the temple noticed this woman. Her gift was too small to matter to men, but it mattered to God. In a world obsessed with status and recognition, Jesus sees faithfulness in obscurity. Nothing done for His glory is ever wasted. Man measures the amount; God measures the motive. Faithfulness never escapes His notice.

2. God measures differently than we do.

We value gifts that are large and impressive; God values hearts that are humble and surrendered. He delights in costly obedience more than comfortable charity. The widow's gift didn't change the temple budget, but it changed heaven's perspective.

3. True giving flows from trust.

This woman didn't give because she had extra; she gave because she trusted God to provide. Generosity that pleases God always grows out of faith.

4. God honors the heart that holds nothing back.

Her two coins represent what Jesus desires from all of us, not wealth, but willingness. When we surrender all to Him, whether in money, time, or obedience, we display the beauty of worship.

VI. The Contrast of Two Worshipers

Mark intentionally places this story right after Jesus' warning about the scribes. The scribes *devoured widows' houses*; this widow *offered her house to God.* They took all they could get; she gave all she had.

The contrast could not be sharper:

Through her, Jesus redefines greatness in the kingdom. It's not about power, wealth, or prestige; it's about faith-filled obedience. God doesn't need impressive givers; He's looking for surrendered hearts. The kingdom moves forward not through the proud, but through the poor in spirit.

VII. The Application to Us

Examine your motives.

Do you give to be seen or because you've seen the grace of God?

Evaluate your measure.

Are you giving out of comfort or out of trust? Generosity begins where self-reliance ends.

Embrace God's economy.

Heaven counts differently. In God's math, two pennies given in faith outweigh millions given for show.

Experience the joy of surrender.

Faithful giving is not loss—it's freedom. When you give yourself wholly to God, you discover He is more than enough.

God doesn't want your leftovers; He wants your life. And when you give Him your all, you'll never regret a single thing you've laid down.

VIII. The Heart of Worship

This passage closes not only a chapter of Scripture but a chapter of confrontation. After exposing false religion, Jesus honors true worship. The scene begins with hypocrisy and ends with humility. And as the temple grows silent and the coins stop clinking, one woman's faith still speaks.

You can't outgive God, but you can trust Him enough to try. The widow didn't give to get; she gave because she already had — she had God. This widow reminds us that the most accurate measure of worship is not what we offer, but how much we trust. Giving to the glory of God means resting in the truth that He gave everything for us first.

Conclusion

Jesus' final act of teaching in the temple is not a sermon on tithing; it's a picture of the gospel. The widow gave all she had to live on; Jesus will soon give

His life for all who trust Him. Her faith foreshadowed His sacrifice. When we give to the glory of God — whether with time, resources, or obedience —we echo her faith and reflect His heart.

The greatest giver in the Bible isn't the widow, it's the Savior. She gave her livelihood, but He gave His life. So give, not to earn favor but to express faith. Give not from comfort but from devotion. And know that the eyes of the Lord still see, still measure, and still delight in every act of worship done for His glory.

Reflection & Response

How does your giving of time, resources, or devotion reflect your trust in God?

What might it look like to give "all you have to live on" in faith this week?

In what areas is God calling you to surrender from abundance into sacrifice?

Chapter 13

It Is Not the End of the World as We Know It

Mark 13:1–13

As Jesus leaves the temple for the last time, one of His disciples makes an admiring remark: *"Look, Teacher, what wonderful stones and what wonderful buildings!"* (v. 1).

The temple was the pride of Israel, the heart of worship, a marvel of architecture, and a symbol of national identity. Yet Jesus looks at those same walls and says something shocking: *"Do you see these great buildings? There will not be left here one stone upon another that will not be thrown down."*

The disciples are stunned. For them, the destruction of the temple could only mean one thing: the end of the world. But Jesus teaches that the fall of Jerusalem, though catastrophic, is *not* the end. It's the beginning of the birth pains, the unfolding of God's plan that leads toward His ultimate restoration. Jesus wasn't giving His disciples a timeline; He was giving them perspective. The world's collapse isn't the end of God's story; it's part of it.

I. The Prediction of Destruction (vv. 1–2)

"Do you see these great buildings? There will not be left here one stone upon another that will not be thrown down."

The temple was massive, Herod's masterpiece, with stones weighing tons. For Israel, it was the visible proof of God's presence and permanence. But Jesus declares it will fall. This prophecy was fulfilled in A.D. 70 when the Romans besieged Jerusalem, burned the temple, and dismantled it stone by stone.

But Jesus' point isn't just about architecture. He's teaching that earthly glory fades. What people admire most can crumble overnight. Only the kingdom of God endures. Everything we build eventually falls, but what God builds lasts forever.

II. The Private Question (v. 3–4)

"Tell us, when will these things be, and what will be the sign when all these things are about to be accomplished?"

Later, on the Mount of Olives overlooking the city, Peter, James, John, and Andrew ask privately what everyone else is thinking: *When?* They assume that one event —the temple's fall —means the end of the age. But Jesus separates the two. Some things will happen soon (the fall of Jerusalem); others will unfold across history.

Their question reveals something deeply human: when we see instability, we want certainty. We long for control in a world that feels like it's collapsing. Jesus doesn't give dates. He gives direction.

III. The Call to Discernment (vv. 5–8)

"See that no one leads you astray. Many will come in my name, saying, 'I am he!' and they will lead many astray."

Before talking about signs of the end, Jesus warns against deception. False messiahs and false hopes will always rise. When fear grows, so does deception. He also speaks of wars, earthquakes, and famines — real, terrifying events — but then adds, *"This is not the end."*

These are the "beginning of the birth pains." Like contractions before birth, they are painful yet purposeful signs that something new is coming. The world's chaos isn't random; it's the groaning of creation awaiting redemption (Romans 8:22). When the world trembles, believers shouldn't panic. Every shaking reminds us that our foundation is not of this world.

IV. The Call to Faithfulness (vv. 9–11)

"But be on your guard. For they will deliver you over to councils, and you will be beaten in synagogues, and you will stand before governors and kings for my sake, to bear witness before them."

Jesus moves from the temple's fall to the trials His followers will face. The destruction of Jerusalem will mark the beginning of persecution, not the end of the mission. The disciples would soon experience everything He describes: arrests, trials, beatings, and betrayal. Yet all of it would serve a divine purpose, *to bear witness.*

When the world opposes the gospel, it becomes the stage for the gospel. God turns persecution into proclamation. Every courtroom becomes a pulpit when a faithful believer speaks the truth. Jesus also promises His presence: *"Do not be anxious beforehand... for it is not you who speak, but the Holy Spirit."* That's comfort for every believer facing pressure for their faith. God never calls us to stand alone; His Spirit gives both courage and words.

V. The Cost of Following Christ (vv. 12–13)

"And brother will deliver brother over to death, and the father his child, and children will rise against parents and have them put to death. And you will be hated by all for my name's sake."

Allegiance to Jesus will cost some relationships, reputations, and even lives. But Jesus' promise stands: *"The one who endures to the end will be saved."* Endurance doesn't earn salvation; it proves it. Persevering faith shows the reality of the Spirit's work within.

Endurance is not gritting your teeth; it's trusting God when everything else falls apart. In every age, believers have faced hostility. From the apostles in the first century to persecuted Christians today, the message is the same: don't mistake hardship for abandonment. God is still working His plan.

VI. The Lesson for Today

This passage isn't meant to fuel speculation about timelines; it's intended to strengthen faith in turbulent times.

Don't confuse shaking with ending.

The world's instability isn't proof of God's absence; it's proof of His unfolding plan.

Don't follow fear; follow truth.

False teachers prey on panic. Stay rooted in Scripture, not sensational headlines.

Don't retreat from witness.

When trials come, God uses them to display His gospel through your endurance.

Don't lose heart.

Jesus promised suffering, but He also promised His Spirit and final victory.

The end of the world as we know it isn't the end of God's plan; it's the beginning of His kingdom.

Conclusion

As Jesus looks at the magnificent temple, He sees what the disciples can't, that it will fall, but His word will not. The temple may crumble, kingdoms may rise and fall, but the gospel will advance. The call of Mark 13:1–13 is not to predict but to persevere. To live faithfully when the world feels fragile. To remember that the collapse of what is temporary only clears the way for what is eternal. So, when everything around you shakes, don't fear, it's not the end of the world as we know it. It's the beginning of God's unshakable kingdom.

Reflection & Response

How do you typically respond when life feels uncertain, panic, or perseverance?

In what areas is God calling you to endure faithfully rather than escape quickly?

How can you anchor your hope in the unshakable kingdom rather than the temporary world?

It Is Not the End of the World as We Know It – Part 2

Mark 13:14–23

Jesus continues His teaching on the Mount of Olives, expanding on His earlier warnings about the temple's destruction and the coming trials. In this section, His tone intensifies. He moves from general birth pains to a specific moment of crisis, the *"abomination of desolation."*

For His disciples, this prophecy was not meant to cause panic but to prepare them for perseverance. While it describes dark days of deception and distress, Jesus' purpose is pastoral: to strengthen His followers for endurance and trust in God's sovereign plan.

Jesus doesn't tell us these things to make us afraid, but to make us faithful. The end of the world as we know it is not the end of God's kingdom; it's the beginning of His victory.

I. The Abomination of Desolation (v. 14)

"But when you see the abomination of desolation standing where he ought not to be (let the reader understand), then let those who are in Judea flee to the mountains."

This phrase, *the abomination of desolation*, comes from Daniel's prophecy (Dan. 9:27; 11:31; 12:11). It refers to something so wicked that it desecrates God's holy place.

Historically, it first occurred when Antiochus Epiphanes defiled the temple in 167 B.C. by setting up an altar to Zeus. But Jesus points forward to another event, the coming destruction of Jerusalem in A.D. 70, when Roman armies surrounded the city and desecrated the temple once again. This would be a moment of judgment on unbelieving Israel and a warning to all generations that the kingdoms of man cannot stand against the purposes of God.

Mark adds, *"let the reader understand,"* reminding us that these words require spiritual discernment. Jesus is describing a near fulfillment, the fall of Jerusalem. The abomination of desolation is a picture of ultimate rebellion, when man tries to take the place of God. It's not just history; it's humanity's heart apart from Him.

II. The Call to Flee (vv. 14–18)

"Then let those who are in Judea flee to the mountains. Let the one who is on the housetop not go down, nor enter his house, to take anything out. And let the one who is in the field not turn back to take his cloak."

Jesus' instruction is clear and urgent: when this moment comes, don't stay and fight, *flee.*

For the disciples and early believers, this warning proved literal. When Roman forces advanced on Jerusalem, Christians remembered Jesus' words and escaped to the mountains of Pella. His words remind us that obedience to God's Word is often the difference between life and death. When judgment comes, salvation is found in faith and obedience, not in self-preservation.

Faith isn't shown in how fast you run but in who you listen to. The ones who trusted Jesus' words were the ones who survived. Then Jesus adds, *"Alas for women who are pregnant and for those who are nursing infants in those days! Pray that it may not happen in winter."* His compassion shines through even in judgment. God's justice is never cold; His heart grieves for the suffering of His people.

III. The Great Tribulation (vv. 19–20)

"For in those days there will be such tribulation as has not been from the beginning of the creation that God created until now, and never will be. And if the Lord had not cut short the days, no human being would be saved. But for the sake of the elect, whom he chose, he shortened the days."

Here, Jesus describes the unimaginable suffering that would accompany those events, what history would later call the destruction of Jerusalem.

Josephus records that famine, violence, and devastation overwhelmed the city. It was a horrific foreshadowing of the final judgment yet to come upon the whole earth. But even in this chaos, notice the mercy of God: *"The Lord had not cut short the days... for the sake of the elect."* God limits the suffering of His people. His sovereignty is not suspended in tribulation; it is displayed through it.

The same God who allows the storm also sets its boundaries. He knows precisely how much His people can bear. This truth steadies believers in every generation. When we face tribulation, we can trust that God's power and compassion remain constant. The suffering is temporary; His salvation is eternal.

IV. The Danger of Deception (vv. 21–22)

"And then if anyone says to you, 'Look, here is the Christ!' or 'Look, there he is!' do not believe it. For false christs and false prophets will arise and perform signs and wonders, to lead astray, if possible, the elect."

Tribulation not only brings pain, but also deception. Jesus warns that false teachers and false messiahs will exploit chaos to gain followers. They will even perform *"signs and wonders."* In other words, deception won't always look evil; it may appear spiritual, persuasive, or miraculous. The goal is to draw people's trust away from Christ and toward counterfeit saviors.

Jesus' warning is urgent: *"Do not believe it."* Stay anchored to truth. When the world grows dark, spiritual counterfeits multiply. Satan doesn't just attack with persecution; he distracts with imitation. When the earth shakes, don't run to the first person promising safety; run to the Savior who promised suffering and glory. Even the elect—true believers—would be deceived *if it were possible.* But God preserves His own. Our perseverance is not a result of our strength but His sustaining grace.

V. The Comfort of His Control (v. 23)

"But be on guard; I have told you all things beforehand."

Jesus ends this section with both warning and comfort. Nothing catches Him off guard. He tells His followers what to expect so they will not be shaken when it happens. The purpose of prophecy is not curiosity but confidence, not to fill our charts but to anchor our hearts.

Jesus didn't tell us everything, but He told us enough. Enough to trust Him, enough to stay faithful, and sufficient to know that He's in control even when the world isn't. By saying, *"I have told you all things beforehand,"* Jesus assures His people that history is not spiraling out of control; it's unfolding under His authority. Every generation of believers can cling to that promise: what appears to be chaos is actually God's plan moving toward consummation.

VI. Lessons for Us

Trust the Word of Christ above the noise of the world.

When confusion surrounds us, Scripture must shape our perspective more than speculation or fear.

Expect suffering, but cling to hope.

Tribulation is real, but it's temporary. God shortens the days for His elect; His mercy sets the limits.

Stay alert, not anxious.

"Be on guard" means living with readiness, not restlessness. Christ's followers don't panic—they persevere.

Hold fast to the true Christ.

False saviors will always arise, but none can match the One who already conquered sin and death.

Conclusion

In this passage, Jesus paints a sobering picture of judgment, tribulation, and deception. But woven through it is a thread of grace: God knows, God reigns, and God preserves His people. The world may crumble, nations may rage, and false voices may shout, but the Word of Christ stands firm.

Reflection & Response

What false hopes or fears most easily distract you from trusting Christ's Word?

How can you stay alert and discerning without living in anxiety or despair?

Where do you see God's mercy limiting suffering or preserving faith in your own life?

It's the End of the World as We Know It – Part 1

Mark 13:24–31

The conversation on the Mount of Olives has taken a sobering turn. Jesus has warned His disciples about persecution, deception, and the desolation that would fall upon Jerusalem. But now, His tone shifts from the darkness of tribulation to the light of hope.

When it feels like the world is falling apart, remember, it's not falling apart; it's falling into place. These verses pull back the curtain on what follows the chaos of human history. Jesus speaks not merely of destruction but of redemption. The message is unmistakable: the end of the world is not the end for the people of God; it's the beginning of His kingdom's glory.

I. Cosmic Upheaval and the Coming of the Son of Man (vv. 24–26)

"But in those days, after that tribulation, the sun will be darkened, and the moon will not give its light, and the stars will be falling from heaven, and the powers in the heavens will be shaken. And then they will see the Son of Man coming in clouds with great power and glory."

Jesus describes the end of the age in imagery that is both poetic and terrifying: darkened skies, falling stars, the heavens themselves trembling. The cosmic disorder reflects the moral and spiritual disorder of a world in rebellion against its Creator.

For centuries, humanity has lived under the illusion of control, governing, building, and boasting. But when the true King returns, creation itself reacts. The sun and moon fade, the stars fall, and the only light that remains is His glory.

When Jesus returns, no one will wonder if it's really Him. His glory will silence every skeptic, and every eye will see Him. This is not merely symbolic language; it points to a real event. The first coming of Christ was marked by humility; He came in weakness, born in a manger. His second coming will be marked by majesty. He will come in clouds, with power and great glory. The world that once rejected Him will see Him enthroned. The same Son of Man who was mocked and crucified will return as Judge and King.

II. The Gathering of the Elect (v. 27)

"And then he will send out the angels and gather his elect from the four winds, from the ends of the earth to the ends of heaven."

After judgment comes restoration. The Son of Man not only reigns, but He also redeems. His angels will gather His people from every direction, demonstrating the completeness of His salvation. This is the moment believers long for, the reunion of all who belong to Christ. Every tear shed in faith, every act of perseverance, every sacrifice for the gospel will find its reward.

The same Savior who scattered us to the ends of the earth for the mission will one day gather us to Himself for eternity. The scope of this promise reminds us that God never loses one of His own. Not one believer is forgotten or left behind. The elect from every nation, tongue, and tribe will be brought home safely.

III. The Lesson of the Fig Tree (vv. 28–29)

"From the fig tree learn its lesson: as soon as its branch becomes tender and puts out its leaves, you know that summer is near. So also, when you see these things taking place, you know that he is near, at the very gates."

The fig tree was a familiar sight to the disciples, a sign of seasonal change. Jesus uses it as a parable for spiritual awareness, just as budding leaves signal the coming of summer, so the signs He described signal His nearness. But notice what He doesn't say: He doesn't tell them to speculate, panic, or predict. He tells them to be discerning and ready.

Jesus doesn't call us to date-set; He calls us to disciple-making. The point of prophecy is not calculation, it's preparation. This balance is essential. The signs remind believers that history is moving toward God's appointed conclusion. Yet our focus is not on predicting the end, but on persevering in the present.

IV. The Certainty of Fulfillment (v. 30)

"Truly, I say to you, this generation will not pass away until all these things take place."

This verse has puzzled many readers. What did Jesus mean by *"this generation"*?

Some understand it as referring to the disciples' own generation, which would indeed witness the destruction of Jerusalem in A.D. 70, the beginning of the fulfillment of these prophecies. Others see it as referring to the generation alive at the time of His return, the people who will witness the completion of all He describes.

Either way, the point remains: *what Jesus says will happen, will happen.* His words are certain. His promises are unstoppable. No prophecy of Jesus has ever failed. The same voice that calmed storms and raised the dead will bring this world's story to its conclusion. The temple fell just as He said it would. History unfolded just as He foretold. And His return will be no different, guaranteed by the truthfulness of the One who cannot lie.

V. The Permanence of His Word (v. 31)

"Heaven and earth will pass away, but my words will not pass away."

Here is one of the most breathtaking claims in all of Scripture. Everything visible, mountains, oceans, galaxies, will fade, but Jesus' words will remain. He speaks not as a prophet repeating divine revelation, but as God Himself declaring it. His authority surpasses creation. The heavens may dissolve, but His Word endures forever.

This statement anchors the believer's hope. In a world where everything feels temporary, God's Word stands permanent. Everything else has an expiration date, but the promises of Christ do not. Every prophecy, every warning, every assurance will come true. When everything else is shaken, the Word of Christ remains unshaken.

VI. Lessons for Us

Be confident, not confused.

The chaos of the world does not mean God has lost control. Every falling star and trembling nation is under His sovereign hand.

Be watchful, not worried.

Jesus didn't tell His disciples to fear the future but to live faithfully in the present.

Be grounded in His Word.

The world changes daily, but the Word of God remains forever. Build your life on what cannot be shaken.

Be hopeful in His return.

For the believer, the end is not destruction—it's restoration. The coming of Christ is the beginning of eternity.

Conclusion

The world as we know it will end. The lights will go out. The heavens will shake. The kingdoms of men will fall. But Jesus' Word will stand. The same Lord who spoke the world into existence will speak it into renewal. For those who belong to Him, this isn't the end; it's the start of everlasting joy.

When the sky grows dark and the nations tremble, lift your eyes because your redemption is drawing near. This is the end of the world as we know it and the beginning of the one we've been waiting for.

Reflection & Response

How does the certainty of Christ's return shape the way you live now?

What areas of your life are built on what is temporary rather than on His unshakable Word?

How can you encourage others to live with confidence, not confusion, about the end times?

It's the End of the World as We Know It – Part 2

Mark 13:32–37

After speaking of cosmic signs and His glorious return, Jesus brings His teaching to a close with one clear command: *"Stay awake."* The emphasis now shifts from what will happen to how believers should live while they wait.

Jesus never told His followers to predict the day of His return; He told them to prepare for it. The disciples had asked *when* these things would be, but Jesus ended by reminding them that only the Father knows the hour. The question, then, isn't *when He will come.* But *will we be ready when He does?*

I. The Mystery of the Timing (v. 32)

"But concerning that day or that hour, no one knows, not even the angels in heaven, nor the Son, but only the Father."

These words correct both presumption and panic. No angel, no prophet, not even the incarnate Son in His earthly humility, knew the precise timing of the end. That knowledge rested solely with the Father.

This statement anchors us in humility. If the Son Himself entrusted the timetable to His Father, how much more should we? The goal of prophecy isn't to satisfy curiosity but to cultivate faithfulness. Speculation has filled libraries and cable channels, but it has never produced holiness. Jesus' words invite trust, not timelines. The future belongs to the Father, and that is enough.

II. The Call to Watchfulness (vv. 33–34)

"Be on guard, keep awake. For you do not know when the time will come. It is like a man going on a journey, when he leaves home and puts his servants in charge, each with his work, and commands the doorkeeper to stay awake."

Here, Jesus turns from mystery to mission. The Master has gone away, but His servants have work to do. Every believer has been assigned a task while the Lord is absent. The danger isn't ignorance, it's indifference. Knowing the Master will return is one thing; living like He will return is another.

Watchfulness doesn't mean staring at the sky; it means staying faithful. The image of the doorkeeper underscores responsibility. His job isn't glamorous but vital: stay awake, stay alert, and be ready to open when the Master comes. So it is with us. Our task is not to predict but to prepare; not to calculate but to cultivate faithfulness.

III. The Uncertainty of His Arrival (vv. 35–36)

"Therefore stay awake—for you do not know when the master of the house will come, in the evening, or at midnight, or when the rooster crows, or in the morning—lest he come suddenly and find you asleep."

Jesus lists the four watches of the night, covering every possible hour. The point is unmistakable: His return will be unexpected. In the ancient world, soldiers stood guard through these same night watches. Sleep on duty wasn't merely careless; it was catastrophic. Likewise, spiritual drowsiness is deadly for the believer.

To "sleep" spiritually means to drift into complacency, to live as though Christ's return were a distant theory rather than an imminent reality. The greatest danger for the church isn't persecution, it's distraction. Satan doesn't need to destroy you if he can keep you comfortable. The antidote to apathy is awareness. Christ could return at any moment, and that reality should shape every decision, every word, every act of obedience.

IV. The Command for All Believers (v. 37)

"And what I say to you I say to all: Stay awake."

Jesus ends this discourse with a single, all-encompassing command. It was not only for Peter, James, John, and Andrew, but for every disciple in every generation. "Stay awake" means to live in constant readiness, cultivating a heart that is alert, prayerful, and steadfast in obedience.

This call transcends time and circumstance. Whether the end comes in our lifetime or a thousand years from now, faithfulness is always the correct response. The Christian life isn't a sprint to predict the finish line; it's a marathon of obedience until the Master returns. The believer who stays awake doesn't waste the waiting. He serves, loves, prays, gives, and endures, knowing that every act of faithfulness is preparation for the King's arrival.

V. Lessons for Today

Stop Speculating—Start Serving.

The question Jesus answers is not *When will He come?* but *What should we do until He comes?*

Stay Alert in a Distracted World.

Busyness and entertainment lull many to spiritual sleep. True watchfulness requires discipline of mind and devotion of heart.

Live Ready, Not Restless.

Readiness is not anxious pacing but faithful labor. The servant at peace is the one found doing his Master's will.

Rest in the Father's Sovereignty.

Since only the Father knows the day and hour, we can rest in His wisdom. The timing of Christ's return is not a problem to solve but a promise to trust.

VI. The Hope Behind the Command

Jesus' final word, *"Stay awake,"* isn't meant to exhaust but to encourage. Watchfulness isn't driven by fear of judgment but by love for the returning King. We're not waiting for the world to end; we're waiting for Jesus to come.

This passage closes the Olivet Discourse not with despair but with hope. The same Christ who will come in power and glory has already come in grace and truth. Until He appears, His people are called to walk in light, bear fruit, and keep their lamps burning.

Conclusion

Jesus' words in Mark 13 draw together warning and comfort. The end will come, but not in panic or confusion for those who belong to Him. He doesn't want sleepy saints but steady servants, men and women who live every day as if it could be the day.

So we stay awake, not out of dread, but out of devotion. The One who left His house will return to it. The Master who gave His servants work will reward their faithfulness. And when that day dawns, all waiting will give way to worship. The end of the world as we know it is not the end for God's people; it's the beginning of forever with Him.

Reflection & Response

Where has comfort or distraction dulled your spiritual alertness?

What "work" has the Master given you to do in this season?

How can you cultivate daily habits that keep your heart awake to His return?

Chapter 14

Three Hearts Toward Jesus
Mark 14:1–11

As the cross draws near, the hearts of those around Jesus are being revealed. Some are hardened in hatred, some are softened in worship, and one is quietly preparing for betrayal. This passage paints a vivid contrast between three hearts toward Jesus—the hateful heart of the religious leaders, the humble heart of Mary, and the hypocritical heart of Judas. The closer Jesus gets to the cross, the clearer it becomes who truly loves Him. Mark invites us not only to observe these hearts but to examine our own.

I. The Hateful Heart – The Plot of the Religious Leaders (vv. 1–2)

"It was now two days before the Passover and the Feast of Unleavened Bread. And the chief priests and the scribes were seeking how to arrest him by stealth and kill him, for they said, 'Not during the feast, lest there be an uproar from the people.'"

The religious leaders had long opposed Jesus, but now their hatred reaches its climax. They wanted Him dead. They plotted in secret, not because they were wise, but because they were afraid, afraid of the people, fearful of losing power, terrified of being exposed. Their hypocrisy is staggering. The very men entrusted with leading God's people in worship are plotting murder during the holiest week of the year.

The Passover was meant to celebrate deliverance from death, and yet here are men plotting death. Theirs is the hateful heart, a heart that resists truth and loves control more than God. It's a reminder that religion without repentance leads not to life but to hypocrisy and hardness. They could celebrate Passover but miss the true Lamb of God standing before them.

II. The Humble Heart – The Devotion of Mary (vv. 3–9)

"And while he was at Bethany in the house of Simon the leper, as he was reclining at table, a woman came with an alabaster flask of ointment of pure nard, very costly, and she broke the flask and poured it over his head."

Mark takes us from the plotting of the priests to the quiet beauty of Bethany. Inside Simon's house, Mary performs one of the most moving acts of worship in all Scripture. She takes a flask of pure nard, worth nearly a year's wages, and breaks it open, pouring it over Jesus. The fragrance fills the room, an act of extravagant devotion that would never be forgotten.

What Mary did in a moment of devotion would be remembered for centuries. Mary's act shows a humble heart—a heart that treasures Jesus above all else. She doesn't care about appearances or cost. She doesn't hold back. She gives everything because she sees Jesus as worthy of everything. This is not reckless emotion; it's reverent love. Her anointing prepares Him for burial, even if she doesn't yet fully understand its significance. While others talk, she acts. While others criticize, she worships.

The disciples, led by Judas, rebuke her: *"Why was the ointment wasted like that?"* But Jesus defends her: *"She has done a beautiful thing to me."* What others call waste, Jesus calls worship. Her devotion becomes the model of discipleship, loving Jesus with unreserved affection and costly obedience.

"Wherever the gospel is proclaimed in the whole world, what she has done will be told in memory of her." And so it is.

III. The Hypocritical Heart – The Betrayal of Judas (vv. 10–11)

"Then Judas Iscariot, who was one of the twelve, went to the chief priests in order to betray him to them. And when they heard it, they were glad and promised to give him money. And he sought an opportunity to betray him."

While Mary's devotion fills the air with fragrance, Judas's heart fills with greed. The contrast could not be sharper. He had walked with Jesus, heard His teaching, seen His miracles, and shared His table. Yet now he sells Him for thirty pieces of silver, the price of a slave.

Judas represents the hypocritical heart, a heart that follows Jesus outwardly but never loves Him inwardly. You can walk with Jesus and still not worship Him. You can serve in ministry and still not love Him.

What began as disappointment with Jesus's mission ends in betrayal of His person. Judas was looking for a Messiah who would conquer Rome, not die on a cross.

When Jesus didn't fit his expectations, his allegiance collapsed. The religious leaders rejoiced, thinking their problem was solved. Judas rejoiced, thinking he'd gained profit. But both were wrong. God was using even their sin to fulfill His plan of redemption. The sovereignty of God weaves even the threads of betrayal into the tapestry of redemption.

IV. Three Hearts Revealed

In these verses, we see humanity's complete response to Jesus Christ:

The hateful heart resists Him.

The humble heart worships Him.

The hypocritical heart betrays Him.

Every person fits into one of these categories. Neutrality is impossible. Mary's act shows us what true discipleship looks like: a heart overflowing with gratitude and love. The priests and Judas show us what it means to reject Him, hearts hardened by pride and greed.

The question isn't which group you admire, it's which heart you possess. This story prepares us for the cross. The plotting, the worship, the betrayal all point toward the sacrifice of the One who is worthy of it all.

V. Lessons for Us

True worship is costly.

Mary's devotion challenges us to give to Jesus not out of convenience but out of commitment.

Religious activity without love is dangerous.

The priests were busy with Passover plans while blind to God's presence.

Sin begins in the heart before it shows in action.

Judas's betrayal didn't start with silver; it began with selfishness.

Christ is worthy of wholehearted devotion.

Every sacrifice made for Him is never wasted.

Conclusion

As Mark's gospel moves toward the cross, these three hearts set the stage. Hatred seeks His death. Hypocrisy plots His betrayal. But humility prepares Him for burial. Mary's fragrant worship lingers long after the scene ends, a living reminder that Jesus is worthy of our best, our first, our all. There will always be critics who say it's too much. But if it's for Jesus, it's never too much. Which heart do you have toward Jesus today?

Reflection & Response

Where has your devotion to Jesus become hesitant or half-hearted?

What would "costly worship" look like in your own life right now?

How can you guard your heart against drifting toward hypocrisy or indifference?

Conspiracy and Communion: Lessons from the Last Supper

Mark 14:12–26

The night before the cross is filled with tension. Shadows lengthen across Jerusalem. The religious leaders are plotting, Judas is scheming, and yet Jesus is preparing a table. Amid conspiracy, Christ offers communion. While the world conspires to destroy Him, He serves a meal that proclaims salvation. Even as men planned His death, Jesus planned our deliverance. This passage shows two simultaneous realities: human treachery and divine sovereignty. Sin is at work, but so is grace.

I. A Meal Prepared by Providence (vv. 12–16)

"And on the first day of Unleavened Bread, when they sacrificed the Passover lamb, his disciples said to him, 'Where will you have us go and prepare for you to eat the Passover?'"

The Passover meal commemorated Israel's redemption from Egypt. Each year, a lamb was slain, and a family gathered to remember God's deliverance. But this Passover would be different. The true Lamb of God was about to be slain, not to deliver from Pharaoh but from sin and death.

Jesus sends two disciples with mysterious instructions: they will meet a man carrying a jar of water who will lead them to a prepared upper room. Everything unfolds exactly as He said. This is no coincidence; it's providence. Even as His enemies plot, Jesus controls every detail. Nothing was random that night. Every direction, every detail, every step was part of God's design. The disciples thought they were preparing a meal for Jesus. In reality, Jesus was preparing a sacrifice for them.

II. A Betrayal Foretold (vv. 17–21)

"And when it was evening, he came with the twelve. And as they were reclining at table and eating, Jesus said, 'Truly, I say to you, one of you will betray me, one who is eating with me.'"

Imagine the silence that fell over that table. The disciples had eaten with Him, traveled with Him, and now they hear the unthinkable: one of them will betray the Master. Each asks, *"Is it I?"* a question that reveals both uncertainty and humility. They knew the weakness of their own hearts. But Jesus knows exactly who it is. *"It is one of the twelve, one who is dipping bread into the dish with me."*

To share a meal was a sign of friendship. Betrayal at the table was the deepest kind of treachery. Judas had been in the inner circle but never in the inner life. He had proximity to Jesus but no purity of heart. Jesus adds a sobering warning: *"The Son of Man goes as it is written of him, but woe to that man by whom the Son of Man is betrayed!"* Here, divine sovereignty and human responsibility meet. Judas's betrayal fulfills Scripture, yet his guilt remains his own. Even in betrayal, God's plan moves forward. Sin is real, but it never frustrates God's purposes.

III. A Covenant Instituted (vv. 22–24)

"And as they were eating, he took bread, and after blessing it broke it and gave it to them, and said, 'Take; this is my

body.' And he took a cup, and when he had given thanks he gave it to them, and they all drank of it. And he said to them, 'This is my blood of the covenant, which is poured out for many.'"

In the middle of betrayal, Jesus gives a new covenant meal. He transforms the Passover into the Lord's Supper, shifting the focus from Israel's deliverance from Egypt to humanity's deliverance from sin. The bread represents His body, soon to be broken. The cup represents His blood, poured out for many. Together, they proclaim the heart of the gospel, substitutionary sacrifice.

Jesus didn't just give them symbols; He gave them Himself. When He says *"for many,"* He speaks of a global redemption, a sacrifice sufficient for all who will believe. The disciples didn't yet understand the cross, but they would. Every time they broke bread together after the resurrection, they would remember that night, the calm before the storm, the grace before the agony.

IV. A Promise of Victory (v. 25)

"Truly, I say to you, I will not drink again of the fruit of the vine until that day when I drink it new in the kingdom of God."

Even as He speaks of suffering, Jesus points to triumph. The cross will not be the end of the story. There will be another meal, another cup, in the kingdom of God. This is the hope embedded in the Lord's Supper. Every time we gather at the table, we look backward to the cross and forward to the coming kingdom.

Every communion service proclaims two truths: He died for us, and He's coming again for us. Jesus is about to leave the table for Gethsemane, yet His eyes are set on glory. The promise of future fellowship sustains Him through present pain.

V. A Hymn of Faith (v. 26)

"And when they had sung a hymn, they went out to the Mount of Olives."

Before facing arrest, trial, and crucifixion, Jesus sings. The hymn they sang was likely the Hallel, Psalms 115–118, praising God for His steadfast love and salvation. Think of it: the Savior of the world sings about deliverance hours before being delivered into death.

Only Jesus could sing about salvation while walking toward sacrifice. This final act before Gethsemane shows us that worship isn't dependent on circumstances. True worship flows from trust in the Father's will. When we sing at the Lord's table, we join the same song, praising the One who faced betrayal and the cross with a hymn on His lips.

VI. Lessons from the Table

God's sovereignty is unshaken by sin.

Human conspiracy never overrides divine control. Every event of this night moved according to plan.

Christ's love extends to sinners.

Judas shared the bread; Peter would soon deny Him, yet Jesus still served them all.

Worship and remembrance go hand in hand.

The Lord's Supper is not ritual but relationship, remembering what He has done and rejoicing that He will come again.

Grace shines brightest against the backdrop of evil.

The darker the night, the clearer the light of Christ's mercy appears.

Conclusion

At the Last Supper, two stories intertwine, one of human betrayal, the other of divine blessing. Conspiracy and communion meet in the exact moment, and grace triumphs over sin. While Judas plots, Jesus prays. While men prepare to arrest Him, He prepares to redeem them.

The table reminds us that our sin was great, but His grace is greater. Every time we come to the Lord's table, we declare that truth again, that what began as a night of treachery became the dawn of salvation. The Passover pointed to the cross; the cross points to eternity. And one day, the same Jesus who sang that night will welcome us to a new table in His kingdom.

Reflection & Response

When you come to the Lord's table, what do you remember most—your sin or His grace?

How does the Lord's Supper strengthen your confidence in God's providence and control?

What might it look like to worship like Jesus—singing even in the face of suffering?

The Fall and Rise of Peter and the Disciples

Mark 14:27–31; 66–72

The cross is coming into view. The Passover meal is finished, the hymn has been sung, and Jesus and His disciples are on their way to the Mount of Olives. The tone shifts from the quiet of the upper room to the weight of the coming storm.

In this passage, we see failure and faithfulness colliding, the weakness of man and the unwavering grace of Christ. Peter and the disciples will fall, but Jesus already promises their rise. The story of Peter's failure is not about how far a man can fall; it's about how far grace will go to restore him.

I. The Fall Foretold (vv. 27–31)

"And Jesus said to them, 'You will all fall away, for it is written, "I will strike the shepherd, and the sheep will be scattered." But after I am raised up, I will go before you to Galilee.'"

Jesus doesn't speak this as a warning to shame them but as a prophecy to strengthen them. He quotes Zechariah 13:7, showing that even their failure is woven into God's sovereign plan. He says plainly: *"You will all fall away."* Not one of them would stand firm. But immediately, He gives a promise: *"After I am raised up, I will go before you to Galilee."*

The Shepherd will be struck, but He will rise and gather His scattered sheep. The same lips that predict their failure also proclaim their forgiveness. Before Peter ever failed, Jesus had already planned his restoration. Peter, unwilling to accept this, speaks up: *"Even though they all fall away, I will not."* He doesn't just distance himself from the world; he distances himself from the other disciples. It's pride disguised as loyalty.

Jesus answers with precision: *"Truly, I tell you, this very night, before the rooster crows twice, you will deny me three times."* Still, Peter insists, *"If I must die with you, I will not deny you."* And all the others join in. They mean it, but they don't yet know their weakness. This is the fall foretold. Jesus knows their limits, yet He loves them still. He doesn't retract His mission or reject His men. He walks forward knowing they will fail—and that His resurrection will restore them.

II. The Fall Fulfilled (vv. 66–72)

Between verse 31 and verse 66 lies the darkest night in human history. Jesus is arrested, tried, mocked, and beaten. The disciples scatter, and Peter follows at a distance.

"And as Peter was below in the courtyard, one of the servant girls of the high priest came, and seeing Peter warming himself, she looked at him and said, 'You also were with the Nazarene, Jesus.' But he denied it."

Three denials unfold, each one deeper than the last. A servant girl's question becomes a crowd's accusation. And each time, Peter insists he doesn't know the man. The last denial cuts deepest: *"He began to invoke a curse on himself and to swear, 'I do not know this man of whom you speak.'"* Peter, the one who swore allegiance, swears ignorance. The sound of his denial echoes into the night, and then, suddenly, the rooster crows.

The rooster's crow wasn't condemnation, it was conviction. It was grace calling Peter back to Jesus. Luke tells us that Jesus turned and looked at Peter. In that moment, their eyes met: the Savior bound in chains, the disciple bound in guilt. And Peter remembered His words. He went out and wept bitterly.

That's the moment of breaking, the sound of repentance. This is not the end of Peter's story. It's the beginning of his restoration. We all know that courtyard. We've all denied Christ, not necessarily with words, but with silence, compromise, or cowardice. Yet the same grace that found Peter finds us. The rooster's crow is not the final word; the resurrection is.

III. The Rise Finished (v. 28; 16:7)

We can't end Peter's story in the courtyard, because Jesus didn't. The promise in verse 28 must be fulfilled: *"After I am raised up, I will go before you to Galilee."* When the angel greets the women at the empty tomb in Mark 16:7, his words are intentional: *"Go, tell his disciples and Peter that he is going before you to Galilee."*

Did you catch that? *"And Peter."* The only disciple mentioned by name, the one who fell hardest, the one who denied Him most loudly, is singled out for grace. Jesus had not forgotten him. The Shepherd had risen and was gathering His sheep again. Grace always puts your name in the sentence where you least deserve it.

Galilee becomes the place of restoration. It's where Peter will see Jesus again, not in condemnation but in commission. The one who denied Christ will be the one who declares Him at Pentecost. The one who fell asleep in fear will stand up in faith. Peter's failure was real, but it wasn't final. This is the rise finished not because Peter stood tall, but because Jesus stood in his place. The gospel doesn't erase our failures; it redeems them. The same Lord who predicted Peter's fall prepared his future.

IV. Lessons from Peter's Story

Failure is never the end for those held by grace.

Jesus knew Peter's weakness and chose him anyway. Our sin may surprise us, but it never surprises Him.

Conviction is grace at work.

The rooster's crow was mercy calling Peter back, not shame pushing him away.

Restoration begins where pride dies.

Peter's pride said, "I will never fall." His tears said, "I can't stand without You."

Christ finishes what we fail to start.

The Shepherd who was struck has gathered His sheep again and still goes before us.

Conclusion

The story of Peter and the disciples is a story of grace that refuses to let go. They fell, but Jesus rose.

Their faith failed, but His faithfulness never wavered. Peter's denial wasn't the end of his discipleship; it was the doorway to deeper dependence. The man who once said, *"I will not fall,"* would one day say, *"Humble yourselves under the mighty hand of God."*

The same voice that told Peter, 'You will fall,' also told him, 'You will be restored.' We all have moments of compromise and regret. But the good news is that grace meets us there. The one who looked at Peter looks at us with the same mercy, inviting us to rise again in His strength. So hear this promise again: *"After I am raised up, I will go before you."*

That's not just for Galilee, it's for you.

Reflection & Response

How has God used failure to deepen your dependence on His grace?

What "rooster's crow" moments has He used to awaken your heart?

How does Peter's restoration remind you that grace always has the last word?

The Agony in Gethsemane
Mark 14:32–42

The shadow of the cross has fallen. The Passover meal is over, Judas has departed, and Jesus now leads His disciples to a place called Gethsemane—a familiar grove on the Mount of Olives where He often went to pray. But this time will be different. This night, the weight of redemption will press upon Him like the heavy stone that crushed the olives to release their oil. In that garden, Jesus experienced agony unlike any other.

Gethsemane was the place where Jesus felt the full weight of bearing the sin of the world, and He bore it alone. This passage unfolds the most significant struggle ever faced by a human soul, and through it, we see the depth of Christ's obedience and the cost of our salvation.

I. Jesus' Agony in Prayer (vv. 32–36)

"And they went to a place called Gethsemane. And he said to his disciples, 'Sit here while I pray.' And he took with him Peter and James and John, and began to be greatly distressed and troubled. And he said to them, 'My soul is very sorrowful, even to death. Remain here and watch.'"

Jesus enters Gethsemane not as a stoic Savior, but as a suffering Son. The language Mark uses — *"greatly distressed and troubled"* — speaks of deep anguish. He tells His disciples, *"My soul is very sorrowful, even to death."* In this moment, Jesus stands at the edge of the abyss. The eternal plan of redemption is about to be accomplished, but it will cost Him the Father's fellowship and His very life.

He moves a little farther into the garden and falls to the ground. The weight of the cup, the wrath of God for sin, presses upon Him. *"Abba, Father, all things are possible for you. Remove this cup from me. Yet not what I will, but what you will."* This is not rebellion but reverence.

Jesus prays as a Son who loves His Father, trusting His goodness even in sorrow.

The cup wasn't merely physical suffering. It was divine judgment, the full outpouring of God's wrath against sin. Jesus would drink it down to the dregs so we could be spared. In that cry— *"Abba, Father"*—we see both intimacy and anguish. He knows all things are possible for the Father, yet He submits completely to His will. Obedience in suffering is the truest test of love. The garden reminds us that redemption wasn't cold calculation; it was costly compassion.

II. Jesus' Agony in Instruction (vv. 37–39)

"And he came and found them sleeping, and said to Peter, 'Simon, are you asleep? Could you not watch one hour? Watch and pray that you may not enter into temptation. The spirit indeed is willing, but the flesh is weak.'"

Three times Jesus prays. Three times the disciple's sleep. The same men who swore allegiance just hours earlier now drift into weariness. Their indifference compounds Jesus' grief. He longed for their prayers, but they could not stay awake. Still, He doesn't lash out. He instructs them.

Jesus doesn't scold them as soldiers who failed a mission; He warns them as a Shepherd who loves His sheep. His command is clear: *"Watch and pray."* Prayer is the only way to resist temptation, yet they sleep through their opportunity for strength.

Peter especially needed that warning. Within hours, his confidence would collapse under the pressure of fear. Had he prayed when Jesus told him to, he might have stood when temptation came. The disciples' failure reveals a truth about us all: our good intentions are not enough. The spirit is willing, but the flesh is weak. Without dependence on God, even the strongest believer will fall.

Prayer doesn't make us strong in ourselves; it keeps us dependent on the One who is strong. Jesus returns to prayer again, repeating the exact words, submitting once more to the Father's will. In agony, He teaches us what surrender looks like: honest lament, humble trust, and holy obedience.

III. Jesus' Agony in Victory (vv. 40–42)

"And again he came and found them sleeping, for their eyes were very heavy, and they did not know what to answer him. And he came the third time and said to them, 'Are you still sleeping and taking your rest? It is enough; the hour has come. The Son of Man is betrayed into the hands of sinners. Rise, let us be going; see, my betrayer is at hand.'"

After the third prayer, the struggle ends, not because the suffering is gone, but because submission is complete. Jesus rises from the ground, resolved. The trembling is replaced with triumph. Jesus didn't leave Gethsemane defeated; He left determined. Prayer didn't remove the cup; it prepared Him to drink it.

When He says, *"It is enough; the hour has come,"* it signals the turning point. What was once dreaded as "the hour" of suffering is now embraced as the hour of salvation. The sleeping disciples symbolize humanity's helplessness. Jesus alone stays awake, stands firm, and walks forward into the darkness that we might live in the light.

Even His words — *"Rise, let us be going"* — show that Gethsemane is not just a place of agony but of victory. The battle was won before the arrest ever happened. Through prayer and submission, Jesus conquers where Adam fell. In Eden, humanity chose its will over God's; in Gethsemane, Jesus chose God's will over His own. The first garden brought death; this garden brings life.

IV. Lessons from Gethsemane

The path of obedience often passes through agony.

God's will is not always easy, but it is always good.

Prayer prepares the heart for trial.

Jesus faced the cross with courage because He faced the Father in prayer.

Dependence, not determination, sustains discipleship.

The disciples' sleep shows the weakness of self-confidence; Jesus' strength shows the power of surrender.

Victory comes through submission.

True strength is not in avoiding the cup but in accepting it for God's glory.

Conclusion

Gethsemane was not a failure of faith but the fulfillment of love. Jesus embraced the Father's will so that sinners might be redeemed. As He rose to meet His betrayer, He did so with the calm of one who had already conquered. The agony of the garden was victory before the cross.

If not for Gethsemane, there would be no Golgotha. If not for Jesus' prayer, there would be no pardon. The next time you walk through your own garden of sorrow, remember this: Jesus has already prayed the hardest prayer, faced the deepest pain, and triumphed through perfect obedience. When your heart says, *"Father, remove this cup,"* grace helps you finish the sentence: *"Yet not my will, but Yours be done."*

Reflection & Response

What does Jesus' prayer in Gethsemane teach you about obedience in suffering?

How can prayer become your first response, not your last resort, in times of testing?

In what area of your life is God calling you to say, "Not my will, but Yours be done"?

The Kiss of Betrayal

Mark 14:43–52

Betrayal hurts most when it comes from someone close. It's one thing to be opposed by an enemy; it's another to be betrayed by a friend. Jesus has just finished praying in Gethsemane. The disciples are weary, and the hour of His suffering has arrived. Into the stillness of the night comes the sound of footsteps, torches, and voices.

This passage teaches us that Jesus was betrayed, misunderstood, and abandoned so that sinners like us could be redeemed. As we walk through these verses, we see three movements, each exposing human sin and revealing divine grace.

I. Jesus Is Betrayed (vv. 43–46)

"And immediately, while he was still speaking, Judas came, one of the twelve, and with him a crowd with swords and clubs, from the chief priests and the scribes and the elders. Now the betrayer had given them a sign, saying, 'The one I will kiss is the man. Seize him and lead him away under guard.' And when he came, he went up to him at once and said, 'Rabbi!' And he kissed him. And they laid hands on him and seized him."

Mark emphasizes the word *immediately*. There's no delay between Jesus' submission to the Father's will and the arrival of His betrayer. The calm of prayer gives way to the chaos of betrayal. Judas comes with a crowd armed with swords and clubs, a small army to arrest a teacher who never resisted anyone. It's a picture of human fear trying to overpower divine peace.

But the greatest sting is not in the crowd, it's in the kiss. In the ancient world, a kiss was a greeting of affection and respect. For Judas to use that gesture to mark Jesus for arrest was an act of calculated deceit. Judas disguised hatred with a symbol of love. Jesus allows the kiss. He does not flinch or pull away. He lets betrayal run its course, not because He is powerless, but because He is purposeful. This is part of the Father's plan.

When we feel betrayed by friends, family, or even fellow believers, we remember that Jesus knows that pain. He endured the sting of disloyalty to redeem disloyal hearts like ours. Judas' kiss brings confusion and sorrow, but it does not derail God's purpose. The betrayal of Jesus becomes the very means of our salvation.

II. Jesus Is Misunderstood (vv. 47–49)

"But one of those who stood by drew his sword and struck the servant of the high priest and cut off his ear. And Jesus said to them, 'Have you come out as against a robber, with swords and clubs to capture me? Day after day I was with you in the temple teaching, and you did not seize me. But let the Scriptures be fulfilled.'"

Peter, ever impulsive, acts out of fear and zeal. John's gospel tells us he's the one who swung the sword. In one moment, he goes from sleeping in prayer to striking in panic. Peter misunderstands what kind of kingdom Jesus came to bring. The cross, not the sword, will win this battle. The crowd misunderstands, too. They come armed for war as if arresting a criminal, when in fact they're seizing the Prince of Peace. Their fear exposes their blindness.

And yet, Jesus doesn't resist. He asks, *"Have you come out as against a robber?"* His calm dignity in that moment exposes their folly. He reminds them, *"Day after day I was with you in the temple."* He was never hiding; their hostility was. Then he adds the phrase that has anchored every event of this chapter: *"But let the Scriptures be fulfilled."* Jesus' life is not spiraling out of control. The betrayal, the sword, the arrest, all of it unfolds according to divine design.

Heaven never misunderstands Jesus. Even when the world doesn't get it, the Father does. That's a comfort to every believer who's ever been misjudged or misrepresented. When others don't see your heart or misread your motives, remember, Jesus was misunderstood, too. He endured it without bitterness, trusting the Father to vindicate Him.

III. Jesus Is Abandoned (vv. 50–52)

"And they all left him and fled. And a young man followed him, with nothing but a linen cloth about his body. And they seized him, but he left the linen cloth and ran away naked."

With these verses, Mark captures the complete loneliness of Jesus' suffering. The disciples scatter. The "young man" (perhaps Mark himself) flees in shame. The detail of the linen cloth underscores vulnerability; everyone is exposed, except the One who will soon be stripped to bear our sin.

In the garden, everyone ran, but Jesus stood. Everyone was faithless, but Jesus was faithful. Jesus knew this would happen. Earlier, He told them, *"You will all fall away."* Yet even in their failure, He promised restoration: *"After I am raised, I will go before you."* That's grace. The same Savior who stands firm while others flee is the One who will welcome them back when they return.

The lonely image of Jesus standing in the garden while His followers disappear into the darkness foreshadows the isolation of the cross. Abandoned, but not defeated; forsaken, but never faithless. Jesus was betrayed by a friend, misunderstood by the crowd, and abandoned by His disciples, but He did it all to bring us near to God.

We sometimes imagine that if we had been there, we would have stayed. But the truth is, we would have fled, too. The good news is that Jesus endured abandonment so that the Father would never abandon us.

IV. Lessons from the Garden

Betrayal cannot break God's plan.

Judas's kiss accomplished what God had already decreed. Evil may strike, but grace always prevails.

Zeal without understanding leads to harm.

Peter's sword reminds us that passion must be guided by truth.

Faithfulness stands when fear scatters.

The disciples ran, but Jesus remained. He is the steadfast Savior we could never be.

When misunderstood or betrayed, trust the Father's plan.

Jesus faced deceit and desertion with calm submission. So can we.

Conclusion

The story of Gethsemane ends not with victory in human terms but with the quiet triumph of obedience.

Jesus stands alone, yet He stands secure in the Father's will. He was betrayed with a kiss so that we could be embraced by grace. He was misunderstood so that we could be known completely. He was abandoned so that we could be accepted forever.

The kiss of betrayal became the doorway of redemption. As the torches fade and the crowd leads Him away, Jesus walks the path none of us could walk. And because He did, no believer will ever walk alone again.

Reflection & Response

How has Jesus' endurance through betrayal strengthened your trust in His grace?

In what ways have you misunderstood His will or resisted His plan?

How does knowing that Jesus stood firm when others fled shape the way you follow Him today?

Guilty as Charged: Truth on Trial

Mark 14:53–65

The courtroom is one of the most sobering places on earth. It's where truth is tested, motives are examined, and justice is rendered. In Mark 14, the Son of God stands in such a room—not as the judge, but as the accused.

After His arrest in Gethsemane, Jesus is led before the Sanhedrin, the highest religious council in Israel.

This was not a fair trial—it was a setup. The verdict was predetermined. Truth itself was on trial.

The innocent One is condemned so the guilty can be declared righteous. That's the gospel in a courtroom.

We'll see three movements in this passage: Jesus' innocence confirmed, His identity declared, and His condemnation endured—all so that sinners could go free.

I. Innocence Confirmed (vv. 55–61)

"Now the chief priests and the whole council were seeking testimony against Jesus to put him to death, but they found none. For many bore false witness against him, but their testimony did not agree."

The Sanhedrin wasn't searching for truth—they were searching for justification to execute Jesus. They wanted evidence, not of guilt, but of control.

Mark highlights their desperation. Witness after witness comes forward, but their stories don't line up. The truth refuses to cooperate with their lies.

It's like trying to fry an egg in a Teflon pan—nothing sticks.

No charge will hold. Their accusations slide off the stainless integrity of the Son of God. Even their fabricated claim—that Jesus would destroy the temple and rebuild it in three days—was twisted and misunderstood.

"Yet even about this their testimony did not agree."

Here is the irony: they can't find evidence to condemn Him because there isn't any. The spotless Lamb stands before sinful men, silent and pure.

And when the high priest presses Him—*"Have you no answer to make?"*—Jesus remains silent. He fulfills Isaiah 53:7: *"He was oppressed and afflicted, yet He opened not His mouth."*

This silence is not weakness; it's wisdom. The One who could have defended Himself with a word chooses restraint for the sake of redemption. Jesus' silence shouts the loudest truth of all, that He came not to win an argument, but to secure our salvation.

The court that should have upheld justice instead exposes its corruption. The Innocent One stands quietly, allowing injustice to play out, so that God's greater justice might be accomplished at the cross.

II. Guilty as Charged (vv. 61b–62)

"Again the high priest asked him, 'Are you the Christ, the Son of the Blessed?' And Jesus said, 'I am, and you will see the Son of Man seated at the right hand of Power, and coming with the clouds of heaven.'"

Finally, the silence breaks, not to defend himself, but to declare the truth. This is the pivotal moment of the trial. The high priest's question pierces to the heart of Jesus' identity: *"Are you the Christ, the Son of the Blessed?"*

And Jesus answers with divine clarity: *"I am."* Those two words echo through Scripture. They are the very name of God revealed to Moses in Exodus 3:14: *"I AM*

WHO I AM." In that courtroom, Jesus affirms that He is the Messiah, the eternal Son of God, the rightful King of heaven and earth. Then He adds, *"You will see the Son of Man seated at the right hand of Power, and coming with the clouds of heaven."* He quotes Daniel 7:13-14, a prophecy describing the Son of Man receiving everlasting dominion. The One standing in chains will soon sit in glory.

They thought they were judging Him, but one day He will judge them. This is the great reversal of the gospel. The world puts truth on trial, but truth will have the final word. The One condemned by men will one day condemn sin and death forever. By claiming His identity, Jesus seals His own earthly fate. The high priest tears his robe in outrage and declares, *"You have heard his blasphemy!"* But in tearing his robe, he unknowingly tears open the veil of God's redemptive plan. Jesus stands *guilty as charged*—not because He sinned, but because He claimed deity. And in that claim, He secured the salvation of all who would believe.

III. Unjustly Condemned (vv. 63–65)

"And they all condemned him as deserving death. And some began to spit on him and to cover his face and to strike him, saying to him, 'Prophesy!' And the guards received him with blows."

The trial ends in mockery and violence. The judges become the criminals, and justice is trampled underfoot. They spit on the very face of God. They strike Him, blindfold Him, and demand that He identify His attackers. The irony drips from every word; they mock Him as a false prophet even as they fulfill the prophecies of His suffering.

Every blow that landed on His face was another stamp on our pardon. What looks like defeat is actually the fulfillment of divine purpose. The Innocent One is condemned so the guilty might be declared righteous. The courtroom of heaven renders its verdict at the cross: guilty, on Jesus, not us. He bears the sentence we deserve, satisfying God's justice once and for all. The Sanhedrin's injustice becomes the stage for God's most incredible display of mercy. The trial was rigged, but redemption was real.

IV. Lessons from the Trial

Truth cannot be silenced.

The world may twist or suppress it, but Jesus' identity stands unshaken.

God's plan uses even injustice for His glory.

Human courts condemned Him, but divine justice was being accomplished.

Jesus' silence was not defeat—it was substitution.

He took our place in the dock, bearing the accusations of sinners so we could be free.

Our hope rests in His verdict.

Because Jesus was condemned, believers are now declared righteous before God.

Conclusion

In the courtroom of the Sanhedrin, truth was twisted, justice was mocked, and innocence was condemned. Yet through that injustice, salvation was secured. Jesus was found guilty so that we could be forgiven. He stood silent so that our voices could sing of mercy. He was condemned by men so that God could accept us.

At the cross, the gavel fell, not on the guilty, but on the innocent Lamb who bore our sin. When you face moments where truth seems silenced or injustice seems to win, remember this: God's purposes are never thwarted. The Judge of all the earth always does what is right. And one day, the same Jesus who stood accused will return, not as the defendant, but as the Righteous Judge.

Reflection & Response

What does Jesus' silence before His accusers teach you about trusting God's justice?

How does this trial deepen your gratitude for the gospel?

In what ways might you be tempted to remain silent when truth is on trial today?

Chapter 15

Justice Denied: A Scandalous Gospel

Mark 15:1–15

Few moments in Scripture reveal the corruption of human justice more clearly than Jesus' trial before Pilate. Here, the perfectly righteous Son of God stands accused, silent, and condemned by men who know the truth but refuse to uphold it.

Mark 15 shows us a courtroom scene dripping with irony: the innocent is condemned, the guilty is freed, and justice is denied so grace can be displayed. This is the most scandalous miscarriage of justice in history, and the most glorious display of mercy.

I. A Scandalous Act (vv. 1–5)

"And as soon as it was morning, the chief priests held a consultation with the elders and scribes and the whole council. And they bound Jesus and led him away and delivered him over to Pilate."

The Sanhedrin had already decided Jesus' fate. They just needed Rome to rubber-stamp the execution. Pilate, the governor, represents worldly power, cold, political, self-preserving. The accusations fly: sedition, rebellion, blasphemy. Jesus, the true King, stands before a petty official of Caesar's empire.

"And Pilate asked him, 'Are you the King of the Jews?' And he answered him, 'You have said so.'" Jesus does not defend Himself. His silence is striking. Mark says, *"Pilate was amazed."* The calm of Christ exposes the chaos of human pride. Pilate was used to men begging for their lives. Jesus stood before him, not as a victim, but as a victor. Every court needs evidence. Every verdict demands proof. Yet here, the only proof is innocence, and still the Judge of all the earth is treated as a criminal.

II. A Scandalous Heart (vv. 6–10)

"Now at the feast he used to release for them one prisoner for whom they asked. And among the rebels in prison, who had committed murder in the insurrection, there was a man called Barabbas."

Mark introduces us to Barabbas, a violent rebel whose very name means "son of the father." The irony couldn't be more apparent: the false son goes free while the true Son of the Father is condemned. Pilate sees an opportunity. Maybe if he offers this notorious criminal, the people will choose Jesus. But the crowd is no longer thinking for themselves; the religious leaders have stirred them up.

"The chief priests stirred up the crowd to have him release for them Barabbas instead." Why such hatred? Verse 10 tells us: *"For he perceived that it was out of envy that the chief priests had delivered him up."* Envy begins as comparison, grows into resentment, and ends in destruction.

Their hearts are on trial as much as their hands. The problem isn't lack of evidence; it's lack of humility. They can't stand a Messiah who threatens their authority, so they choose a murderer over the Savior. In doing so, they expose the scandal of the human heart: given a choice between Jesus and sin, we often choose sin.

III. A Scandalous Substitution (vv. 11–15)

"And Pilate, wishing to satisfy the crowd, released for them Barabbas, and having scourged Jesus, he delivered him to be crucified."

This is the climax of the injustice. Pilate knows Jesus is innocent; Luke records him saying it three times: *"I find no guilt in this man."* Yet political pressure outweighs moral courage. Pilate washed his hands, but he couldn't cleanse his heart.

The crowd shouts for blood. Pilate caves. Jesus is scourged, a brutal beating that leaves Him near death. Barabbas walks free, bewildered perhaps, while Jesus bears the punishment reserved for him. This is substitution in its most vivid form: the innocent condemned, the guilty released.

Barabbas represents every sinner. We are the ones guilty of rebellion, deserving death; we are Barabbas, yet Jesus takes our place. This is where injustice becomes redemption. The scandal of the cross is that the Judge dies for the criminal.

IV. A Scandalous Gospel

The cross exposes both the depravity of man and the depth of God's mercy. Human justice failed spectacularly that day, but divine justice was satisfied eternally. At the cross, compassion and truth met, righteousness and peace kissed each other. (Psalm 85:10)

What looks like chaos is actually all according to the divine decree. Every lie, every lash, every cry of "Crucify Him!" plays a part in God's redemptive plan. Barabbas's release isn't just a historical footnote; it's a theological portrait. He walks out of prison because Jesus takes his place. We, too, walk free because Christ bore our sins.

"He was pierced for our transgressions, crushed for our iniquities; the punishment that brought us peace was upon Him, and by His wounds we are healed." (Isaiah 53:5)

The crowd's injustice became heaven's instrument of grace. That's the scandal of the gospel: the innocent condemned so the guilty can be justified.

V. Lessons from the Trial

Human justice is limited, but divine justice is perfect.

Earthly courts fail; God's court never does.

Envy and fear can close our eyes to truth.

The priests' jealousy and Pilate's cowardice mirror the danger of a heart that values reputation over righteousness.

Substitution is the heart of salvation.

Jesus didn't die as a martyr; He died as our substitute.

The gospel is both scandalous and sufficient.

Scandalous because grace offends the proud; sufficient because it saves the humble.

Conclusion

On the surface, Mark 15:1–15 reads like the record of a corrupt trial. But beneath the injustice is the justice of God. Jesus is silent before His accusers so He can speak for us before the Father. He is condemned so that we can be acquitted. He is scourged so we can be healed. He is delivered over so we can be delivered out.

What the crowd meant for evil, God meant for good—the salvation of many souls. Barabbas went free that day, but the real wonder is that we did too. The innocent died in the place of the guilty, and that is the scandalous beauty of the gospel.

Reflection & Response

How does Barabbas's freedom help you understand substitutionary atonement?

What areas of your heart are prone to envy or fear that distort truth?

How can remembering Christ's unjust trial give you confidence when you face injustice?

You Shall Bruise His Heel, Part 1

Mark 15:16–32

Genesis 3:15 foretold it from the beginning: *"He shall bruise your head, and you shall bruise his heel."* In Mark 15, we see that prophecy fulfilled. The serpent strikes, and the heel of the Son of God is bruised.

Here, Jesus bears the full weight of the curse. The One who spoke the world into being is mocked, beaten, and crucified. His suffering is not accidental—it is intentional, redemptive, and foretold.

In the garden, Adam wore the crown of blessing and lost it through sin. On the cross, Jesus wore the crown of thorns and restored what Adam lost. As we walk through this passage, we witness the Savior wearing, feeling, and being treated as the curse for us.

I. Jesus Wore the Curse (vv. 16–20)

"And the soldiers led him away inside the palace (that is, the governor's headquarters), and they called together the whole battalion. And they clothed him in a purple cloak, and twisting together a crown of thorns, they put it on him."

The Roman soldiers mock Jesus' kingship. They dress Him in purple, the color of royalty, and place a crown on His head, but it's a crown of thorns. Every detail drips with irony.

The thorns recall Genesis 3:18, where the ground was cursed to bring forth "thorns and thistles." Now those very thorns are pressed into the brow of the Creator. He wears the symbol of the curse so He can remove its sting from us. That image captures the tenderness of redemption. The Son of God allows the curse to rest on His head so sinners can be crowned with mercy.

The soldiers bow before Him in mockery: *"Hail, King of the Jews!"* They strike Him and spit on Him. Their laughter fills the air, but heaven sees glory in the moment. This is the King who conquers not by force but by sacrifice. They meant to humiliate Him, but even their mockery fulfilled prophecy. Every insult became an instrument in God's redemptive plan. When they strip off the purple robe, they reveal His torn flesh. The King of glory stands humiliated, wearing the curse for His people.

II. Jesus Felt the Curse (vv. 21–25)

"And they compelled a passerby, Simon of Cyrene, who was coming in from the country, the father of Alexander and Rufus, to carry his cross."

The crossbeam, likely weighing over a hundred pounds, is laid upon Jesus' shoulders. But His body, already weakened by scourging, collapses under the weight. The soldiers grab a man from the crowd, Simon of Cyrene, to carry it for Him.

Mark alone identifies Simon as "the father of Alexander and Rufus," a detail that points to their later presence in the early church (Romans 16:13). The man pressed into service that day may have gone home a believer, his sons following Christ after him.

They led Jesus to *Golgotha*, "the Place of a Skull." There, they offer Him wine mixed with myrrh, a narcotic meant to dull pain, but He refuses it. Jesus will feel the curse fully. He will drink the cup of wrath unmixed. He wasn't looking for a way to escape pain; He was embracing the will of His Father.

The soldiers drive nails into His hands and feet. Each strike echoes through creation. The One who flung stars into space is now fastened to wood by human hands. They lift Him up, fulfilling His own words: *"When I am lifted up, I will draw all people to Myself."* (John 12:32)

The inscription above His head reads: *"The King of the Jews."* What they intend as mockery, God declares as truth. Jesus feels the curse in His body, but beyond the pain is a more profound agony, the holy One being treated as unholy, the righteous One bearing sin.

III. Jesus Was Treated as a Curse (vv. 26–32)

"And with him they crucified two robbers, one on his right and one on his left."

The innocent Savior hangs between two guilty men. Even here, prophecy is fulfilled: *"He was numbered with the transgressors."* (Isaiah 53:12) The crowd passes by, wagging their heads, echoing Satan's temptation: *"Save yourself and come down from the cross!"* The chief priests and scribes mock Him: *"He saved others; He cannot save himself."*

Love held Him there. The nails didn't keep Him on the cross—grace did. They taunt Him: *"Let the Christ, the King of Israel, come down now from the cross that we may see and believe."* But had He come down, there would be no salvation to believe in. Their words fulfill Psalm 22:7-8: *"All who see me mock me; they make mouths at me; they wag their heads; 'He trusts in the Lord; let Him deliver Him.'"*

Even those crucified with Him join in the scorn. The Son of God hangs alone, surrounded by sinners He came to save. At this moment, the serpent's strike seems complete. The heel of the Savior is bruised, bloodied, pierced, and nailed. Yet even in apparent defeat, the victory is unfolding.

They thought the cross was a sign of weakness, but it was the weapon of redemption. Through mockery, pain, and rejection, Jesus fulfills the Father's will. The curse is not just worn and felt; it is entirely borne.

IV. Lessons from the Cross

Jesus took the curse we deserved.

Every thorn, every nail, every insult reminds us that sin's price was paid in full.

Humility is the way of Christ.

The One who wore a crown of thorns calls us to carry our own cross with joy.

The curse became our blessing.

Galatians 3:13 says, *"Christ redeemed us from the curse of the law by becoming a curse for us."*

What looked like defeat was divine design.

The bruised heel would soon crush the serpent's head.

Conclusion

At Golgotha, justice met mercy and wrath met grace. The bruised heel of Christ becomes the means by which the serpent is crushed and sinners are set free. He wore the curse, felt the curse, and was treated as the curse so that we could wear His righteousness.

Every thorn, every mockery, every strike of the hammer was not a tragedy; it was triumph. As you meditate on the cross, remember: the bruised heel was not the end of the story. The One who was cursed would rise to bless, and the serpent who struck would soon be silenced forever.

Reflection & Response

What part of Jesus' suffering most reminds you of the cost of redemption?

How does seeing Christ bear the curse deepen your gratitude and humility?

What does it mean for you personally that "the bruised heel crushed the serpent's head"?

You Shall Bruise His Heel – Part 2

Mark 15:33–41

The cross is both the darkest and the brightest moment in human history. In it, we see the full weight of sin and the full wonder of grace. Genesis 3:15 foretold that the serpent would bruise the heel of the promised Seed, but the bruising would not be the end.

In this section of Mark, Jesus suffers the final blows of the curse. The sky darkens, the Son cries out, and the Savior gives His life. Yet even in death, the glory of God shines through. The serpent struck His heel, but the heel that was bruised would soon crush the serpent's head. As we witness these sacred moments, we'll see how Christ's death opens the way for sinners to live.

I. From Darkness to Death (vv. 33–37)

"And when the sixth hour had come, there was darkness over the whole land until the ninth hour."

From noon until three o'clock, the world goes dark. Creation itself seems to shudder as the Creator bears judgment for sin. The darkness is not merely atmospheric; it is theological. It is the darkness of divine wrath and separation.

Jesus cries out in Aramaic, *"Eloi, Eloi, lema sabachthani?"*— "My God, my God, why have You forsaken Me?" quoting Psalm 22:1. He is not losing faith in the Father; He is experiencing the full reality of sin's alienation. The Son endures the wrath we deserve so that we might know the mercy He secured. At the cross,

Jesus experienced what it meant to be cut off, so that we would never have to be.

Then, with a loud cry, Jesus declares victory: *"It is finished."* And Mark writes, *"He breathed His last."* This is not defeat. It is completion. The serpent's strike has landed, but the Savior's work is done. The debt is paid, the curse is carried, and redemption is accomplished.

II. Access Granted (v. 38)

"And the curtain of the temple was torn in two, from top to bottom."

As Jesus breathes His last, God tears the veil that separated the Most Holy Place from the rest of the temple. For centuries, that thick curtain had declared, *"Keep out!"* No one could enter God's presence except through a mediator. Now, torn from top to bottom, it proclaims, *"Come in!"* The way to God is open. The tearing begins at the top, showing that this act comes from heaven, not earth.

God Himself ripped open the barrier. The price was paid, and the door to His presence flung wide open. The torn veil is God's announcement that fellowship with Him is now possible through the blood of Jesus. What the darkness concealed, the torn curtain reveals. Spurgeon once said, *"The rending of the veil was the loud proclamation that the mercy seat is now uncovered, and God invites sinners to draw near."* Through Christ, access is granted forever.

III. New Life Received (v. 39)

"And when the centurion, who stood facing him, saw that in this way he breathed his last, he said, 'Truly this man was the Son of God!'"

Here stands a Roman centurion, hardened by countless executions. Yet something about this death is different. He has seen many men die in fear or rage, but never like this. The centurion's confession, *"Truly this man was the Son of God!"*, is astonishing. A Gentile soldier becomes the first human voice after the cross to proclaim Christ's divinity. The cross that seemed to silence Jesus becomes the very thing that reveals who He is.

He didn't see weakness; he saw a victor. He didn't see a criminal; he saw the Son of God. This is the power of the gospel. The death of Jesus opens blind eyes, softens hard hearts, and brings life where there was only death. Even in the final breath of the Son of God, grace is drawing sinners near.

IV. Conviction Strengthened (vv. 40–41)

"There were also women looking on from a distance, among whom were Mary Magdalene, and Mary the mother of James the younger and of Joses, and Salome."

When the disciples had fled, these women stayed. They could not stop the suffering, but they refused to turn away. They had followed Him from Galilee, served Him in life, and now they witnessed His death in love. Faithfulness is not always flashy. Sometimes it's simply remaining when others run. These women stand as living proof that true discipleship endures even in the shadows of sorrow.

When faith costs you something, that's when it means the most. Their devotion strengthens our conviction. They model the quiet courage of those who keep loving, keep believing, and keep looking to Christ even when all seems lost.

Conclusion

At Calvary, the heel of the Savior is bruised. Darkness covers the land, the veil is torn, a Roman confesses, and a group of faithful women stand near the cross. What looked like tragedy was triumph. The serpent struck, but his wound was self-inflicted. He died not because He was overpowered, but because He was obedient. The bruised heel will soon crush the serpent's head. The cross is not the end of the story; it is the foundation of it.

Reflection & Response

What does the darkness at Calvary teach you about the weight of sin and the holiness of God?

How does the torn veil give you confidence to draw near to God today?

What do you learn from the centurion's confession about the power of Christ's death?

How do the women at the cross inspire you to remain faithful in moments of loss or fear?

You Shall Bruise His Heel – Part 3

Mark 15:42–47

The cross has fallen silent. The crowds have gone home. The sky has cleared, but the weight of what has happened still hangs in the air. Jesus of Nazareth is dead. Mark slows the pace here. Every word reminds us that the gospel rests not on myth or imagination, but on fact. The death and burial of Christ are real, historical, and witnessed by credible people. If Jesus did not truly die, then He did not truly rise. But because His death and burial were real, our hope is sure. This passage moves from the crucifixion to the tomb. The bruised heel of the Savior lies still, but the victory beneath the surface is already at work.

I. A Literal Death (vv. 42–45)

"And when evening had come, since it was the day of Preparation, that is, the day before the Sabbath, Joseph of Arimathea, a respected member of the council, who was also himself looking for the kingdom of God, took courage and went to Pilate and asked for the body of Jesus."

Joseph of Arimathea steps into the scene as an unlikely disciple. A wealthy and respected member of the Sanhedrin, he had likely remained silent when the council condemned Jesus. But now, when the others have scattered, he finds courage. He approaches Pilate, the Roman governor who had ordered the crucifixion, and requests the body. This was a risky move. To align oneself with an executed criminal could mean social exile or worse. But Joseph's courage springs from conviction. He is *"looking for the kingdom of God."*

Pilate is surprised to hear that Jesus is already dead. Crucifixion usually took days. To confirm, he summons the centurion. The Roman officer who oversaw the execution gives his testimony: the prisoner is indeed dead. This detail matters. Mark is establishing historical certainty. Rome knew how to execute criminals, and its soldiers knew how to confirm death. There was no mistake, no fainting, no resuscitation. Jesus truly died.

His death fulfills prophecy, Isaiah 53:9 says, *"They made his grave with the wicked and with a rich man in his death."* Condemned among sinners, He is now claimed by the righteous. The Son of God was no apparition; He breathed His last and entered death's domain. Jesus didn't just appear to die; He entered death fully so that He could conquer it completely.

II. A Literal Burial (vv. 46–47)

"And Joseph bought a linen shroud, and taking him down, wrapped him in the linen shroud and laid him in a tomb that had been cut out of the rock. And he rolled a stone against the entrance of the tomb."

Mark records the careful details of Jesus' burial. Joseph lowers the lifeless body from the cross. Imagine the weight of that moment, the torn flesh, the cold stillness, the hands that once healed, now motionless. He wraps the body in linen, a gesture of honor and love. John's gospel tells us that Nicodemus assists him, bringing spices for the burial. Two men who had once followed Jesus in secret now step into the open when courage costs the most.

The tomb is newly cut out of rock, likely Joseph's own. The body is placed inside, and a large stone is rolled over the entrance. The sound of that stone sealing the tomb would have echoed like a final note of sorrow. The Son of God, who had nowhere to lay His head in life, was laid in a borrowed tomb in death.

Outside, the women watch. Mark names them again: Mary Magdalene and Mary, the mother of Joses. These same women who witnessed the crucifixion now witness the burial. Their presence anchors the story in eyewitness truth. They saw where He was laid. They will be the first to see the empty tomb. Every believer who faces death can take comfort in this: Jesus has been there. The tomb is no longer a place of finality; it's a passageway to resurrection.

III. A Lasting Gospel

The death and burial of Jesus are not incidental details; they are the bedrock of our faith. Paul wrote in 1 Corinthians 15:3-4:

"Christ died for our sins in accordance with the Scriptures, that He was buried, that He was raised on the third day in accordance with the Scriptures."

Without His death, there is no forgiveness. Without His burial, there is no resurrection. Without both, there is no gospel.

Because He truly died, our forgiveness is real.

The debt of sin is fully paid. The justice of God is satisfied.

Because he was truly buried, our victory is certain.

Death has no hold on those who belong to Him. The grave that received Christ is now powerless to keep His people.

Because He entered the tomb, our resurrection is assured.

As surely as He went down, He will rise—and all who are united to Him will rise with Him.

The tomb is not a symbol of defeat; it's the seedbed of life. Mark's closing verses prepare us for what comes next. The women stand by, the stone is rolled in place, and the world grows still. It's as though all creation holds its breath. The bruised heel has been crushed by death, but the serpent's perceived victory will be short-lived. The One who sanctified the grave will soon step out of it.

Conclusion

The burial of Jesus is often overlooked, but it stands as one of the most powerful testimonies of God's faithfulness. What began in a garden with Adam ends in another garden with Christ. The first Adam brought death to all; the second Adam goes down into death to bring life to all who believe. As Chapter 15 closes, the silence of the tomb is not the sound of defeat—it is the prelude to resurrection. The heel is bruised, but the head of the serpent is about to be crushed forever.

Reflection & Response

What does Jesus' literal death and burial reveal about the reliability of the gospel?

How does Joseph's courage inspire you to act faithfully when following Christ costs you something?

Why is it significant that the same women who saw the burial would later witness the resurrection?

How does knowing Jesus sanctified the grave change the way you view death as a believer?

Chapter 16

He Shall Bruise Your Head

Mark 16:1–8

From the first promise in Genesis 3:15 to this moment in Mark 16, all of Scripture has been moving toward one climactic event: the crushing of the serpent's head. For chapter fifteen, we've seen the heel of the Savior bruised: the mockery, the nails, the spear, the tomb. But on this morning, the bruised heel of Christ strikes the fatal blow. Death is defeated. Hope is reborn. The gospel reaches its glorious crescendo.

The resurrection of Jesus Christ is the Father's exclamation point on the statement, "This is my beloved Son." Mark 16:1–8 invites us into the moment when despair gave way to joy, and silence turned to proclamation.

I. Devoted Disciples (vv. 1–3)

"When the Sabbath was past, Mary Magdalene, Mary the mother of James, and Salome bought spices, so that they might go and anoint him."

The same women who stood by the cross now return to the tomb. While the male disciples are hidden behind locked doors, these women show steadfast devotion. They come early, in love and sorrow, bringing what they can, spices for a body they think is still in the grave. Their dedication is tender but

341

incomplete. They intend to honor the dead, not worship the risen.

The women didn't come expecting a miracle; they came expressing love. As they approach the tomb, they ask the practical question: *"Who will roll away the stone for us from the entrance of the tomb?"* They had seen its size the night before, and they knew they lacked the strength to move it. Yet they came anyway. That's faith in its simplest form, doing what you can while trusting God to handle what you can't. Their concern about the stone reveals the same tension we feel today. We often worry about barriers God has already removed.

II. Empty Tomb Eyewitnesses (vv. 4–6)

"And looking up, they saw that the stone had been rolled back—it was very large. And entering the tomb, they saw a young man sitting on the right side, dressed in a white robe, and they were alarmed."

God has already done what they feared could not be done. The stone is gone. The tomb is open. Inside, they see not a corpse but a messenger—an angel in radiant white—seated where the body of Jesus had been. The women are startled. But the angel speaks the greatest words ever uttered to fallen humanity:

"Do not be alarmed. You seek Jesus of Nazareth, who was crucified. He has risen; he is not here. See the place where they laid him."

Three phrases that changed the world: *"He was crucified. He has risen. He is not here."* The cross was real. The death was inevitable. The resurrection is historical.

342

The tomb was open not to let Jesus out, but to let witnesses in.

The angel's words authenticate everything Jesus claimed to be. His resurrection is the Father's divine endorsement of His Son. It's as if heaven declares: *"Everything He said is true. Everything He promised is yours."* The bruised heel has struck back, and the serpent's head is crushed beneath the triumph of life.

III. Missional Messengers (vv. 7–8)

"But go, tell his disciples and Peter that he is going before you to Galilee. There you will see him, just as he told you."

The angel commissions the women: *"Go, tell."* Grace always moves outward. Those who have seen the empty tomb cannot keep silent. And then comes the phrase that still melts hearts: *"and Peter."* Those two words are a sermon on grace all by themselves.

Peter — the one who denied Him three times — is singled out by name. The resurrected Lord is already pursuing the fallen disciple. The message of Easter is not just "He is risen," but "He is risen for you." Mark tells us the women fled the tomb in trembling and astonishment. Fear and joy often mingle in the presence of glory. The silence of verse 8 is temporary because the story didn't end there. The gospel of Mark was always meant to drive us forward, to tell what the women soon would: *"He is risen indeed."*

IV. Theological Reflection: The Serpent Crushed

The resurrection is not just an event in history; it is the turning point of eternity. Through the cross and the empty tomb, Jesus has crushed the serpent's head. In Genesis 3, sin brought death. At Calvary, death met its match. The serpent bruised the heel of Christ, but Christ's heel came down with power.

The resurrection:

Authenticates the person of Christ — proving He is the Son of God.

Vindicates the work of Christ — showing His death satisfied divine justice.

Transforms the people of Christ, giving new life, hope, and mission to His followers.

The empty tomb is God's receipt, stamped across history: Paid in full. The resurrection is the assurance that death shall die. The Lord's resurrection is our hope; His ascension is our glorification. This is the gospel: the crucified Savior lives. The stone is rolled away. The serpent is crushed. And the kingdom of God will stand forever.

Conclusion

Mark's gospel ends abruptly but is not unfinished. It stops where faith begins, at the empty tomb. The women came in grief, left in awe, and eventually proclaimed the good news that still reverberates through the centuries: *"He is risen."* The bruised heel of Christ has crushed the serpent's head. The curse has been broken. The tomb is empty. If the story ended at the cross, there would be sympathy without salvation. But because the tomb is empty, we have victory and vindication forever.

Reflection & Response

What does the resurrection prove about Jesus' identity and mission?

How do the women's actions challenge you to live and serve with devotion?

What does the phrase "and Peter" reveal about the heart of God?

How does the resurrection give you courage in the face of fear, doubt, or death?

Conclusion

Beholding the Christ, Following the King

The gospel of Mark begins with the bold announcement that Jesus is the Son of God, and it ends with an empty tomb and the command to go and tell. Between those two bookends lies the most incredible story ever told: the story of God Himself stepping into our world to redeem it.

Mark does not aim to satisfy curiosity but to summon faith. His gospel reveals Jesus not as a distant figure of history, but as the living Christ who still calls, still heals, still forgives, and still reigns. From the first miracle to the final commission, every scene invites us to behold His glory and to follow Him on the path of discipleship.

Throughout this gospel, we've seen Jesus' authority displayed over creation, sickness, sin, and death. Yet the greatest display of His power came through surrender. The cross was not a moment of defeat; it was the place where love triumphed over sin and life conquered death. Mark draws us to that moment again and again so that we would never forget: *the Son of Man came not to be served, but to serve, and to give His life as a ransom for many* (Mark 10:45).

But Mark's story does not end at the cross. The risen Christ sends His followers into the world with a message of hope that still resounds today: "He has risen; He is not here" (Mark 16:6). The empty tomb stands as the ultimate proof that Jesus is who He claimed to be, the Son of God, the Savior of sinners, the Lord of life.

To behold the Christ is not merely to admire Him; it is to follow Him. Discipleship means more than believing certain truths about Jesus; it means ordering our lives around Him. It means walking by faith when the road is difficult, trusting His authority when the world resists it, and serving others as He served us. It means daily surrender, because only those who lose their lives for His sake will truly find them.

If you have walked through this gospel and seen Jesus more clearly, then the call is simple and yet life-altering: follow Him.

Follow Him when the crowd turns away. Follow Him when obedience costs you something. Follow Him when faith feels weak and the future uncertain. Follow Him because there is no greater joy than knowing and serving the risen Christ.

My prayer is that this study through Mark has not only informed your mind but transformed your heart. May you, like the Roman centurion at the foot of the cross, see clearly what so many others missed and proclaim with conviction: *"Truly this man was the Son of God"* (Mark 15:39). May you live every day in light of that truth, trusting His grace, resting in His power, and reflecting His glory to the world. And may your life echo the invitation of this gospel: **Behold the Christ.**

www.ingramcontent.com/pod-product-compliance
Lightning Source LLC
Chambersburg PA
CBHW060405130626
46555CB00005B/1991